Refactoring in Java

Improving code design and maintainability for Java developers

Stefano Violetta

BIRMINGHAM—MUMBAI

Refactoring in Java

Copyright © 2023 Packt Publishing

Group Product Manager: Kunal Sawant
Publishing Product Manager: Teny Thomas
Senior Content Development Editor: Rosal Colaco
Technical Editor: Vidhisha Patidar
Copy Editor: Safis Editing
Project Manager: Prajakta Naik
Project Coordinator: Manisha Singh
Indexer: Pratik Shirodkar
Production Designer: Ponraj Dhandapani
DevRel Marketing Coordinator: Shrinidhi Manoharan
Business Development Executive: Kriti Sharma

First published: December 2023

Production reference:1081223

Published by Packt Publishing Ltd.
Grosvenor House
11 St Paul's Square
Birmingham
B3 1RB, UK.

ISBN 978-1-80512-663-8

www.packtpub.com

I dedicate this book to Cristina, the love of my life, and my children, Alessandro and Andrea.

I believe, in life, the most important thing is to keep learning and getting better.

Thanks for showing me something new every day.

– Stefano

Contributors

About the author

Stefano Violetta is a creative backend engineer, bringing over 15 years of experience in software development and architecture. He has worked in a diverse range of companies, spanning from startups to industry giants like eBay. Stefano takes pride in crafting meticulously written code to build sophisticated applications that align with their intended purpose, ensuring functionality and meeting the precise needs of users. Or at least, he tries to! Beyond the world of software, Stefano enjoys immersing himself in reading and watching movies during his free time.

About the reviewers

Giuseppe Bonocore is a senior IT professional, with more than 15 years of experience in the software industry, with different roles. His competencies include cloud technologies, modern software architectures, data, and AI. He has a master's degree in computer science. He is passionate about open source and the impact of digitalization on organizations and has been speaking at many important technical conferences. In 2021, he published a book about cloud-native applications development. His professional experiences include Salesforce, Red Hat, Accenture, and Docomo Digital, covering many technical leadership roles and deploying huge transformation projects across Europe.

Siddhesh Nikude is a software craftsperson who believes in improving the world's software development by writing better software and teaching others how to do it. He carries over 10+ years of experience and prefers calling himself a generalist.

Siddhesh started his career as a smart card developer, where he was introduced to Clean Code and XP. It was then he started working in an iterative and incremental approach to notice effective results. Not only does it improve the design and safety of the software, but it also improves the lives of the people working on it. He has worked in a variety of roles from developer to transformation coach on a variety of projects. He has mentored teams in B/TDD, mutation and micro testing, CI/CD pipelines, XP/Lean practices, Clean Code and SOLID principles, DORA metrics, Monte-Carlo simulation, Scrum, Delivery Automation, Test Pyramid, User Stories/Slicing, and Chartering. As a developer, he has worked with Java, Kotlin, Go, TypeScript, React-Native, and so on.

Table of Contents

Part 1: Introduction to Refactoring

1

2

Part 2: Essence of Refactoring and Good Code

3

4

5

Refactoring Techniques   107

6

Metaprogramming   145

7

Static and Dynamic Analysis   167

Part 3: Further Learning

8

Crafting Quality Every Day   191

Preface

In a time when it seems there is no other topic but artificial intelligence, it may seem strange to write a book that gathers the key practices for writing good, maintainable, and, in a word, clean code. As I write this, tools are becoming well-known – perhaps they are already well-known – that assist the developer and help write code, suggesting how to complete the line of code they are writing or even writing some short methods. Opinions at the moment are very polarized, between those who fear becoming obsolete in a few weeks and those who believe their natural intelligence is superior to any artificial intelligence.

As often happens, we will probably find ourselves somewhere in the middle. While it's true that AI can assist us in small, very specific tasks, analyzing small portions of code around the line we are writing and completing the work for us, there is still quite some time before it will write all the code for us, that is scalable, maintainable, and expandable, and without bugs – if that moment ever arrives, by the way. Writing good code involves making decisions that go beyond mere syntax and involve understanding the specific requirements and nuances of a given problem, which no AI can grasp.

Well-written code is clear, readable, and easy to understand. This is crucial for collaboration in a team, as other developers (or even yourself in the future) need to comprehend and modify the code. AI can assist in generating code, but it might not always produce code that is easy to maintain.

Bugs are inevitable in software development. Writing clean and well-organized code can significantly ease the process of debugging. Clear code is easier to navigate, making it simpler to identify and fix issues. AI tools can help with debugging, but they may not catch every type of error or understand the specific logic of your code as well as a human can.

The technical skills of a programmer are still very important and will be for a long time; writing clean code and refactoring one's codebase will be pivotal qualities, that will make us better and more valuable professionals.

Who this book is for

This book is primarily for those who write code; we believe it is particularly useful for those who have been doing it for a short time, but even experienced professionals sometimes forget how to do certain things – or perhaps think that the context doesn't allow for alternative approaches. We bring no secret recipes, no magic formula, just a compendium of the main techniques and tricks for refactoring your code, writing clean code, and above all, understanding if something is wrong and fixing it. We also try to avoid ending up in unpleasant situations with small adjustments to implement every day. All in one book.

Our job is very complex, much more than it seems, and this complexity is challenging to convey to those who don't speak our slang; there are many aspects to consider, and there are several variables at play, both technical and not. Even after the end of a course of study, one often begins to face the world of work having to learn many other new things.

This is a book that I would have wanted when I started my career: a sort of map of a very vast and, for many, still unexplored territory.

What this book covers

Chapter 1, What is Refactoring?, starts with the fundamental concepts, explaining what is meant by refactoring and why it is important. Faced with many possible opportunities for refactoring, let's learn to understand how to give each opportunity the right importance, i.e., which one to refactor first. We also understand when it is not necessary to refactor.

Chapter 2, Good Coding Habits, covers the topic of writing high-quality code by day-to-day habits. What is good code? What is bad code? We will delve into this and briefly explore the concept of clean code. We'll talk about the SOLID principles of software design, and also about the importance of (not using) side effects and mutability and common causes of bad code.

Chapter 3, Code Smells, is about the most frequent "red flags" that you can step into when going through your codebase; those red flags should immediately catch the eye of a professional. Recognizing them (and thus avoiding them) is a crucial part of our skills.

Chapter 4, Testing, is about the importance of the testing phase. Why is it important and why do you have to test as often as you can? We'll learn about unit testing and how we can be sure that most of our codebase is covered by tests. We'll go into Test Driven Development.

Chapter 5, Refactoring Techniques, is an overview of the main "tricks" that we can adopt to get rid of the code smells we discovered in *Chapter 3*. We'll learn to write better methods and move code when necessary; we'll organize data and simplify both conditional logic and method calls. We'll also discuss generalization.

Chapter 6, Metaprogramming, is about... not writing code! In other terms, we can use well-tested and well-grounded frameworks and libraries to write the code for us, avoiding reinventing the wheel.

Chapter 7, Static and Dynamic Analysis, talks about how we can be sure we're on the right path. The chapter delves into the concept of code analysis and program analysis, also exploring some tools that can be very useful in understanding how far we are from the quality threshold we want to set.

Chapter 8, Crafting Quality Every Day, tells us about the little and big actions that we can put in place during our day-to-day work routine. From code versioning to code formatting, from code reviews to pair programming, we can incorporate a lot of small but constant effort to keep our codebase clean and maintainable.

Chapter 9, Mastering Software Architecture, lifts our gaze and talks about the architecture of a software project. It explains what architecture is and what it is made of; it tells us about the main architectural patterns. Just as we did for individual pieces of code, we discussed which are the main architectural red flags to avoid.

To get the most out of this book

The code samples provided in this book are just code snippets, generic enough to be run with the most recent Java versions, provided by any vendor. All the most common operating systems (Windows, macOS, and Linux) will work. The build and dependency management tool used is Maven.

The suggested configuration is Java 17 and Apache Maven 3.8:

Software/hardware covered in the book	Operating system requirements
Java 17	Windows, macOS, or Linux
Maven 3.8	Windows, macOS, or Linux

GitHub repository

If there's any errata, it will be updated in this GitHub repository: `https://github.com/PacktPublishing/Refactoring-in-Java`

Conventions used

There are a number of text conventions used throughout this book.

`Code in text`: Indicates code words in text, database table names, folder names, filenames, file extensions, pathnames, dummy URLs, user input, and Twitter handles. Here is an example: "A parameterized SQL query is created using `PreparedStatement`, where ? is a placeholder for the user input."

A block of code is set as follows:

```
String userInput = getUserInput();
String sqlQuery = "SELECT * FROM users WHERE username = ?";
PreparedStatement preparedStatement = connection.
prepareStatement(sqlQuery);
preparedStatement.setString(1, userInput);
ResultSet resultSet = preparedStatement.executeQuery();
```

Any command-line input or output is written as follows:

```
They're not equal
They're equal
```

Bold: Indicates a new term, an important word, or words that you see onscreen. For instance, words in menus or dialog boxes appear in **bold**. Here is an example: "We can see a **START** node, from which starts an edge that goes into a conditional node."

> **Tips or important notes**
> Appear like this.

Get in touch

Feedback from our readers is always welcome.

General feedback: If you have questions about any aspect of this book, email us at customercare@packtpub.com and mention the book title in the subject of your message.

Errata: Although we have taken every care to ensure the accuracy of our content, mistakes do happen. If you have found a mistake in this book, we would be grateful if you would report this to us. Please visit www.packtpub.com/support/errata and fill in the form.

Piracy: If you come across any illegal copies of our works in any form on the internet, we would be grateful if you would provide us with the location address or website name. Please contact us at copyright@packt.com with a link to the material.

If you are interested in becoming an author: If there is a topic that you have expertise in and you are interested in either writing or contributing to a book, please visit authors.packtpub.com.

Share Your Thoughts

Once you've read *Refactoring in Java*, we'd love to hear your thoughts! Scan the QR code below to go straight to the Amazon review page for this book and share your feedback.

https://packt.link/r/1805126636

Your review is important to us and the tech community and will help us make sure we're delivering excellent quality content.

Download a free PDF copy of this book

Thanks for purchasing this book!

Do you like to read on the go but are unable to carry your print books everywhere?

Is your eBook purchase not compatible with the device of your choice?

Don't worry, now with every Packt book you get a DRM-free PDF version of that book at no cost.

Read anywhere, any place, on any device. Search, copy, and paste code from your favorite technical books directly into your application.

The perks don't stop there, you can get exclusive access to discounts, newsletters, and great free content in your inbox daily

Follow these simple steps to get the benefits:

1. Scan the QR code or visit the link below

https://packt.link/free-ebook/9781805126638

2. Submit your proof of purchase
3. That's it! We'll send your free PDF and other benefits to your email directly

Part 1: Introduction to Refactoring

We will start by defining what is meant by "refactoring" and why it is an important practice in software development. We will also cover the benefits of refactoring and the situations in which it is appropriate to use it. We will delve into the specific areas of code that developers should consider refactoring, providing guidance on how to identify and prioritize areas for improvement.

Then we'll cover the topic of writing high-quality code by day-to-day habits, which each professional should interiorize. We're going to start by discussing what distinguishes good code from bad code and briefly explore the concept of clean code. Then we'll delve into the SOLID principles of software design, the importance of (not using) side effects, mutability, and common causes of bad code.

This part has the following chapters:

- *Chapter 1, What is Refactoring?*
- *Chapter 2, Good Coding Habits*

1
What is Refactoring?

Picture this. It's your first day at a new job, and you're filled with excitement and eager to showcase your skills. Your new colleagues are enjoyable to be around, the company seems fine, and you're itching to get started. Your "onboarding buddy" begins showing you the project that you'll be working on for the next several months or even years. The concepts behind it are promising, and the business itself is stable. However, the code base is an enormous, chaotic mess—like a smoking, tangled plate of spaghetti. Well, perhaps you don't need to imagine it. It's likely you've been in that situation before. Maybe you're even experiencing it right now.

As soon as you open your IDE, you're greeted with a plethora of modules with very similar names. Once you enter a module, you're met with a daunting number of classes, some of which run hundreds of lines. These classes often house methods with vague names such as "manageThis" or "processThat," and they tend to be burdened with an excessive number of parameters. Suffice it to say, this isn't the most conducive environment for grasping the inner workings of your new project. Brace yourself for a few challenging weeks – or even months – of work, as the code base and architecture of the project are far from optimal. Lack of documentation or poor code commenting can make things even more challenging when dealing with existing code issues. However, if the code itself is well written and follows good architecture practices, it can compensate for the lack of documentation (which is definitely not something desirable) and minimize the need for excessive comments (we'll delve into this in the book).

Let me be clear: it's not about blaming. Every one of us – and by "us," I mean a large group of people I could call "The Software Development Community" – has a slightly different way of solving the very same problem. And everyone, at least once in their lifetime, thought "I would have done it better." But again, every one of us knows – or will know – that it's a lot about circumstances. If a certain module or piece of code was completed quickly but poorly, it is likely because someone requested it to be completed quickly. Sometimes, we come across situations where contradictory requirements are given to us or when priorities change due to internal or external events that take place. This request may have been made due to a valid business reason, a critical security concern, or any other reason that they deemed important. No one is lazy; (almost) nobody works poorly. It's just a matter of circumstances. We've all felt that pressure.

The techniques and concepts that fall under the broad umbrella of "refactoring" help prevent you from ending up in that situation, ensuring that your code doesn't become that plate of spaghetti. These techniques, and, more importantly, the mindset associated with refactoring, can also assist you in improving the existing code base, gracefully navigating the swamp you find yourself in, without feeling overwhelmed. In this chapter, we will explore the meaning of refactoring and, in reality, how elusive it can be. I will try to narrate, also based on my experience, the motivations behind refactoring – motivations that will probably be familiar to you. I will then give you some advice on how to organize your refactoring sessions and how to prioritize the various parts that need to be fixed in your code.

But let's start slowly, trying to agree on what we mean by the term that gives the title to this book.

In this chapter, we'll cover these topics:

- What do we mean by refactoring?
- Why you should consider refactoring
- When you should refactor
- What you should refactor

What do we mean by refactoring?

If we should give a strict definition of refactoring, we could be in some trouble, because it is often interpreted in different ways. The most common meaning, anyway, is related to code rewriting. Code refactoring is the process of restructuring and improving existing code without changing its behavior. Code is rewritten so that it is easier to understand and easier to modify.

We could also give a "recursive" definition of refactoring: a series of refactorings applied to the software without changing its behavior.

Let me highlight this again because it's very important: the software will return the very same results as before, no more and no less. It will just be written differently. The main (maybe the only) target you have to achieve is to make your code easier to understand, and this is one of the most important yet most difficult tasks to accomplish.

Refactoring could also be bounded with another couple of concepts.

It can be viewed as a way of iteratively improving the design of a software system. As the system evolves, its design can degrade and become outdated, leading to issues such as increased complexity, reduced maintainability, and reduced flexibility. Refactoring helps to address these issues by making incremental changes to the design of the system, improving its overall quality and maintainability. Moreover, refactoring can be used as a technique for discovering the underlying design of a system. By identifying patterns and commonalities in the code, developers can gain insights into the design of the system and identify areas for improvement. We'll deepen this concept in the following paragraph.

Refactoring and clean code

Refactoring is also closely tied to the concept of clean code. We'll go into details in the next chapter, but we can briefly say that clean code refers to code that is easy to read, understand, and *maintain*. Refactoring is one of the primary ways in which developers can ensure that their code remains clean. By continuously improving the design of their code through refactoring, developers can eliminate code smells (a code smell is a sign of a potential problem in the source code – we'll deep dive into this later on in the book) and improve the overall quality of the code base. Refactoring helps to keep the code base *maintainable* and extensible, reducing the risk of issues. Refactoring can help to ensure that the code base remains aligned with the principles of clean code. When your code is not clean enough – and we will see what this means in the following chapter – what you have to do is just stop and refactor.

Misconceptions about refactoring

There are various concepts that may resemble refactoring but are not synonymous with it. Exploring these concepts can contribute to a better comprehension of refactoring.

Refactoring is not about optimization. However, refactored code could have better performance.

Let me explain a little bit better. The main purpose of refactoring is to make your code easier to read, not to – for instance – reduce its cyclomatic complexity. (Cyclomatic complexity is a way to measure how complex a program's flow is. It counts the number of different paths or decision points in the code. The higher the complexity, the more complicated the code becomes. It's a useful tool for gauging code maintainability and finding areas that could use some simplification or extra testing.) It's quite the opposite! Improving your code's performance will probably reduce its readability… and it's OK because the purposes are different. Refactoring is one thing; improving performance is another. Nonetheless, it is also true that more readable code could be, in some cases, also more efficient.

Here's a very simple example.

Suppose you have this (very old-school) method:

```
public static int sumArray(int[] arr) {
    int sum = 0;
    for (int i : arr) {
    sum += i;
    }
    return sum;
}
```

As you can easily see, this method just takes an array of int elements and sums them, scanning the array one element at a time. We could try to make this method faster, without changing its behavior, by writing the following:

```
public static int sumArray(int[] arr) {
    int sum = 0;
```

```
int i = 0;
int len = arr.length;

while (i < len - 1) {
sum += arr[i++] + arr[i++];
}

if (i == len - 1) {
sum += arr[i];
}
return sum;
}
```

The refactored method uses a while loop instead of a for loop and increments the loop counter by 2 in each iteration. This allows the method to process two elements of the array at a time, effectively reducing the number of iterations needed to sum the array. This is a bit more efficient, but it is not more readable for sure. We reached the goal of optimization, but we did not refactor the code. How could we reach both goals? For instance, using a plain, simple one-liner such as this:

```
public static int sumArray(int[] array) {
    return IntStream.of(array).parallel().sum();
}
```

This method uses the IntStream class from Java 8's Stream API to perform a parallel sum operation on the elements of the array. The parallel() method enables parallel processing, allowing multiple threads to work on different portions of the array simultaneously. The sum() method then calculates the sum of all the elements in the array.

Refactoring is not "fixing bugs." This is much like the matter of complexity we just saw: you could fix a bug by refactoring a piece of code but it would be almost accidental. Or, better, it would be like killing two birds with a stone: if you can fix a bug *and* refactor a piece of code, it's a big win! But remember – it's generally advised not to mix different code actions in a single code change, even though it frequently happens.

Refactoring can actually *help* you solve bugs, but we'll see it later on.

Most important, refactoring is not "adding features." When you're adding functions to your software, you should not change existing code, but just add capabilities. On the contrary, when you refactor, your northern star shouldn't be to change the existing behavior. As a software professional, you will probably find yourself switching between these two aspects. The important thing is that you are aware of what you are doing: you structure the code better, then you add new functionality; once the new functionalities are tested and proven to be working, you can refactor again; and so on. It's like you're wearing two hats (using Kent Beck's metaphor) and you keep swapping them: you can and you should, but remember which one you're wearing at each moment.

In certain situations, there might be pressure from the business to prioritize adding new features instead of allocating time for refactoring, which may be seen as having no immediate value or merely serving the IT department. As a result, attempting to incorporate refactoring tasks discreetly within feature releases can lead to a blurring of roles. This means that you are not maintaining separate focuses or responsibilities (you're not *wearing two hats*), thus creating a mixture of objectives.

Now that we know, more or less, what refactoring means, we are ready to get the reasons behind it.

Why you should consider refactoring

We just saw that refactoring is highly coupled with the concept of clean code. Hence, we could say that one of the most important outtakes of refactoring your code is to improve its readability. In other words, refactoring makes your code easier to understand.

Even if the main goal of writing code is to tell a machine to do what you want, exactly the way you want it, it's important to underline something that we tend to forget, sometimes: you have to be understood not only by computers, but first and foremost you have to be understood by human beings. And one of those human beings is you: your future self! In my experience, I've found myself a lot of times asking, "Why?!" looking at a piece of code I wrote, maybe just weeks before.

Although it may seem simple or even naive, the idea of writing readable code is often overlooked due to the urgency of making our programs work. While this is certainly important, we must also remember that a significant portion of our work as software professionals is devoted to maintenance. In my experience, the opportunity to start a project from scratch is rare; more often than not, we inherit code from someone else and must maintain or build upon it. By prioritizing readability, we can benefit in many ways.

Although it's important to write code that is easy to understand in the future, it's also helpful to transform complex and unreadable code into clear and organized code. Just like Indiana Jones or Lara Croft, developers often have to delve deep into the projects they are working on to comprehend the intentions of their programmer ancestors. However, this can be significantly more challenging if the code is difficult to read. By refactoring the code, you can gain confidence in the functionality of the code you'll be working with.

Another good reason for having readable code is when the code is intended to be open sourced. Whether it is due to a personal interest in collaborating with open source projects, a company's approach or using it as a showcase for professional profile building, having readable code becomes even more crucial in these scenarios.

Another situation where readable code is valuable is when your code undergoes peer review or is used for training junior team members. In such cases, having code that is easy to follow and comprehend helps ensure effective collaboration and knowledge transfer within the team.

I also like readable code because I have a very bad memory. I am unable to hold more than a certain amount of information in my head; actually, I don't want it. There's no need if you can retrieve the information by simply reading the code like it was a piece of prose. It's not fair to expect my future self or colleagues to recall details that could easily be included in the code, such as why a particular approach was taken, why certain information was sourced from a particular location, or why one solution was chosen over another. One of the most frequent questions I ask myself when dealing with legacy code is, "Is this a mistake or is it intentional?"; readable code (coupled with the correct amount of tests, code comments, and coding standards, but we'll see this later) is the right choice to remove doubts.

There are many techniques to make the code more readable, and we will expand on them later in this book. There is something else I'd like to highlight first: readability can be something very subjective. What is readable for me may not be for my teammates. Some prefer one-liners, and others prefer to isolate a couple of lines in a single method. You may prefer to make explicit the type of every single variable; I prefer to use the `var` keyword. My suggestion is simple: talk to your teammates and agree on a trade-off. Remove from the discussion objective improvements (for example, using streams in place of classic loops) and agree on a general "code style" level (you could use a coding standard document or a unique formatter for your IDE, but we'll deep dive into this later). It is important to keep the code consistent in all of the project classes.

Improving the design of your software

Refactoring helps you improve the design of your software. If you don't do it, the design will (not so slowly) decay; it will be more difficult to understand, for instance, where to put new features or how to implement them. Refactoring is like "tidying up" your project once a new functionality is guaranteed. If you don't do it, you will probably fall into pitfalls, one of which is, the ancient monster that lies in almost every software company. Reducing duplicated code is not just a matter of "doing things properly" (even if doing things properly should be the norm) but has a direct benefit: when you have to modify that code, you will modify it only once. Believe me when I say that this very basic concept is not always respected. I will quote Martin Fowler here, in his book *Refactoring: Improving the Design of Existing Code*: "*By eliminating the duplicates, you ensure that the code says everything once and only once, which is the essence of good design.*"

If code is poorly designed or implemented, you'll have to do extra work to add functionalities, fix bugs, or improve performance: that extra work is due to something called **technical debt**. Technical debt happens when you prioritize speed over long-term benefits in your design or implementation choices. Just like a loan, it accumulates interest over time, making it harder to maintain and improve the software later. Constant refactoring improves design and quality; a better design reduces technical debt.

Maintainability and scalability

As we said before, software development is a lot about maintainability. If refactoring helps you keep a good design, that is a clear understanding of what each piece of code does and where to put any new code. In a situation such as this, maintainability is facilitated: by improving code organization and structure, it becomes easier to identify and fix issues or add new features over time. If you take care of your software and refactor when you think it's necessary (see the next subsection), the consequent good design will help you to scale your code. While improving performance isn't the main reason for refactoring, it often ends up being a nice bonus. If a certain functionality is properly isolated, for instance, it will be likely easier to parallelize it or to remove it and put it in another service, using a remote call to retrieve information from it.

Understanding, avoiding, and fixing bugs

Good design means that each part of your code does one thing, and it does it well. But things can go bananas, sometimes; bugs are just around the corner. One of the first things to do when you fight against a bug is to understand what's happening and where. Refactoring helps to understand the code (because you have to rewrite or restructure it a little bit without changing the external behavior), and thus you get to know the code better. If you know and understand your code, it will be faster to spot bugs or implement fixes.

Let me give you some advice: try to avoid having "restricted areas" in projects you're working on. In this case, a restricted area refers to a library, module, or another part of your code base that you rely on and understand its purpose, but you're afraid to touch because it's really fragile. You know what it does, but not exactly how it does it. It's like a big mess that no one in your company wants to deal with. The more complex and old the system is, and the more people have worked on it, the harder it becomes to understand the code base. Sometimes these restricted areas are unavoidable, especially if the previous developers didn't leave any documentation. It's not a big deal if you have some of these areas, but it's best to minimize them as much as possible. Refactoring can help, but there are certain conditions that need to be met, such as having good test coverage (but we can talk about that later).

Faster development

All of the previous considerations bring us to one, big deal: refactoring helps to do things faster. It may sound a bit counterintuitive, but if you think about it a little bit, it becomes crystal clear. Having well-designed, bug-free, understandable software means keeping good quality software. And of course, the main goal of having high-quality software is to add functionality faster, to scale it quickly, and to fix bugs in the blink of an eye.

Keep in mind that writing software is a craft. As software developers, we are like artisans who shape and mold our applications and engineer and assemble our services. Even though we don't use physical tools such as hammers and wrenches, we are still artisans. The main difference is that what we create is flexible and adaptable. We have the ability to revisit our work, improve upon it, and make it more receptive to change. By doing so, we can establish a solid foundation to build upon whenever we need to expand our work.

If there is no proper design, engineering tasks turn into an endless cycle of quick fixes and hacks. If you continue to approach projects in this way, relying on one temporary solution after another, it is only a matter of time before the project becomes unmanageable.

If your manager is more focused on schedules and timelines rather than technical aspects or quality in general (yes – that can happen), highlighting faster development as a key benefit of refactoring can be a compelling selling point.

When you should refactor

At this point, we have a clear understanding of what refactoring is and why it holds such significant importance or, I would even go as far as to say, it is crucial in our daily work. You may be wondering when is the appropriate time to engage in this activity. There are several factors to consider when deciding on the timing of refactoring. It is no secret that refactoring can be time-consuming, so how can we effectively incorporate it into our workflow? When is the optimal time to execute this activity?

Let me start with some fundamental advice based on our experience: it's always a good idea to do some minor refactoring whenever you have the chance, even if it means integrating it into your current task. For example, while running tests or performing static code analysis, you might come across a variable named *x*. That name doesn't convey much meaning, does it? So, you'll spend some time trying to figure out what that variable represents, only to discover that it contains a user's name. You went through the trouble of deciphering it, but why should others have to do the same thing? Why should you have to go through the same hassle 3 weeks later when you revisit the code? Just take a moment to rename the variable `username`. It's a simple and almost effortless task (your IDE can do that) that can save others time and effort. I try to maintain this mindset at all times, which aligns with my "lazy" attitude of achieving maximum results with minimal effort.

The "Rule of Three"

The **Rule of Three** suggests that code should not be duplicated more than twice and that once duplication occurs for the third time, it should be extracted into a reusable module or function. It is unclear who originally stated this principle as it has been widely used and adapted by various software developers and teams over the years (it was popularized by Martin Fowler, who credits it to Don Roberts). A more effective way to state the same is *three strikes and you refactor*.

Preparatory refactoring for smooth feature implementation

When adding a new feature to your code base, it is often helpful to engage in **preparatory refactoring**. This means taking the time to analyze parts of your code base that will be affected by the new feature and making necessary changes beforehand. I'll borrow Martin Fowler's excellent analogy for preparatory refactoring: it's like taping off electrical sockets, door frames, and skirting boards when painting a wall. The taping itself isn't painting, but it makes the painting process quicker and easier.

During the analysis phase of preparatory refactoring, you may notice areas where a small change in the code could lead to significant improvements in speed or efficiency. For example, you may realize that using a method parameter instead of a literal or a class hierarchy instead of a `switch` statement would improve the flexibility and adaptability of your code. By making these changes through refactoring, you can make your code more open to change in the future and ultimately make development easier overall.

Refactoring for bug fixing

It is often overlooked, but fixing a bug can present a great opportunity for a refactor. This is because a significant portion of bug-fixing-related refactoring is aimed at improving the readability of your code. By making your code more understandable, you can identify the root cause of the bug sooner and fix it more efficiently. The bug had been present all along, but it went unnoticed due to the lack of readability in your code. So, it's always a good practice to take the time to refactor when fixing bugs to prevent them from happening again in the future.

> **Important note**
>
> Let me be a bit clearer here: refactoring and bug fixing are two different things. It's important to fix the bug first and then focus on improving the code. They may be related but separate steps, and one doesn't automatically include the other.

Comprehension refactoring

You don't need a bug to make your code cleaner and more understandable; you can refactor your code while trying to understand it or – we all have been there – remember what you were trying to do 2 months ago. I will repeat this concept several times because I think it's one of the most important in our job: writing code is not only talking to a set of machines; it is more about talking to our future selves and our colleagues. Martin Fowler refers to this technique as **comprehension refactoring**. The idea can be likened to organizing one's wardrobe, where the goal is to have a clear and complete view of all available clothing options to select the best-fitting outfit. In the same way, comprehension refactoring involves streamlining code to improve its readability and comprehensibility.

The "Boy Scout Rule"

And then comes one of my favorite concepts related to software engineering, which is borrowed from the camping world and should also be applied in real life. Leave code better than you found it; at least, leave it as clean as it was. Do not leave it worse. Just like when you go camping or you picnic on a green field, you must think that that green field is not yours – you're just borrowing it; do not leave your trash. If you find some trash, take some time to pick it up.

Going back to our world, if you find some code that is – let's say – understandable but that you think could work better (for instance, parametrizing a function or using another library method with a better signature), just do not ignore the problem and fix it. Pick up that small amount of trash you found along your path. At the same time, remember that you were doing something else; your task was not to pick up the trash but to enjoy your day in the open air (just to continue this joyful metaphor). So, find a trade-off between your actual task and this litter-picking refactoring; something I found useful, sometimes, is just to keep note that someone will have to clean that piece of code: how you do it (a Jira task, a `git pull` request, a Post-it on your monitor) depends on how your team works. But this is the kind of small-step refactoring that you will find very useful and, I would say, almost mind-changing.

Planned refactoring

At this time, it could seem that refactoring must be an activity included in your software developer routine, something "opportunistic;" and of course it is. You should refactor code as part of your daily activity. Writing software can be seen as adding functionalities upon functionalities, resulting in a never-ending stack of features and, thus, code modules, but developers know that most of the time it's easier just to change existing code to add a new feature. You should never think about software as "done;" it is alive, and it is ever-changing. The moment software stays the same for too much time, there's probably a problem: it could be too hard to change or to extend (not enough refactoring has been done), or maybe it has been replaced by something else (and so, my advice is… dismiss it).

What I'm trying to say here is that it is not always possible to write excellent code on the first try; sometimes you have to stop, rewatch what you've done, and… try to do it better. Sometimes, you'll even have to plan to refactor because you understand that changes are too hard to make on the existing code base; the concept is similar to the preparatory refactoring we mentioned before, but it is like a level up because you plan the refactoring. You should do it rarely, because this means that you didn't include small refactorings into your daily activity, but it can happen. In this case, plan with attention: sometimes it could be better, for instance, to use separate branches or commits for new features and refactorings; someone else says that this would separate the refactoring from its purpose. I don't really have a suggestion here: just do what fits best for your team.

Long-term refactoring and "Branch by Abstraction"

Although most refactoring tasks can be completed in just a few minutes or hours, certain activities may require several weeks of effort to complete. These typically include tasks such as isolating specific logic into a separate component or replacing one library with another. To address these more complex tasks, it can be helpful for a team to establish a practice of performing refactoring whenever they approach a "danger zone" that has been identified as in need of improvement. One useful technique for achieving this is called **Branch by Abstraction**, which can be used to change a library or service call in a gradual and controlled manner.

Branch by Abstraction consists of five phases.

Imagine that you need to replace the outdated `FaultyPay` payment service that you integrated into your system several years ago. Naturally, you don't want to cause your customers any problems or inconvenience during the transition process. Here, you can see that there is a call and response between the client code and `FaultyPay` service:

Figure 1.1 – A very basic situation: our client code calls a legacy system and gets a response

After you identified the service you want to replace, you build an abstraction layer to allow continued communication between the systems that are being replaced and the entities requesting that service. This abstraction layer acts as a contract, exposing functionality while concealing the implementation details:

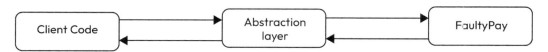

Figure 1.2 – An abstraction layer, often represented by a Java interface, is inserted between the client code and the component that needs to be eliminated

Then, start replacing the legacy system by systematically building the replacement system (we'll call it ShinyPay) and gradually integrating each rebuilt feature into the abstraction layer as they are completed. It is important to keep in mind that during this process, all traffic – both from the new and the old system – will be passing through the abstraction layer. It is also important to note that you could also choose (if this is possible – it is not always) to migrate one function at a time:

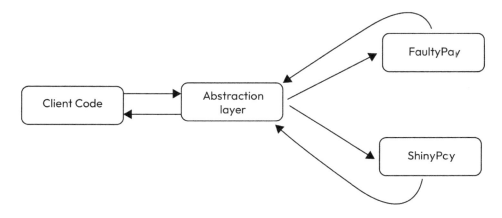

Figure 1.3 – Once the replacement component is prepared, it can be connected to the abstraction layer

The abstraction layer can also be used to fine-tune the service, such as directing only a portion of the traffic or specific features to the new component (feature toggle). It could also be possible to migrate one method at a time. It is important to ensure that both the legacy and the new system adhere to the same contract.

At this point, the code in the old system (`FaultyPay`, in our example) becomes obsolete, so you can delete it:

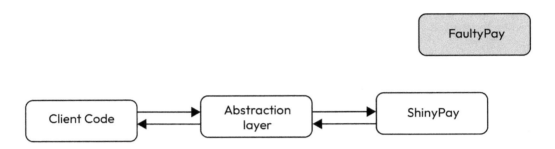

Figure 1.4 – The previous implementation (FaultyPay) is disconnected from the system; all traffic and functionalities are now exclusively directed toward the new implementation (ShinyPay)

Once all of the legacy code has been removed, you have the option to dismantle the abstraction layer. Alternatively, you may choose to retain this layer for the purpose of extensibility or future-proofing:

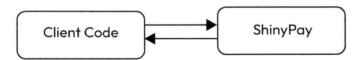

Figure 1.5 – We have returned to the ideal situation but with our new component! If we have been careful, skilled, and lucky, nobody has noticed anything (meaning there has been no disruption)

This approach has several obvious advantages. Apart from the primary advantage of enabling seamless migration of large features in continuous integration, there are several additional benefits of using the Branch by Abstraction technique:

- The release schedule is completely independent of architectural changes, making it easy and cost-effective to pause and resume the migration process as needed. This is because the new implementation is safeguarded by the system, allowing for quick adaptation to urgent requests or priority features from the leadership team or customer service department or to fix bugs. In contrast, when using a standard feature branch, it can be more challenging to resume a migration that has been paused.

- The potential for merge conflicts is also limited to the abstraction layer only, which can significantly reduce the scope of conflicts that may arise. Without the abstraction layer, a code base refactor sitting in a feature branch for an extended period could generate a wide range of merge conflicts that might be difficult to resolve completely.

- Instead of switching completely to the new system, you could choose to turn new features on and off when you need to. These "specific switches" are called **feature toggles**. A feature toggle, also known as a feature flag or feature switch, is a technique that allows developers to enable or disable specific features or functionality in an application, at runtime and without modifying the code base. By using feature toggles, developers can release new features to a subset of users, test them in production environments, or enable/disable features based on certain conditions or user segments. This approach provides flexibility, allows for gradual rollouts, and reduces risk associated with deploying new features.

Refactoring in a code review

A **code review** is a process of reviewing the source code. It is usually done by other developers or peers who are more or less familiar with the programming language and the project's requirements. We'll cover code reviews in detail in *Chapter 8*.

The purpose of a code review is to ensure that the code is written in a clear, concise, and efficient manner and that it meets the project's requirements and coding standards. Code reviews can help to identify and fix potential bugs or security issues, as well as improve the overall quality and maintainability of the code.

During a code review, the reviewer examines the code line by line and provides feedback on issues such as code structure, syntax errors, performance, and readability. The review may also involve discussions and suggestions for improvement, as well as questions and clarifications about the code's functionality and design. Code reviews are an important part of the software development process and are typically conducted before the code is merged into the main code base or released to customers.

Martin Fowler suggests that code reviews are a great time to do some refactoring. If you want to understand someone else's code (as we've already said), the best way is to refactor it. Otherwise, you might only get bits and pieces of it and give vague feedback. Refactoring helps you get a clearer picture. By the way, there's something called **pair programming** (and something called **mob programming**) that takes code review to the next level. We'll talk about it more in this book later.

What you should refactor

Sometimes in my career, we've come across situations where I wanted to make changes to different parts of my project. Maybe there was something that wasn't working properly or something that I didn't fully understand, or simply something that could be improved. It's important to decide which parts to focus on and prioritize. And in some cases, it might even be better to leave things as they are and not make any changes at all.

There's no hard and fast rule when it comes to refactoring, but with a little thought, you can come up with a solid plan that meets your specific needs. Remember – in our profession and in life, we often have to make compromises.

Recently, I came across a helpful concept in Gary Keller's book, *The One Thing* (*Bard Press, 2013*). While it's not specifically related to software development, it can be applied to our needs. The idea is this: "What's the one thing you can do, such that by doing it, everything else will be easier or unnecessary?" While this is a broad question with many implications that we can't discuss here, it can be a useful starting point for deciding what to do with our code base. This approach is super helpful when it comes to refactoring code. So, when you're starting a new task or feature, take a look at your code and ask yourself if there's anything that, if improved, would make the rest of the project work a lot easier or completely unnecessary.

The question is focused on what you can do, which forces you to think in actionable terms. It's not about what you would do if certain conditions were met, but rather what you're capable of doing right now. By identifying the one thing that can make everything else easier or unnecessary, we can focus our efforts on the most critical task at hand. It's like distilling the essence of our job down to its core: doing the minimum necessary to achieve the maximum impact. This approach can be particularly valuable in software development, where there are often many different areas that could benefit from refactoring or improvement, but we need to prioritize and focus our efforts to achieve the greatest impact.

Let me give you an example to illustrate this point. Picture yourself working at a travel company that's doing well, but facing challenges in handling a complex ecosystem with multiple travel providers and their solutions. The trouble is, there's some outdated code causing problems, and the booking process occasionally fails. The system technically works without any bugs, but it's outdated, difficult to maintain, lacks proper documentation (in one word: its *legacy*), and definitely not ready to handle the expected surge in traffic. We really need to refactor it, or else the company won't be able to handle all the upcoming new customers. Meanwhile, there's an internal team responsible for managing website content, and they're struggling with a tool they only use twice a month. It's incredibly confusing and impractical, making even simple tasks time-consuming. We absolutely have to refactor that tool to make it more user-friendly for the team. While both issues are important, it's clear that the first problem with the legacy code and booking process should be addressed first, because travel booking is the core business of the company and because those people would be free to deal with something else.

Anyways, let's face it – refactoring legacy code can be overwhelming, especially when you're pressed for time and resources. While "the one thing" rule is a fantastic approach, it's also pretty broad. So, let me show you something more precise that can help you decide which parts of the code base require your attention the most.

Impact analysis

Impact analysis is like detective work in software refactoring. It's all about figuring out how changes to one part of the code base will affect other parts of the system.

So, first, the developers identify code modules that need to be refactored or updated. Then, they investigate the connections and relationships between these modules and other parts of the software, such as external libraries, user interfaces, and interfaces.

By understanding these dependencies, the developers can get a good sense of how changes will ripple through the system. They can pinpoint areas that might be particularly tricky to change and take steps to reduce the chances of bugs or other issues cropping up.

Basically, impact analysis is a crucial tool in the software refactoring toolkit. It helps developers make changes in a more thoughtful and careful way so that the code remains stable and easy to maintain in the long run.

Performing an impact analysis involves thoroughly assessing the potential effects of making changes to a system or project. Here's a breakdown of the steps:

1. **Preparation**: Define the change, clearly stating what you want to do. Collect data about the proposed change.

2. **Identify affected areas and dependencies**: Brainstorm which parts of the system will be impacted by the change and how the change will affect other components in the system.

3. **Identify affected elements in each area**: Evaluate how the change will impact functionality, performance, security, and other aspects. Identify potential risks and problems that could arise from the change.

4. **Evaluate**: Conducting an evaluation, the team identifies both positive and negative impacts of the proposed change.

5. **Deal with negative consequences**: With a clearer understanding of the negative impacts, the team can now focus on addressing them. They have the opportunity to consult with team members and stakeholders to discuss whether the change should proceed or not. Additionally, conducting regression testing becomes crucial in this scenario.

Risk assessment

Risk assessment is a fancy way of saying "figuring out what could go wrong." In software refactoring, it's all about taking a hard look at the code base and identifying potential risks before making changes.

When assessing risk, developers consider a range of factors, including the complexity of the code, the likelihood of introducing bugs, and the potential impact of any issues that might arise. There may be impacts on data (some pieces of code are maybe dealing with crucial information such as personal or financial data), possible downtimes (some pieces of code, in case of issues, may bring down the entire system or some core functionalities), business issues (pieces of code that if broken could cause financial issues or contract infringements), or security breaches. They may also look at the time and resources available for the refactoring project and the potential impact on users and stakeholders.

Once risks have been identified, developers can take steps to mitigate them. For example, they might create test cases to ensure that the refactored code works as expected, or they might make changes in small increments to reduce the chances of something going wrong. We will talk more deeply about test coverage later in this book.

Overall, risk assessment is an important part of software refactoring because it helps developers make informed decisions about how to proceed. By taking the time to consider potential risks and plan accordingly, they can ensure that the refactoring project is successful and that the code base remains stable and maintainable over time.

Value estimation

Value estimation in software refactoring is all about figuring out whether a particular refactoring project is worth the time and resources required to complete it.

When estimating value, developers consider a variety of factors, such as the current state of the code base, the potential benefits of the refactoring, and the potential costs and risks involved. They might also take into account factors such as user feedback, performance metrics, and the needs of stakeholders.

Once the potential value of a refactoring project has been estimated, developers can decide whether it makes sense to move forward. In some cases, the potential benefits might not outweigh the costs, and the project may be shelved or postponed. In other cases, the benefits may be significant enough to justify the investment, and the project may move forward.

Value estimation is an important part of software refactoring because it helps developers prioritize their efforts and make strategic decisions about how to allocate resources. By focusing on projects with high potential value and avoiding those with lower potential value, developers can ensure that they are making the most efficient use of their time and resources.

Prioritization matrix

A **prioritization matrix** (also known as the **Eisenhower Matrix**) is a tool used in software refactoring to help developers prioritize their efforts and make informed decisions about which refactoring projects to tackle first. It typically involves a matrix with two axes, one representing the level of urgency given to a project and the other representing the potential impact on the system.

Each project is evaluated based on these two factors and then plotted on the matrix accordingly. Projects that require the least effort and have the greatest potential impact are considered the highest priority, while those that require more effort and have a lower potential impact are considered lower priority.

Using a prioritization matrix can help developers make strategic decisions about which projects to tackle first, based on the potential benefits and costs of each project. By focusing on the highest priority projects first, developers can make the most efficient use of their time and resources, and ensure that they are addressing the most critical issues in the code base:

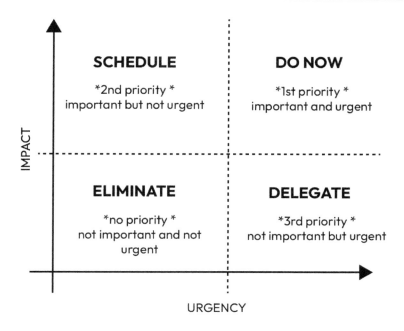

Figure 1.6 – You should put your activities in a prioritization matrix
in order to choose the right priority for execution

The higher priority should be assigned to activities that have high urgency and impact. Lower priority (or no importance at all) should be given to activities that are not urgent and will have no impact.

Further considerations

There's more to think about when it comes to refactoring. I'll jot it down here just to cover all our bases, but honestly, it might be a bit beyond the scope of this chapter. Once you've figured out which parts of your code base to prioritize for refactoring, the next step is to create a detailed plan that includes the scope, goals, steps, and timeline for the project. It's also crucial to communicate this plan to everyone involved, such as your team, manager, clients, and users. You need to explain why you're refactoring, what you'll be doing, how you'll be doing it, and when it'll be done. It's important to set clear expectations and manage them throughout the refactoring process.

The final step is to execute the plan with discipline and diligence. Stick to best practices such as making small and frequent changes, running tests before and after each change, committing and documenting each change, and reviewing and verifying each change. Keep an eye on how the refactoring is affecting things such as code quality, system performance, and user feedback. Measure the outcomes and compare them with your goals and expectations.

Refactor or rewrite?

There are various opinions on this matter, which I have observed to be a common source of disputes among teammates and colleagues. The truth is there is no simple answer. It's just one of those things where there are a ton of conflicting opinions out there, and it's tough to figure out what to believe. But I'll do my best to share some of those opinions with you and offer up some advice, for whatever it's worth.

There are situations when it's simply not justifiable to refactor your code. Perhaps it's plagued with too many bugs, the design is overly complicated, and comprehending it is nearly impossible. Going through it's like trying to solve the Rubik's Cube blindfolded – or, quoting a former colleague of mine, like counting money with a fan blowing nearby. In such cases, rewriting it from the ground up may be the better option, and it's something that many software developers find enjoyable. After all, it's often more comfortable to create something new than to take small, incremental steps that are still tied to what was previously done.

On the other hand, we often fall into the trap of wanting to rewrite everything, thinking that what's already there is terrible, when in reality, we may not have put in the effort to fully understand it. It's important to remember one of the fundamental rules of programming, according to American developer Joel Spolsky: *it's harder to read code than to write it*. Let's not immediately denigrate the legacy code we come across in our code bases, which typically wasn't written by us (our own code is, of course, beautiful). Legacy code has a history; it has been thoroughly tested and integrated with all necessary use cases and has often demonstrated good performance. We should respect legacy code.

It's a really complicated decision, and as I said, there's no general rule. Perhaps, a very simple rule to adopt could be to try to evaluate the cost (both in terms of time and complexity) of rewriting and refactoring code and choose the option that seems best to you. Note that I didn't say "the option that costs less," because it's often an investment. Another useful thing could be to break down the part under examination into smaller parts (the good old "divide and conquer") and choose to refactor (or rewrite) only that part, so as not to be "stuck" for too long.

If you decide to rewrite a piece of code, a module, or an entire component, let me give you a heartfelt piece of advice: don't get too attached to what has already been done. Let me explain. Surely, it will be useful to try and understand what the code does and the individual steps that make up the logical flow. It will be equally useful to understand how users currently behave and which business cases are currently implemented. However, I have often found that what is currently present does not correspond to the real needs of users; perhaps it never did, or perhaps needs have changed over time. Perhaps half of that software is simply no longer needed. So, it's fine to read what exists and try to rewrite it better or differently, but often this reverse-engineering process can be quite complicated, time-consuming, and, especially, error-prone. Instead, try to identify what users need, possibly with the help of the Product Owner (to know what a PO exactly is, you can refer to `https://www.scrum.org/resources/what-is-a-product-owner`).

This may actually encounter some resistance, which depends on the mentality of the company you are working for. Many times, I have been told: It must have the same logic as before, but it must work better. This is obviously a great way to cover one's back, but it almost never leads to effective results. It forces engineers to do huge reverse-engineering work, which in light of (often) changing user needs can be partially useless; it does not allow the team (both the so-called tech part and the so-called product part, assuming such differentiation makes sense) to focus on the importance of individual features, in order to prioritize activities and perhaps avoid unnecessary ones. So, I suggest you always start from the needs – from the why, before the how. Think about the goal before how to get there.

Summary

This chapter delves into the concept of refactoring and its elusive nature. It examines the underlying motivations for refactoring and offers insights into organizing effective refactoring sessions, as well as prioritizing different areas requiring attention in your code. Furthermore, it emphasizes the significance of integrating refactoring seamlessly into your regular activities. In conclusion, the chapter provides a comprehensive summary and presents a range of techniques to successfully incorporate refactoring into your professional routine.

In the upcoming chapter, we will discuss a set of recommended practices that are considered "good habits" for software professionals to adopt in their work.

Further reading

- *Martin Fowler, Refactoring, Addison-Wesley Professional*
- **How do you prioritize which legacy code to refactor first?** https://www.linkedin.com/advice/0/how-do-you-prioritize-which-legacy-code-refactor
- **Refactor vs. rewrite: Deciding what to do with problem software**: https://www.techtarget.com/searchapparchitecture/tip/Refactor-vs-rewrite-Deciding-what-to-do-with-problem-software
- **Things You Should Never Do, Part I**: https://www.joelonsoftware.com/2000/04/06/things-you-should-never-do-part-i/
- **Feature Toggles (aka Feature Flags)**: https://martinfowler.com/articles/feature-toggles.html
- **BranchByAbstraction**: https://martinfowler.com/bliki/BranchByAbstraction.html

2
Good Coding Habits

In a book about refactoring, I believe it's necessary to talk about well-written code. These are two obviously closely related aspects that almost overlap. The lack of good code or solid architecture is among the main reasons for refactoring; refactoring is the means through which we aim to improve the writing of a method, a class, a project, or an architecture.

To understand clearly what we're talking about, it's important to try to explain what good code is and, by exclusion, what is considered poorly written code. It may seem excessive to try to define what good code is because, in reality, it should be – or should be treated as – something quite intuitive. We should almost have *spider senses* that tingle when we see code that is hard to understand or overly complicated. If you don't have spider senses developed yet, don't worry! They will grow with experience (and this book could help you get there).

Nowadays, good code is often synonymous with *Clean Code*, that is, a collection of informal rules gathered in the book of the same name by Robert C. Martin (we're going to speak about Clean Code a lot). In this chapter, we'll try to summarize in broad terms what Clean Code means, what its fundamental principles are, and why we should all strive for Clean Code every day of our professional lives.

Clean Code is often accompanied by and closely related to the so-called SOLID principles, for which the computer science community has shown great inventiveness regarding acronyms. But they also provide *solid* (do software developers love dad jokes?) foundations for writing excellent code.

In this chapter, we'll cover the following topics:

- What is good code?
- Clean Code
- Write SOLID code
- Side effects and mutability
- Causes of bad code

A small disclaimer

I don't claim to present the ultimate truth about anything. I know that some of what I'll write is the subject of debate, and there are plenty of programmers out there ready to question everything (and I say that as a good thing). The intention is to share what I believe are healthy habits to practice every day, to avoid getting stuck and, most importantly, to find joy in our beautiful craft as artisans.

Characteristics of good code

Once again, I must disappoint you. I struggle to find a clear, precise, and universally agreed-upon definition of what good code is. It is a highly subjective concept that heavily depends on the context. Online and in textbooks, you can find numerous definitions that differ slightly from each other. However, I strongly believe that there are some foundations on which we can all agree. I will try to summarize the various interpretations of good code and provide some feedback based on my experience, for what it's worth.

Good code is readable

Obviously, this is the first thing. Pretty intuitive, right? Well, yes, but it's one of the aspects that I've often found to be underestimated. Sometimes we are so focused on achieving the end result, on delivering a product at all costs, that we forget about what comes after; we forget that – as already mentioned – code must not only speak to machines but also and above all to other programmers. And those other programmers are also our future selves! Doing things quickly is not the only reason for which code lacks readability: for instance, sometimes we could have performance issues to handle. Anyways, if you have other aspects to handle, my small piece of advice is to make sure to at least strike a balance between readability and those aspects.

To give a definition of readable code, we don't need to rely on the code itself. Plain language is enough. Just imagine for a moment that you're at your own home and you need to assemble one of those beautiful, satisfying, low-budget Swedish furniture pieces that we have to assemble ourselves, like a wardrobe. Instead of the crystal-clear visual instructions that we are familiar with, we find a text that says the following:

Take the white wooden piece with dimensions A x B, which we will now refer to as L. Take another wooden board with dimensions B x C, which we'll call M. Take the tool consisting of a metal rod with a cross-shaped end. Take a screw that fits into the holes of both L and M; it must be not too short and not too long. Using the cross-shaped end of the aforementioned tool, rotate the screw clockwise so that they inextricably join, forming a single partial structure that we'll call P.

This text is obviously incomprehensible. I suffered a lot in writing it. Don't fall into the trap of thinking that code is different from prose language. I mean, of course, it's different, but in an abstract way, you should consider them as the same thing. Imagine, when you write code, writing in prose. You should aim for prose writing, in a way, so that your code is as readable as possible. When a piece of code is readable even by someone who knows nothing about the project or has basic programming skills, then you have succeeded. The excerpt from the previous instruction manual could be rewritten as follows:

Take the wooden board labeled "left side" and screw it together with the one labeled "back" using a Phillips screwdriver.

This excerpt can certainly be further improved. But the starting point is definitely understandable; it's understandable to me and it's understandable to others, and that's how your code should be. Readable code is code that can be improved and expanded upon.

Good code is reliable

If I have to think of a definition for "reliable," it brings to mind a friend of mine who, when they say they will do something, they do it and only that. Nothing more, nothing less. So, think of reliable code as your friend who always agrees to help you in the best possible way—no surprises, as Radiohead used to sing. I could give you an example of unreliable code not so far from certain things I have encountered in the past. For instance, imagine you have an entity in your domain represented like this:

Student
id: String
name: String
surname: String
taxCode: String

Table 2.1 – Example entity

Both `id` and `taxCode` are of type String and are unique within the domain. That means there cannot be two students with the same `id` or the same `taxCode`.

I also have an exposed method from the `Student` interface that is written like this:

```
public String getUniqueIdentifier();
```

Apparently, this signature of this method is correct, because it does not expose the internal structure of the object. But, it could also have been named `getId()` or `getTaxCode()` and that is *exactly* the point. Without looking at the implementation, we don't know if we will get `taxCode` or `id` when using it. When we actually use `getUniqueIdentifier()`, we realize that the behavior is variable and depends on the specific implementation. If we were to use this method within a payment and invoicing system where we specifically need `taxCode`, this method would be unreliable. One possible solution could be to expose two separate getter methods so that we know exactly which information we are reading at that moment. Alternatively, another solution could be to expose an additional method called `getTaxIdentifier()` that specifically returns `taxCode`. This way, you would have separate methods providing clear and unambiguous access to each piece of information without exposing the internal structure.

Good code is hard to misuse

To easily explain the concept of code that cannot be misused, all I have to do is take a look inside my children's room. There are toys, sometimes referred to as "Montessori toys," that involve small wooden objects being inserted into a box with corresponding holes of the right shape for each object. As can be seen from *Figure 2.1*, it is impossible to fit a cylinder into a square, a cube into a circle, and so on.

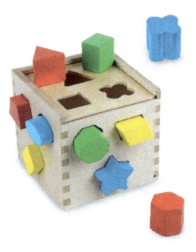

Figure 2.1 – An example of a Montessori toy

The usage is intuitive and provides immediate feedback.

We need to envision writing the code and designing the components in this way: we expect our code to perform certain actions, which may have impacts on external systems or a database. Misusable code could potentially cause significant problems—for instance, it could write incorrect information to a database—or it could simply fail to function properly. When providing our services, which include our code, libraries, and design, we must put ourselves in the shoes of those who will integrate or utilize them.

There are several techniques to make your code non-misusable, and it would take – and indeed there are – entire books on the subject. However, I want to give you a couple of ideas here that can be easily applied even without delving too deep.

Don't be overly generic

One "trick" to make your code non-misusable is to avoid overly generic data types whenever possible. Types like Integer, String, List, and so on, serve as the building blocks for constructing our programs and are very versatile. However, the flip side is that they can sometimes be too generic. Let me give you a couple of examples from my own experience: in a company operating in the travel industry, we deal with a service that returns all available flights based on a user's search. As we need to represent the number of adults, children, and infants for whom a solution is being sought, we chose the following solution (for simplicity, let's omit the handling of null values, possible initializations with default values, etc.):

```
private List<Integer> passengers;
```

So, for example, if we are searching for a flight for 2 adults, 1 child, and 1 infant, the convention would be to populate `passengers` as an array: `[2, 1, 1]`. In my opinion, this choice is very risky. We could insert fewer values than necessary, for example, just one or two. We could insert more values. We could even omit them entirely. Yes, we could introduce some input validation, but why allow input and then return an error later? If this were a library, by the way, I would be forced to read the documentation to understand how to populate that field (there's nothing wrong with reading documentation, of course, but it should be something that could be more intuitive). It would be more intuitive instead to divide the information into a more meaningful structure:

```
private Integer adultCount;
private Integer childrenCount;
private Integer infantCount;
```

Much clearer, isn't it?

We could, in fact, go further and create an ad-hoc structure for our needs, something that cannot lead to confusion. Something like this:

```
public class Passengers {

    private final Integer adultCount;
    private final Integer childrenCount;
    private final Integer infantCount;

    //constructor(s) and getters...
}
```

And that would lead to having a single, understandable field:

```
private Passenger passengers;
```

Use standards for writing good code

Another way to make your code non-misusable is to use standards whenever possible. A couple of examples come to mind, related to handling time. If you need to represent a date, choose a format, document that you are using it, and consistently use it throughout your project. One thing I've seen done very often is trying to represent a time period or duration with an Integer or even a String:

```
private Integer movieDuration = 150; //movie duration in
                                     minutes
```

Starting from **version 8**, Java has introduced the `Duration` class, and I highly recommend using it. It is incredibly versatile and allows you to represent a duration of time unambiguously:

```
private Duration movieDuration = Duration.of(150,
    ChronoUnit.MINUTES);
```

Additional cool thing: the preceding duration serializes according to a convenient ISO standard (ISO-8601), such as `PT2H30M`.

The thing here is simple: don't reinvent the wheel! After all, Java is so widespread also because there are a multitude of libraries available, so I suggest, while we are solving common problems, to avoid recreating basic components and instead rely on language features or open source libraries. One of the first things that I always ask myself is: am I the first one having this issue? The answer is rarely yes.

Use single sources of truth for data and logic

Last piece of advice: use a single source of truth for data and a single source of truth for logic. I must admit that the concepts of a single source of truth are often straightforward to explain but less easy to implement.

Let me try to illustrate what I have in mind with an example. Once again, let's imagine managing a flight search system. Typically, the data can be divided into primary data and derived data. Primary data is essentially the information without which our system couldn't function, while derived data refers to all the other information. In our flight search example, let's say we need to provide, among other details, the duration of a trip from Milan to San Francisco. The trip consists of two flights: one from Milan to Copenhagen and another from Copenhagen to San Francisco. In this example, we can consider the departure and arrival times of each individual flight as primary data. From these, we can derive information about the duration of the trip and potentially the duration of the layover. Managing derived data as primary data, for example by storing it in the database, could lead to inconsistencies. Especially when deriving information from a large volume of data – or when the derivation is complex or involves some external system – the computational cost of such calculations could be high. I would advise you to exercise caution and consider implementing a mechanism called **lazy calculation**. Essentially, this approach involves calculating the derived data only when it is needed, rather than in advance, and saving it in a cache so that it is readily available for future use. In our flight duration example, we would calculate the journey duration using the flight's departure and arrival times (we have also to consider the airport locations and their time zones) without storing it in a database, but at most in a short-term cache or something like that. If we stored it in a database, in fact, we would have to recalculate it every time the flight departure/arrival times change (in industry jargon, every time there is a "schedule change") or we might get inconsistencies.

Just as having a single source of truth is a good practice, having a single source of logic is also beneficial. In the aforementioned case, for instance, we need to calculate the duration of a flight from Milan to San Francisco. While it may not be rocket science, it is not a trivial calculation either, as it involves different time zones and the so-called daylight saving time. It is one of those things that is easy to underestimate and can, more easily than you might think, lead to bugs in production (and there are many flight search websites that have this bug in production at the moment I'm writing). In this case, it is very helpful to write the function once, thoroughly test it, and then consistently use it throughout our code base. This way, we do not stray far from the good old principle of **Don't Repeat Yourself** (**DRY**). In this case, you could write a library, a service, or just a class in your project that deals with the journey duration and use it every time you need it.

Good code is modular

In general, modularity refers to the concept of dividing a system or complex entity into smaller, independent components or modules. It is a principle that can be applied beyond software and is used in various fields and disciplines. Let's consider a shelving unit consisting of individual modules that can be easily assembled and disassembled.

Figure 2.2 – This kind of furniture is composed of a set of identical and reusable modules

Each module serves as a building block, and you can arrange them in various configurations to create different shelving arrangements based on your needs. This modular approach allows for flexibility in adapting the furniture to different spaces and changing requirements. For example, as seen in *Figure 2.2*, it is possible to use the same type of brackets vertically, adapting them to shelves of different lengths.

The components that make up this shelf are easy to use, meaning they have clear interfaces and few points of interaction. If you put yourselves in the shoes of both the designer of this shelf and the person who has to assemble and maintain it, you understand that modularity is essential. If there were a different way to assemble each shelf or bracket, or if there were different brackets for different shelves, the management would be much more complex and prone to errors. We'll say something more about modularity in the text sections.

Dependency injection

Classes often need to use other classes. In well-organized code, we often solve each of these smaller problems with a separate class. However, there isn't always just one way to solve a problem, so it can be helpful to structure our code in a way that allows us to change how we solve these smaller problems. That's where dependency injection comes in handy.

I could give you a quick example relating to our example flight search system. Let's suppose we have `FlightSearcher` which returns, given an itinerary and a description of the people involved, some possible travel plans around Europe and their relative prices. Of course, we are a profitable company so we want to surcharge the original price to get some earnings out of it. A crucial part of the response will be the price given to the customer, calculated through a component called `FlightPricer`:

```
class FlightSearcher {
    private final EuroFlightPricer euroFlightPricer;

    FlightSearcher() {
        this.euroFlightPricer = new EuroFlightPricer();
    }

    Collection<Flight> searchFlights(FlightSearchRequest
flightSearchRequest) {
        ...
    }
}
```

It is clear to see that the `FlightSearcher` components depend on `EuroFlightPricer`. As easily inferred from the name of the `EuroFlightPricer` component, it handles and returns prices in euros. Without blaming the hard-working development team that was under pressure to deliver this feature as quickly as possible to ensure the company's commercial success, it is clear that hardcoding this dependency is not a wise long-term choice. Certainly, ensuring simplicity and readability of the code is guaranteed (for example, there is no need to provide any parameters for the constructor). However, if we were to use another currency or any other logic for calculations in the future, we would need to modify the existing code. The solution is to inject the dependency from the outside:

```
class FlightSearcher{
    private final FlightPricer flightPricer;

    FlightSearcher(FlightPricer flightPricer){
        this.flightPricer = flightPricer;
    }

    Collection<Flight> searchFlights(FlightSearchRequest
flightSearchRequest){
        ...
    }
}
```

It is crucial to note that FlightSearcher now depends on an interface. We will use, in fact, a specific implementation of the FlightPricer interface intended just to handle the euro currency:

```
class EuroFlightPricer implements FlightPricer{
    ...
    @Override
    Collection<Price> getPrices() { ... }

    @Override
    Collection<Discount> getDiscounts() { ... }
}
```

With dependency injection, we can easily reconfigure the FlightSearcher class. This is possible because all the different pricer classes implement the same FlightPricer interface, allowing the FlightSearcher class to depend on it. This means we can use any implementation of FlightPricer, making the code more flexible and adaptable.

This leads to a general technique for making code more modular and adaptable: if we depend on a class that implements an interface with the needed functionality, it's usually better to depend on the interface itself instead of the specific class.

Law of Demeter

The **Law of Demeter**, also known as the principle of least knowledge and sometimes abbreviated as **LoD**, is a software design guideline that promotes loose coupling and encapsulation. According to this principle, an object should have limited knowledge about other objects and should only interact with its immediate neighbors. Let's see some applications of this principle:

- **Avoid chaining method calls excessively**: Instead of accessing methods of multiple objects in a single chain, limit the number of method invocations to maintain loose coupling.

```
// Non-compliant
String result = object1.getObject2()
    .getObject3().getObject4().getValue();
```

While this code works, it could be problematic for several reasons. Firstly, it assumes that each method call will successfully return a non-null object, otherwise, it may encounter a `NullPointerException`. Additionally, it tightly couples the code to the specific structure of the object hierarchy. If the structure changes in the future, this code will need to be modified accordingly.

```
// Compliant
Object2 object2 = object1.getObject2();
Object3 object3 = object2.getObject3();
Object4 object4 = object3.getObject4();
String result = object4.getValue();
```

In this version, the nested object hierarchy is traversed step by step, and each intermediate object is stored in a separate variable. This approach allows for better readability, improved error handling (it would be possible to check for null values), and flexibility in case the structure of the object hierarchy changes.

- **Don't expose the internals of an object by returning references to internal objects**: Instead, provide high-level methods that encapsulate the required functionality. For example, let's suppose we must retrieve all the books from a warehouse that stores several types of goods:

```
// Non-compliant
public List<Item> getItems() {
    return warehouse.getItems();
}
```

This code is technically OK, but the caller is forced to retrieve all the items and then filter to keep only the books. This is unpleasant for several reasons: we query the `Warehouse` for all of the items, but we only need books; the caller must increase its complexity to filter the items; we must expose the internal structure of `Item` to let the client get the `Type` of the `Item` itself, so that it can apply filtering. We're producing, above all else, strong couplings.

```
// Compliant
public List<Item> getItems(String itemCategory) {
    return warehouse.getItemsByCategory(itemCategory);
}
```

In this way, we don't let the client do all the filtering and we only enquire in the warehouse for books. We are not forced to expose the type of the `Item`, because the client just asked for a given category. We should optimize even more this code, for example returning a `Book` class instead of `Item`, but the purpose was just to provide an example for the internal structure exposure, so we'll stop here for now.

- **Avoid passing objects further than necessary as method arguments**: If an object requires access to another object, provide only the necessary information or dependencies:

```
// Non-compliant
public void processOrder(Order order) {
    shippingService.shipOrder(order);
}
```

In this code, the shipOrder method receives all of the order, while it needs only the items of the order itself. It would be better to change the shipOrder signature so that it takes only them.

```
// Compliant
public void processOrder(Order order) {
    shippingService.shipOrder(order.getItems());
}
```

Now, we provide to shipOrder only the necessary information.

It can't be said that the entire developer community fully agrees with the Law of Demeter (refer to the Further reading section), so much so that some think it should be called the *suggestion* of Demeter.

Data cohesion (make related data work together)

Classes help us organize things, but it can become problematic if we group too many things together in a single class. We should be careful about this, but at the same time, we shouldn't forget the benefits of grouping things together when it makes sense.

Sometimes, certain pieces of data are naturally related to each other, and our code needs to handle them together. In such cases, it makes sense to group them into a class or a similar structure. By doing this, our code can focus on the overall concept that the group of items represents, rather than dealing with specific details all the time. This approach promotes modularity in our code and allows changes in requirements to be isolated more easily.

An example of related data grouping is the combination of price and currency. In many applications, when dealing with financial transactions or monetary values, it is essential to consider both the price amount and the currency in which it is expressed.

By grouping the price and currency together into a class or a data structure, we can conveniently handle these related pieces of information as a single unit. This allows us to perform calculations, conversions, and other operations on the price while ensuring that the corresponding currency is correctly accounted for.

For instance, we can create a Price class that encapsulates the price value and the currency code. This class would provide methods to perform arithmetic operations and currency conversions and enforce consistency between the price and currency (and thus, the logic would all be in one place, behaving as a single source of truth).

Another example of related data grouping could involve latitude and longitude coordinates. When working with location-based applications or mapping systems, latitude and longitude values are often used together to specify a specific point on the Earth's surface. By grouping latitude and longitude into a class or a data structure (simply put: `Point`) and encapsulating the latitude and longitude values, we can conveniently handle and manipulate geographic coordinates as a cohesive unit. And again, we could perform various operations such as distance calculations, mapping functionalities, or finding nearby locations (actually, many libraries that deal with geographical calculation do exactly this).

Don't leak implementation details in the return type

In order to keep things organized and easy to work with, it's important to make sure that each layer of abstraction is clean and doesn't reveal how things are implemented under the hood. When implementation details are leaked, it can expose information about lower layers in the code and make it really tough to make changes or customize things later on. One common way this happens is when the code returns a type that's tightly connected to those specific details.

In our hypothetical flight search system, let's consider the scenario where we depend on external suppliers through traditional web service calls. Due to legal requirements, we are obligated to retain all the requests and responses for a specific duration. To address this, we have implemented a service within our code base that handles the storage of these records. We use a cloud storage system, referred to as SkyVault, for this purpose:

```
class PayloadStorageService{
    public SkyVaultClientResponse upload(Payload payload){
    … }
}
```

As we can see, the class spills the beans about using `SkyVault` as our storage service, and it binds the client to this choice. This makes it super hard to change things if we ever want to switch to a different storage service, use a database, or go for any other type of data storage. Changing the code would be very difficult.

One solution to this problem could be to abstract the response in a very trivial way:

```
class PayloadStorageService{
    public UploadResponse upload(Payload payload){ … }
}
```

Besides the return type, there are cases where the implementation is overly visible, creating a tight connection between library or service users and the service itself. For example, the implementation complexities of external systems are exposed instead of being simplified and pushed up to the caller level:

```
class PayloadStorageService{
    public boolean exists(Payload payload) { … }
    public UploadResponse overWrite(Payload payload) { … }
```

```
        public UploadResponse upload(Payload payload) { … }
        …
    }
```

In this case, the client needs to first check if the payload `exists` before calling the `upload` method. If it does exist, they have to use the `overWrite` method instead. This extra step adds unnecessary complexity for the client. It would have been better if this complexity was handled internally within the method itself (unless, of course, overwriting an existing file is somehow important to our specific situation).

Good code is reusable

As engineers, we often solve big problems by breaking them down into smaller ones (the good old *divide et impera*). And guess what? We keep running into the same small problems over and over again across different projects. So, if we or other engineers have already figured out a solution to one of these recurring problems, it just makes sense to reuse it. It saves us time and reduces the chances of introducing bugs because we know the solution has already been tried and tested.

The concept of reusability is closely tied to two key practices: establishing clear layers of abstraction and developing modular code. By implementing clean layers of abstraction and modularizing our code, we naturally break down solutions to subproblems into separate code components that are loosely interconnected. This approach significantly enhances the ease and safety of code reuse and generalization.

Don't make assumptions while writing your code

Don't make assumptions is a good piece of advice for life in general – but I don't want to be your life coach here, so don't worry.

There is no specific definition for an assumption, but I can provide you with a recent example I encountered. Imagine you are responsible for managing an e-commerce system and need to maintain records of purchases. Each purchase is characterized by a set of properties, and each purchase has a unique identifier called the **ID**. It is important to note that this ID is a numeric value that increases sequentially. For instance, if a purchase has ID x, the subsequent purchase will be identified as $x+1$, and so on.

Alongside the purchase management system, there is a typical component found in most companies called a reporting system (in my mind, I can hear a horse neighing, as in the movie *Frankenstein Junior*). This reporting system relies on determining the relative recency of purchases. The logical basis for this comparison is typically a date field such as `created_on` or a similar attribute. However, the reporting system in this case makes the assumption that the ordering of purchases is solely dependent on the `id` field. It assumes that the lower the ID, the more recent the purchase.

Now, let's consider a scenario where the maintainers of the purchase management system needed to migrate data. It became convenient for them to change the ID generation process to use random alphanumeric strings instead of numeric increments. Consequently, the reporting system, which had assumed that the IDs were numerical and sequentially incremental, ceased to function correctly.

Assumptions can lead to bugs when code is reused because the reused code may rely on certain conditions or behaviors that are not met or consistent in the new context. These bugs may kick in many different ways, including the following:

- **Contextual differences**: When code is reused in a different context or environment, the assumptions made during the original implementation may not hold true anymore. The underlying dependencies, data structures, or system configurations might be different, causing the code to behave unexpectedly or produce incorrect results.

- **Implicit dependencies**: Reused code may have implicit dependencies on external factors, such as specific data formats, database schemas, or API responses. If these dependencies are not properly understood or communicated, using the code in a different context can result in compatibility issues and unexpected failures.

- **Assumed constraints**: The reused code might make assumptions about the limitations or constraints of the original system. These assumptions could include factors like data size, frequency of operations, or expected usage patterns. If these constraints are exceeded or not satisfied in the new context, the reused code may not handle the situations correctly, leading to bugs or system failures.

- **Compatibility issues**: Code reuse often involves integrating different components or libraries. If the reused code relies on specific versions or configurations of these components, it may not work as intended when used with different versions or alternative implementations. Incompatible interactions between reused code and other components can introduce bugs or cause system instability.

- **Limited validation**: Assumptions may not have been thoroughly validated during the original implementation. When code is reused, there is a risk that the assumptions were only valid in the original use case but not in other scenarios. Insufficient validation of assumptions can result in bugs that arise when the code is reused in a different context.

If you make assumptions, identify them clearly

I am a man who lives by his own contradictions, and so now I tell you: making assumptions is crucial! The important thing is to do it at the right time, in the right amount, and for the right things. For example, when we find ourselves working on a completely unfamiliar code base, it is vital to make assumptions; otherwise, we would be navigating through every single class, every single line, searching for answers to our countless questions. Another example is debugging: when it comes to fixing bugs, start by making lots of assumptions, especially if you're familiar with the code. Trust your gut feeling. Most of the time, when someone starts explaining the problem to you, you will already know where the bug is hiding. Also, when creating new code, assumptions can be crucial in order to build quickly and effectively. Otherwise, we may end up stuck trying to create code to handle every possible use case, even the ones that are not going to happen.

At times, making assumptions becomes necessary or simplifies the code significantly, outweighing any drawbacks. However, when we make assumptions in our code, it's crucial to remember that other engineers might not be aware of them. To prevent them from inadvertently being affected by our assumptions, we need to enforce them. There are generally two approaches we can adopt to achieve this:

- **Making the assumption "impossible to break"**: If we can structure the code in such a way that it won't compile if an assumption is violated, we ensure that the assumption always remains valid. For example, if a class must be instantiated or initialized in a certain way, keep its constructor private and expose a `create()` method instead.

- **Utilizing an error-signaling technique**: If it's not feasible to make the assumption foolproof, we can implement code that detects when the assumption is violated and employs an error-signaling technique to quickly halt the execution.

If you would like to look more deeply into these aspects, I recommend the book by Tom Long listed in the *Further reading* section.

So far, we've learned what makes code good, the most important things for which are readability and reliability. Good code should be easy to understand and hard to mess up. It's modular, like a well-built piece of furniture that you can use over and over again. Of course, there's some room for debate and personal preference, but I think we can mostly agree on these points. Now, let's move on to another important way to create good code: **Clean Code**.

Clean Code

The most well-known book on Clean Code is called *Clean Code* by Robert C. Martin. Surprisingly, even Martin himself struggles to come up with a single definition for Clean Code. It seems like there are multiple definitions floating around among us developers. In fact, in his book, Martin asks several developers to provide their own "custom" definitions, and he includes all of them so that we can create our own understanding of what Clean Code means.

Clean Code is all about writing code that's easy to understand and follows a logical and disciplined approach. The main goal is to create software efficiently and effectively while ensuring that the code is readable, adaptable, expandable, and easy to maintain.

You could argue that this definition is not objective, and you would be right! For example, "*readable*" is something very personal (and depends also on the seniority and the skillset of those who are approaching the code). More often than you might think, we judge code by our guts. Can I understand it? Then it's readable! Rephrasing from the "*Fundamental Theorem of Readability*" book by Bowsell and Foucher: *code should be crafted in a way that reduces the amount of time someone else would need to comprehend it.*

And when we use the word "*understand*," we set a very high standard. To truly comprehend your code, someone should possess the ability to make modifications, identify bugs, and grasp how it interacts with the rest of your code base. Clean Code is not a set of laws or a set of rules; it is an attitude, a mindset that we all should follow.

As already mentioned, refactoring and clean code are strictly related, since they both aim to improve the quality and maintainability of software.

Why Clean Code?

Exactly as happens with refactoring, when I talk about Clean Code at work to people who don't have a technical background, the reactions vary, but not so much: they range from yawning to rolling their eyes, from looking down to impatient gestures. They perceive someone talking about incomprehensible topics to them, or proposing "changing something that works" or "writing code well," as if there was something other than code that either works or doesn't work (and – let's face it – considering practices such as refactoring as a waste of time and money).

Things such as documentation and comments are definitely important (and we'll get there), but the most crucial thing that should always speak for itself is your code. Write your code as if you're talking in everyday language. Make it understandable not just for now, but also for yourself and others in the future. Remember that a big part of our job is maintenance (which might not be fun, but it's a reality). When your code can speak for itself, it not only improves your technical skills but also enhances the quality of your code. Being able to communicate clearly about your code allows you to seek help and receive valuable suggestions for improvement. Clean code doesn't magically appear; it requires dedicated effort to express your intentions effectively. Aim to write self-explanatory code, organized and structured, so that you don't have to litter it with excessive comments to explain its purpose.

I've already mentioned that your code will be read by someone else, whether it's another person or even yourself. This highlights the need to write Clean Code, as it benefits teamwork. It takes less time to understand what the code does, fix it when issues arise, and add new features. Clean Code promotes code reusability and makes you a more efficient programmer; it facilitates easier and faster maintenance, as it is easier to understand, debug, and modify when needed. Simply put, it makes the team faster. You can use this argument (this *fact*) when a colleague or manager accuses you of wasting time by being picky about the code!

One often underestimated aspect of writing clean code is feeling comfortable with what you're doing. Imagine having to ask someone for help and showing them something messy and shaky, something that is hard to understand and complicated to explain. It would be embarrassing. Moreover, in my opinion, working on a clean project boosts morale. You have the satisfaction of doing things properly, almost something beautiful, you could say. It's what a craftsman should do (forgive the clichéd metaphor). We're not just button pushers; we're artisans. Let's always write code as if we were going to show it to someone else (and actually showing it to someone else, through peer reviews or pair programming, really helps—we'll come on to that later). Clean Code just works better, hence the satisfaction is not only when people look at your code, but also when they use the services it provides and they work properly.

If you think your main job as a programmer is writing code, think again. You actually spend more time reading code, hunting down bugs, identifying issues, and figuring out solutions. Clean Code simplifies all of these tasks. One thing every programmer can unanimously agree on is that Clean Code is undeniably better.

Some principles of Clean Code

Trying to explain Clean Code in its entirety would take a whole book, and guess what? It already exists courtesy of Uncle Bob, Robert C. Martin. However, I do think it would be helpful to provide you with some highlights, especially if you're new to this topic. We'll delve deeper into some of these aspects later on.

KISS – Keep things as simple as possible

KISS (short for **Keep It Simple, Stupid** or **Keep It Stupid-Simple**, depending on how bold you want to be) is one of the oldest rules in clean code. It urges programmers to keep their code as simple as possible. Avoid making things needlessly complicated. In the world of programming, there's never just one way to solve a problem. You can accomplish a task using different languages and various commands. Programmers who embrace the KISS principle always ask themselves if there's a simpler way to tackle a specific problem.

DRY – Avoid repetition

One of the main functions of computer science is to come up with cool acronyms. **DRY** (short for **Don't Repeat Yourself**) is one of them. It's like a more specific version of KISS, emphasizing that functions in Clean Code should do one thing only (and do it well). It's worth noting that the opposite of DRY code is called **WET**, which stands for **We Enjoy Typing** or **Write Everything Twice**.

A very trivial WET code example is the following:

```
public class WETExample {
    public static void main(String[] args) {
        String name = "John";
        System.out.println("Hello, " + name + "!");
        // Some other code...
        System.out.println("Hello, " + name + "!");
    }
}
```

As you can see, in this code, there are many lines that are basically the same. We must try to avoid these repetitions; to continue with the wordplay, we must *dry* this *wet* code.

In its DRY version, the preceding code becomes the following, with no surprises:

```
public class DRYExample {
    public static void main(String[] args) {
        String name = "John";
        greetUser(name);
        // Some other code...
        greetUser(name);
    }

    public static void greetUser(String name) {
        System.out.println("Hello, " + name + "!");
    }
}
```

In the DRY version, we simply isolated the repeated code in a single method. This example was very simple because the repeated line was just a one-line `sysout`, but this was just to explain the concept: imagine how it would be if there were many lines. And that will not only create clean, more readable code but will also reduce the possibility of bugs sneaking in (and security issues, as well).

YAGNI – delete what's useless

The Clean Code principle **YAGNI** (short for **You Aren't Gonna Need It**) follows this simple idea: a developer should only add extra functionality to code when it's actually needed. YAGNI is closely associated with Agile software development approaches. According to the YAGNI principle, instead of starting with a grand plan, you should build the software architecture in small increments to address problems as they arise. This allows for dynamic and individualized problem-solving. Clean Code is achieved when the underlying problem is solved efficiently without unnecessary bells and whistles.

Code should be readable, not concise

Code needs to do its job and be interpreted correctly by the machine. But it's not just the machine that needs to understand it—other developers should be able to comprehend the code too, especially in collaborative projects. That's why readability is always prioritized over brevity in software development. Writing concise code is pointless if it becomes incomprehensible to others. A prime example of producing clean and readable code lies in variable naming.

A variable should have a name that clearly conveys its purpose. Take the following variable, for instance, which is cryptic without the requisite background knowledge and explanation:

```
int x;
```

But also, this somewhat more precisely named variable still leaves some doubt:

```
int elapsed;
```

It should be elapsed... time, OK, but what's the measurement unit? By using the following name for the same variable, its purpose becomes evident:

```
int elapsedTimeInMillis;
```

Our personal opinion on the length of variable names is that I prefer them to be longer rather than too short. It would be ideal to find a middle ground, but it's not always possible. Between the two extremes, I lean towards longer names as they enhance readability. However, it's important to note that lengthy names can sometimes indicate underlying issues.

To summarize, we quickly reviewed what Clean Code is. There are entire books, online courses, and company workshops dedicated to this topic... in short, there is a whole world around it, and I don't expect these few lines to cover everything. My invitation, as usual, is to delve into it as much as possible. There are still people out there who consider Clean Code as an accessory, something that wastes time because the code works even when it's not clean. I hope I conveyed the concept that things don't work that way and that good and clean code brings numerous advantages with relatively low effort if approached methodically. In the next section, we will add another adjective to our code: after good and clean, we will see what is meant by *SOLID* code!

Write SOLID code

If there's one thing the software engineering community excels at, it's coming up with cool acronyms! That's exactly what Michael Feathers did when he took inspiration from a paper by the ever-present Robert C. Martin (aka Uncle Bob) and came up with the term **SOLID principles**. In his essay, Martin recognized that software evolves and gets more complicated over time. But without good design principles, he warned that software becomes rigid, fragile, and hard to work with. That's where the SOLID principles come in—they were created to tackle these issues head-on and make software development easier and more flexible.

The acronym SOLID represents five fundamental design principles:

- **Single Responsibility Principle (SRP)**
- Open-closed principle
- Liskov substitution principle
- Interface segregation principle
- Dependency inversion principle

These principles are widely adopted by software engineers and offer significant advantages for developers. Please note that, unlike what is explained in the other sections, the SOLID principles apply only to object-oriented languages.

Single responsibility principle

The essence of the SRP, as eloquently stated by Robert Martin, is that "*a class should have one, and only one, reason to change.*" By adhering to this principle, each class focuses on a specific task, ensuring that every class, module, or component in the software system has a clear responsibility. In simpler terms, each class should address a single problem.

The single responsibility principle is a fundamental concept already employed by most developers when writing code. It can be applied to various levels, such as classes, software components, or microservices.

By following this principle, several benefits arise: code becomes easier to test and maintain, software implementation becomes more straightforward, and it helps prevent unexpected side effects when making future changes.

Maybe it's worth providing an example:

```
public class User {
    private String username;
    private String password;
    public User(String username, String password) {
        this.username = username;
        this.password = password;
    }
}

public class UserManager {
    public void saveUserToDatabase() {
        // Code to save the user to the database
        // This method is responsible for persistence
    }
    public void sendEmailToUser(String message) {
        // Code to send an email to the user
        // This method is responsible for email sending
    }
}
```

In this example, the `UserManager` class violates the SRP by having two distinct responsibilities: saving the user to the database and sending emails to the user. Ideally, each class should have only one responsibility.

To address the SRP violation, we can refactor the code by separating the concerns into different classes. Here's a possible refactoring:

```
public class User {
    private String username;
    private String password;
```

```
    public User(String username, String password) {
        this.username = username;
        this.password = password;
    }
}

public class UserRepository {
    public void saveUserToDatabase(User user) {
        // Code to save the user to the database
    }
}

public class EmailService {
    public void sendEmailToUser(User user, String message){
        // Code to send an email to the user
    }
}
```

In this refactored code, the UserRepository class is responsible for handling persistence logic, while the EmailService class handles email communication. By separating these concerns into different classes, we adhere to the SRP and make the code more maintainable and flexible.

Open-closed principle

The concept behind the open-closed principle is that when new functionality needs to be added, it's preferable to extend existing, well-tested classes rather than modify them. Making changes to classes can introduce issues or bugs. The goal is to be able to enhance a class's behavior without altering its original implementation.

Adhering to this principle is crucial for developing code that is easily maintainable and adaptable. A class follows the open-closed principle if it satisfies the following conditions:

- **Open for extension**: The class's behavior can be extended or augmented

- **Closed for modification**: The source code of the class remains unchanged and is not directly modified

At first glance, these two criteria might appear contradictory, but as you become more familiar with the principle, you'll realize that it's not as complex as it initially seems.

To follow these principles and make sure your class can be easily extended without changing the code, you need to use abstractions. Inheritance or interfaces that allow for different implementations are commonly used to meet this requirement. No matter which method you choose, it's important to stick to this principle so that your code remains easy to maintain and update.

Let's say you work for a travel e-commerce company that sells various modes of transportation. With a focus on environmental sustainability, you decide to display the CO2 emissions for each mode of transport. Currently, you handle airplanes and trains.

We decided to have the following interface and classes:

```
public interface Co2Calculator{
    Integer calculateCo2Tons();
}


public class AirplaneCo2Calculator implements
    Co2Calculator{
    @Override
    public Integer calculateCo2Tons(){
        //...calculates...
    }
}


public class TrainCo2Calculator implements Co2Calculator{
    @Override
    public Integer calculateCo2Tons(){
        //...calculates...
    }
}
```

We have two implementations of `Co2Calculator`, one used for planes and one for trains. Each of them implements, of course, the same method. This interface would be used in another class – let's call it `EmissionCalculator`, in this way:

```
public class EmissionCalculator {
    public Integer calculateEmissions(Co2Calculator
        calculator) {
            return calculator.calculateCo2Tons();
    }
}
```

Should we decide to introduce a new transportation mode, for example, Bus, it would be easy to do:

```
public class BusCo2Calculator implements Co2Calculator{
    @Override
    public Integer calculateCo2Tons(){
        //...calculates...
    }
}
```

None of the existing code has been touched. Our `EmissionCalculator` class doesn't need to implement new logic when we introduce a new transportation mode.

Liskov substitution principle

Among the five SOLID principles, the Liskov substitution principle can be challenging to grasp. In essence, this principle states that any derived class should be capable of replacing its parent class without causing any issues. Simply put, if class *A* is a subtype of class *B*, we should be able to replace *B* with *A* without disrupting the behavior of our program.

For a very trivial example, let's suppose we must model vehicles (for simplicity, I'm omitting constructors, getters, and setters):

```java
public class Vehicle {
    public void startEngine();
}

public class Airplane extends Vehicle {
    private AirplaneEngine engine;

    @Override
    public void startEngine(){
        engine.start();
    }
}

public class Train extends Vehicle {
    private TrainEngine engine;

    @Override
    public void startEngine(){
        engine.start();
    }
}
```

Introducing a new `Bicycle` entity and making it extend the `Vehicle` class would violate the principle:

```java
public class Bicycle extends Vehicle {

    @Override
    public void startEngine(){
        throw new UnsupportedOperationException(
            "Bicycles do not have engines!");
    }
}
```

In this code, we are forced to implement the method of the `Vehicle` interface, but we are also unable to do it because, you know, bicycles have no engine! So we're forced to cause disruption, for example, throwing an exception. We would not be able to replace a vehicle with a bike without disrupting the behavior of our program, violating the Liskov principle.

Interface segregation principle

The main idea behind the **Interface Segregation Principle** (**ISP**) is to have many small interfaces rather than a few big ones. According to Martin, "*Make fine grained interfaces that are client-specific. Clients should not be forced to implement interfaces they do not use.*"

For software engineers, this means you shouldn't just add new methods to an existing interface. Instead, start fresh and build new interfaces tailored to each client's needs. Using smaller interfaces encourages composition over inheritance and promotes loose coupling. If an interface is too big, it's better to break it down into smaller ones. That way, classes implementing those interfaces just have to worry about the methods they actually care about.

Let's suppose we have the usual transportation selling system, and we have the following interface:

```
public interface FlightManager {
    Long calculateDistance();
    Long calculateEmissions();
    Double calculatePrice();
}
```

This interface seems pretty big, and the fact that its name ends with "*manager*" is too generic and could be a problem (because it lacks specificity and doesn't provide clear information about the responsibilities or purpose of the class or component). It covers a lot of different things. If you were to implement it in a class, you'd have to handle a bunch of different stuff, each with its own level of importance.

What about splitting the `FlightManager` interface into three specific "calculators", one for each concern?

```
public interface FlightDistanceCalculator {
    Long calculateDistance();
}

public interface FlightEmissionCalculator {
    Long calculateEmissions();
}

public interface FlightPriceCalculator {
    Double calculatePrice();
}
```

By doing this, we can have greater flexibility in deciding which classes will implement specific interfaces:

```
public class FlightStatisticsManager implements
    FlightDistanceCalculator, FlightEmissionsCalculator {
    public Long calculateDistance() {
        //implementation here
    }

    public Long calculateEmissions () {
        //implementation here
    }
}

public class FlightPricer implements FlightPriceCalculator{
    public Double calculatePrice() {
        //implementation here
    }
}
```

Now, each specific class only implements the required method(s) and isn't aware of anything that is not its particular concern.

Dependency inversion principle

This principle helps separate software components. Basically, the dependency inversion principle suggests that developers should "*depend on general concepts, not specific implementations.*" Martin also explains that "*higher-level modules should not rely on lower-level modules. Both should rely on abstract concepts.*" Additionally, "*abstract concepts should not rely on specific details. Details should rely on abstract concepts.*"

A common approach to following this principle is to use a dependency inversion pattern, but that's not the only way to achieve it.

To test this principle, let's suppose we have a (simplified) LocationCatalog class, which handles all of the queries about locations in a system. This class takes the "location dictionary" from a database repository:

```
public class LocationCatalog {
    private final LocationDatabaseRepository
        locationRepository;

    public LocationCatalog() {
        this.locationRepository = new
            LocationDatabaseRepository();
    }
}
```

This code will function correctly, allowing us to utilize `LocationDatabaseRepository` without limitations in our `LocationCatalog` class.

So everything's OK now? Not quite. There's an issue, and it lies in tightly coupling these three classes together when declaring `locationRepository` with the new `LocationDatabaseRepository` class.

This not only makes it difficult to test our `LocationCatalog` class, but it also eliminates the possibility of easily swapping out the `LocationDatabaseRepository` class for a different one if needed.

To address this, let's decouple our location manager from `LocationDatabaseRepository` by introducing a more generic `LocationRepository` interface and incorporating it into our class.

```
public interface LocationRepository{ }

public class LocationCatalog{
    private final LocationRepository locationRepository;

    public LocationCatalog (LocationRepository
        locationRepository) {
        this. locationRepository = locationRepository;
    }
}
```

We have successfully eliminated the dependency and now have the freedom to choose any source for our location, be it a file, an external service, or a mocked implementation (particularly useful for testing purposes).

Now we have a good foundation in writing good code: we know what it is, we know about Clean Code, and we know that good code is also SOLID code. Next, let's consider the reliability of code and the fact that reliable code does not produce unwanted effects, also known as side effects.

Side effects and mutability

When something is immutable, it means its *state* can't be changed once it's created. Understanding why immutability is a good thing involves recognizing the problems that can arise from its opposite—mutability.

There are several downsides to having mutable objects or, in general, in being forced to handle mutability (and thus, handling objects' state).

A mutable class that has setup functions can easily be misconfigured, leading to an invalid state; this is a sort of addendum (a *spin-off*) to what we said before ("*good code is hard to misuse*"). If you allow a class to have some kind of really detailed and complicated setup functions, it will be more likely to misuse it, ending up with a wrong or invalid configuration that will end in some malfunctioning in your code.

Another big issue with mutable objects arises when you think about thread safety, a critical concern in multi-threaded or parallel programming because multiple threads can access and modify shared data simultaneously. For more information about what thread safety is, there's an entry in the *Further reading* section. Mutable objects are not thread-safe because they can be modified by multiple threads concurrently without proper synchronization, leading to unpredictable and potentially incorrect behavior.

However the real problem with mutability occurs when a function messes with the input parameters. It's like lending something to a friend. When you lend something, you don't want it to get messed up because you might need it later or want to lend it to someone else (think of a book, a bike, or your favorite Batman action figure). That function holds important information that the function needs, but you might still need it for other things after the function is done.

If a function starts changing the input parameter, it's like scratching your bike or ruining your Batman action figure. Usually, when you pass an object to a function, you expect it to be borrowed and returned as it is. But if the function goes ahead and messes with it, that's not cool. Changing an input parameter is a side effect because it affects something outside the function itself. Typically, functions take inputs through parameters and give back results through return values.

For most engineers, modifying an input parameter is an unexpected side effect that can lead to surprises and confusion. So, it's best to avoid messing with borrowed objects and stick to the convention of using parameters for inputs and return values for results.

A good way to make code non-misusable is to use immutable objects. In Java specifically, a typical immutable object would contain just the fields (with the final modifier), a constructor, and – optionally – the getters:

```java
public class Student {
    private final String name;
    private final String surname;

    public Student(String name, String surname) {
        this.name = name;
        this.surname = surname;
    }

    public String getName() {
        return name;
    }

    public String getSurname() {
        return surname;
    }

    //... toString(), hashCode(), equals(), etc...
}
```

This object is indeed immutable, and it follows a common pattern for implementing immutability. All of its properties are declared as `final`, meaning they cannot be modified after they are initialized. The properties are typically declared in a constructor, which may or may not require all of these parameters, depending on the specific requirements. This object does not provide setter methods, as attempting to do so would result in a compilation error due to the `final` fields. However, it does provide getters for accessing the property values, but this can vary depending on your specific needs. It should be evident that once this object is created, it cannot be modified.

Of course, the same aim can be achieved in a much simpler way using a Java record (introduced in **Java 14**), but that would be a bit out of scope here. The goal is to promote immutability; this implementation is just an example. There's also the builder pattern that we'll introduce in the next section.

Another really common example in Java is the `String` class. A `String` object always represents the same string. Since `String` is immutable, once created, a `String` object always has the same value. To add something to the end of a `String`, you have to create a new `String` object:

```
String s = "a"; // Creates a String object with the value
    "a"
s = s.concat("b"); // Creates a new String object with the
    value "ab"
// The below two operations also result in the creation of
    new String objects:
// s += "b";
// s = s + "b";
```

In general, to make a class immutable, follow these rules:

- Don't provide any methods that modify the state of your object (aka mutators).
- Ensure that the class can't be extended (this is mostly done by making it `final`).
- Make all fields `final` and `private`.
- Ensure exclusive access to any mutable components: it can happen that a field of your class is defined as a mutable object. In this case, be sure that a client cannot obtain references to this object. Initialize it *inside* your class and make defensive copies in constructors and accessors.

You could argue: OK, but I just have that one use case in which I *must* create an object and then change it. A typical example is when you have to create an object and fill its fields in different steps. My suggestion here is to use the builder pattern instead.

The builder pattern

A builder is a design pattern commonly used in object-oriented programming to construct complex objects step by step. It provides a flexible and readable way to create objects with multiple optional parameters or configurations. The builder pattern separates the construction of an object from its representation, allowing the same construction process to create different representations of the object. It provides a clear and intuitive API for constructing objects by providing methods to set values for various properties or parameters. Typically, a builder class is created for each complex object, and it contains methods to set individual properties or configurations of the object. The builder accumulates these settings and finally constructs the object when requested. This approach allows for more readable and maintainable code, especially when dealing with objects that have many optional parameters or configurations. It promotes the idea of *fluent* or chainable method calls, where each method returns the builder instance itself, allowing for a more concise and readable construction syntax.

Let's use a builder to create a "student":

```
public class StudentBuilder {
    private String name;
    private String surname;

    public StudentBuilder() {
        // Default constructor
    }

    public StudentBuilder withName(String name) {
        this.name = name;
        return this;
    }

    public StudentBuilder withSurname(String surname) {
        this.surname = surname;
        return this;
    }

    public Student build() {
        return new Student(name, surname);
    }
}
```

The class provides a default constructor, which doesn't take any parameters. The StudentBuilder class also provides two setter-like methods: withName(String name) and withSurname(String surname). These methods allow setting the name and surname properties of the student, respectively. Each setter-like method updates the corresponding property of the builder instance and returns the builder object itself (this) to support method chaining. Finally, the build() method is used to construct and return a new `Student` object using the values set in the builder. It creates a new `Student` instance with the name and surname obtained from the builder and returns the constructed object. With this builder class, you can construct a `Student` object step by step, setting the name and surname values as needed. Here's an example:

```
Student student = new StudentBuilder()
    .withName("John")
    .withSurname("Doe")
    .build();
```

This code creates a new `Student` object with the name `"John"` and surname `"Doe"` using the builder pattern. By chaining the `withName()` and `withSurname()` methods, you can set the desired values for the name and surname properties, respectively. Finally, the `build()` method constructs and returns the `Student` object with the provided values.

This might seem a bit inconsistent with the message we provided earlier, the one regarding long chains of calls. However, in my opinion, this is a special case where we are simply constructing an object: there is no logic, the return type is always the same, and the alternatives would be equally complex, or worse – a long sequence of "set" methods and/or a constructor with many parameters.

The builder can be implemented in slightly different ways, and what's more, it can be automated. You have the option to use IDE plugins or metaprogramming libraries such as Lombok. We will discuss these alternatives later on in this book.

I hope that, up to this point, I have provided you with some small tools to help combat bad code; not an exhaustive list, but I hope to have at least sparked curiosity. Another thing I have always wondered is: why does bad code exist? Assuming it is not due to laziness or incompetence of individuals, let's quickly explore some contingent causes that contribute to the situation we are trying to address.

Causes of bad code

As I mentioned in the previous chapter, I don't have the intention of blaming those who write bad code. I myself have written bad code; it has happened in the past, it still happens, and it will happen again (I can already imagine my colleagues nodding as they read these lines!). In the vast majority of cases, those who write bad code do so without realizing it because we are human and can only handle a certain number of tasks at once. In our hearts, we have the desire to do a good job, something to be proud of, but in our minds, we have deadlines, and pressure, and we generally work within an ecosystem that we don't fully control. Very often, companies are complex systems that may have clear rules (for example, regarding the methodologies to follow), but they have to deal with an increasingly hectic world, with time-to-market pressures, and the need to compete fiercely. There's a way things should be and the way they actually are. As software engineers, we guide or support the work of the company and often find ourselves interacting with mentalities and needs that are very different from our own. Sometimes, the result is sacrificing quality and experiencing a bit of frustration. Almost always, this leads to having a bad code base. But why does this happen? If we could identify some common causes of bad code, maybe we'd be able to recognize them and avoid them.

Deadlines

This is definitely going to be a controversial point. For many, blaming deadlines as the cause of bad code is just an excuse to hide laziness or incompetence. It's not true that there's no time; it's just that you don't want to put in the effort to think and do things properly. In some cases, that may very well be true. Over the years, though, I've often observed – although I must say, not always and to a lesser extent as time goes on – a disconnect between management and engineers. There's often a tendency to "sell" the solution without paying much attention to how long it will actually take to implement it. As a result, developers end up not negotiating a deadline but simply being subjected to it. So they take shortcuts, maybe cut back on testing, documentation, and overall quality (violating some of the principles seen so far, such as keeping code readable or without repetitions).

On this matter, I'd advise you to take a look at what's called the *project management triangle*:

Figure 2.3 – The project management triangle

It's like an equilateral triangle with sides representing the **Scope**, **Cost**, and **Time** of a project. These three dimensions are interconnected, and changing one of them will affect the overall shape of the triangle, which represents the quality. Furthermore, since the triangle needs to remain equilateral, it's clear that modifying the available time will decrease the cost, and vice versa. By extending the time available, you can increase the project scope, but the costs will also go up accordingly. It's a neat metaphor for how projects, including software projects, work.

The Broken Window theory

Here's another thing to consider: the Broken Window theory. Philip Zimbardo, a psychologist from Stanford, did a very interesting study: he parked a car in a fancy neighborhood for a couple of days and just watched it. Surprisingly, nothing happened. He waited and waited, but nobody touched the car. Then, he decided to break a small window to see if things would change. Within just a few hours, the car was completely stripped; everything was gone – tires, wheels, electronics, steering wheel, seats, mats, even the engine. All that was left was a bare-bones car sitting on cinder blocks.

Now, the same kind of thing can happen with code. You start off with a clean situation; everything's looking good. But as soon as you introduce one bit of bad code, things can quickly go out of control. For instance, you ignore code duplication in a few places, leave inconsistent formatting, and tolerate inconsistent variable naming. Again, you can start adding code without the proper test coverage, or you avoid upgrading your project's dependencies due to fear of issues sneaking in.

Initially, these may seem like minor problems, and developers prioritize adding new features or fixing critical bugs instead. Other team members notice these neglected issues but also follow suit, assuming they are not a high priority. As developers, we're already making some mistakes, so why bother doing it right in this case? Taking shortcuts and doing things the easier, faster way seems tempting. As time goes on, more developers join the project, and the code base grows larger and more complex. The neglected issues start to accumulate, making the code harder to understand and maintain. The lack of consistent conventions leads to confusion, reduces code readability, and introduces errors. Additionally, because the existing issues were not addressed, developers may feel less motivated to maintain code quality. They might think, "If there are already duplicated code snippets, what harm can a few more do?". Eventually, the code base becomes a tangled mess of poorly organized, duplicated, and hard-to-read code. New developers joining the project struggle to make sense of it and find it increasingly difficult to introduce changes without inadvertently introducing bugs or breaking existing functionality.

It's like a snowball effect, and things can get pretty messy in no time. And this kind of mess can produce technical debt; you re-pay technical debt with slowness in developing new features.

No code review process

When we started programming, maybe back in school, it often happened that we did it alone. You wrote the code, tested it in some way, and that was it. The code and the design only needed to make sense to us and no one else.

When working in a team, it's a good idea to implement code review mechanisms. A **code review** is the process of reviewing and examining code to improve its quality, identify issues, and ensure adherence to standards – we'll delve into that in *Chapter 8*. Code reviews are also useful to make the code we write somewhat "consistent" and clear for all team members. When code reviews are absent, the code can become subject to personal preferences, may contain errors, or have room for improvement in terms of performance. Some people see the review process as a distraction from business activities; some developers see it as a hindrance to their own tasks. Sometimes, of course, even reviews cannot address particularly deep-rooted problems. However, they at least help identify major "issues" that may have slipped past the individual developer, who was focused on solving complex problems. It happens more often than you might think.

In *Chapter 8*, we will introduce the **Pair Programming** practice, which can be used as a substitute for code reviews.

Insufficient domain or technical knowledge

Sometimes, the reason behind bad code is simply that the people who worked on it were not aware of the application domain or the technologies being used. These are different aspects but somehow related.

When lacking domain knowledge, it's easy to misinterpret requirements or write the logic in the wrong place (maybe not knowing that it already exists elsewhere). The situation gets worse when the code is already messy, and we have to work on it without really knowing what we're doing. In this situation, even with the purest of intentions, removing an apparently unused if statement or changing how an object is created requires careful consideration (and adequate test coverage, something else we'll tackle later).

Knowledge gaps can also be purely technological. It may be that some of us are new and don't yet have a clear understanding of the technology stack. This often leads to overly complex solutions or, on the contrary, workarounds and hacks. It can happen that the developer lacks certain discipline and the habitual use of good practices that we've tried to explain in this chapter. These practices – contrary to what it may seem – don't exist to slow us down, but actually enable us to produce high-quality code quickly and consistently.

We have tried to investigate some of the most common causes of bad code. I realize that I have relied on my own experience to some extent, but I believe that some of the concepts expressed here are universal and worth considering, such as the Broken Window theory or the project management triangle. The next time a manager asks you to do something well and in less time, you will hopefully have an additional argument on your side!

Summary

Speaking of refactoring, it is crucial to understand what needs to be refactored; in other words, it is necessary to distinguish good code from bad code. In this chapter, we have seen what is typically meant by good code, providing an overview of its characteristics. When these characteristics are lacking, it is likely that refactoring is needed. When discussing good code, we must also talk about Clean Code; we addressed this topic and learned how to recognize it and, hopefully, write it. Good code is usually also SOLID code, and we briefly touched upon the meaning of that as well. Lastly, after understanding what good code is, we investigated some causes of bad code; the hope is that you will be alert if you find yourself in one of the described situations.

In the upcoming chapter, we'll address a set of warning signs—elements in your code that should alert you and prompt contemplation on refactoring your code.

Further reading

- mscharhag, *ISO 8601 durations in Java*: `https://www.mscharhag.com/java/iso8601-durations`

- Tom Long, *Good Code, Bad Code*, Manning

- *Stop calling it bad code*, by Joel Spolsky: `https://blog.pragmaticengineer.com/bad-code/`

- *The law of leaky abstraction*, by Joel Spolsky: `https://www.joelonsoftware.com/2002/11/11/the-law-of-leaky-abstractions/`

- **What does Clean Code mean?** `https://cogut.medium.com/what-does-clean-code-mean-2190e4aed818`

- Robert C Martin, *Clean Code*, Prentice-Hall 2009

- Robert C Martin, *Design Principles and Design Patterns*: `http://staff.cs.utu.fi/~jounsmed/doos_06/material/DesignPrinciplesAndPatterns.pdf`

- **What is thread safety?**: `https://en.wikipedia.org/wiki/Thread_safety`

- **The SOLID principles in pictures**: `https://medium.com/backticks-tildes/the-s-o-l-i-d-principles-in-pictures-b34ce2f1e898`

- *You should break the Law of Demeter*, by Ted Kaminski `https://www.tedinski.com/2018/12/18/the-law-of-demeter.html`

Part 2: Essence of Refactoring and Good Code

Going through code, especially old code, is a big part of a software developer's job. There are certain warning signs, like "red flags," that professionals should notice right away. Recognizing and avoiding these issues is an important skill, and in this section, we'll understand how to spot them.

Now that we've learned what refactoring is and why it's important, let's explore a crucial requirement. Refactoring isn't safe unless you have really good test coverage. We'll find out why having thorough tests is essential.

Next, how do you actually refactor your code? There are some common techniques that can be very helpful. We'll learn how to master them.

After that, we'll delve into metaprogramming. Instead of manually changing code, metaprogramming techniques can automatically analyze and refactor it. For example, metaprogramming can generate code, replace method calls, or dynamically modify class structures. This makes refactoring faster and less prone to errors by reducing the amount of manual work needed.

Lastly, we'll discuss static and dynamic analysis. Static analysis involves examining code without running it and identifying issues like code smells and security vulnerabilities. Dynamic analysis, on the other hand, involves analyzing code by running it, helping find performance bottlenecks and runtime issues like memory leaks.

This part has the following chapters:

- *Chapter 3, Code Smells*
- *Chapter 4, Testing*
- *Chapter 5, Refactoring Techniques*
- *Chapter 6, Metaprogramming*
- *Chapter 7, Static and Dynamic Analysis*

3
Code Smells

The title of this chapter should be self-explanatory or perhaps sounds disgusting, but I think it's important to explain what is meant by the term *code smell*. The sensation is similar to when you open the refrigerator and a strange odor hits your nose, something that shouldn't be there. A bad smell doesn't necessarily indicate a problem, but it's worth taking a look, just in case. There might be an issue, or there might not be, but ignoring it is not a good idea.

In our code base, it's the same. A code smell is a potential problem, a situation in the code that makes us wrinkle our noses. They are very tangible and observable situations, recurring patterns in our projects. They indicate that there is or could be something that needs to be fixed as soon as possible before the problem becomes even bigger. Just like bad code in general, smelly code can lead to widespread inefficiency, limited code extensibility, and comprehension, as well as performance issues and potential bugs.

We need to learn how to recognize and avoid code smells; it's much easier to produce them than one might think, given how absorbed we are in tasks and deadlines. The important thing is, once again, to take the time to review our work and identify potential problems, the bad smells that arise from our lines of code. Over time, with practice and experience, you'll build a mental compass that points out coding pitfalls like a seasoned treasure hunter unearthing hidden gems. Sometimes, it will guide you even before you've finished crafting your code.

There are plenty of code smells that have already been cataloged by our *developer ancestors*; I don't think it's appropriate to list them all here. I'll tell you about the ones that I believe are the most common to encounter and produce. The selection has been made based on purely subjective criteria, so feel free – in fact, I recommend it – to delve deeper into the *Further reading* section. Many of these code smells are related to **clean code** and the **SOLID principles**. If you happened to skip the previous chapter, it might be a good idea to go back and take a look.

We'll start with duplicated code, the nuisance of almost all code bases. It's often caused by the developer's temptation to meet deadlines by resorting to the ultimate shortcut: copy and paste. We'll then move on to long methods and large classes. It's truly disheartening when you encounter a bug on line number *4215* of a class, not because of the bug itself, but due to the humongous number of lines the class contains!

Then, I'll show you that `switch` statements can also be a problem when they are repeated; a typical situation that object-oriented programming can easily solve! When discussing object-oriented programming, why not represent the concepts of our domain through dedicated objects rather than rely on language primitives? There's an anti-pattern called **Primitive Obsession** and we'll tackle it.

In addition to large classes, there are classes or methods that heavily rely on the methods of others; in other words, they just can't mind their own business! We'll explore what **feature envy** methods are and how to address the potential harm they cause. We'll also discuss two anti-patterns closely related to code changes and intertwined with each other: **divergent change** and **Shotgun Surgery**. Depending on where and how many changes we need to make in our code when introducing new features or making modifications in general, we may encounter one or the other.

Last but not least, we'll talk about the so-called **god object**; this anti-pattern is a bit like that friend of yours who insists on doing everything, taking all the responsibilities; but then everyone relies on them for everything, and it's too much for them. Too many responsibilities should not be assigned to a single entity, right? I'll tell you what's wrong with this and how to try to solve the problem.

In this chapter, we'll learn about the following topics:

- Duplicated code
- Long methods
- Large classes
- Switches
- Primitive Obsession
- Middle Man
- Message Chains
- Feature envy methods
- Divergent change
- Shotgun Surgery
- God object

As mentioned before, code smells are, at the end of the day, smells. Just as a bad odor in the fridge doesn't necessarily indicate a problem with your food (think of gorgonzola cheese!), a bad smell in your code doesn't necessarily indicate a problem. However, there is a potential problem that is worth considering. In my view, the most important thing is to be aware of what we have in our code bases. We shouldn't perceive every code smell as the most urgent thing in the world because it probably isn't. However, it is crucial not to underestimate them because by ignoring one code smell after another, we end up with code bases that are either unmaintainable or maintainable at an excessively high cost. This applies not only in economic terms but also to personal frustration.

Duplicated code

Let's start with what Martin Fowler calls the *stink parade* (I can't help but mention it because the term cracks me up) with duplicated code. Duplicated code is intuitively a bad smell, and our software engineer instincts will soon learn to reject it as something that harms us. Let's try to list a few reasons why duplicated code is harmful to the health of our code bases.

Clearly, copy-pasting code is the first thing to avoid, at least in 99% of cases. Taking a piece of code from one class and using it exactly as it is in another is easily avoidable. By pausing for a moment to reflect, it's highly likely that we can extract a method to use instead of the duplicated code. Centralizing the code in this way ensures better code maintainability. Just think about how nightmarish it would be to maintain (e.g., fixing a bug in) every single piece of copy-pasted code scattered throughout the code base (and the scariest part is that the developers might not be aware of all the instances of duplication). A nightmare. A nightmare that is a reality in many places, believe me.

Sometimes, duplicated code exists because the programmer doesn't have a clear understanding of what they are doing, they don't own the source, or they want to change it. In other words, they struggle to grasp the code they are working on. As mentioned before, it's useful to do some refactoring to try to better understand the code we're working with. It's likely that even with this simple (figuratively speaking) approach, you'll already be able to handle what you're working on more effectively.

In general, code quality is compromised by duplicated code; the code becomes longer and sometimes less readable. Sometimes it's impossible to refactor a duplicate code block, but the aim should be to decrease technical debt as much as possible. It helps to make your code of higher quality.

The most basic form of duplicated code occurs when you come across the same expression in two methods within the same class. To solve this, all you need to do is extract a method and call that piece of code from both locations:

```
public void printCharacters() {
    SwCharacter darthVader = new DarthVader();
    SwCharacter obiWan = new ObiWanKenobi();

    System.out.println("Name: " + darthVader.getName());
    System.out.println("LightSaber color: " +
        darthVader.getLightSaberColor());
    System.out.println("Birth place: " +
        darthVader.getBirthPlace());

    System.out.println("Name: " + obiWan.getName());
    System.out.println("LightSaber color: " +
        obiWan.getLightSaberColor());
    System.out.println("Birth place: " +
        obiWan.getBirthPlace());
}
```

The previous snippet presents some repetitions, as you can easily spot. We'll extract a `printDetails` method and use it twice:

```
public void printCharacters() {
    SwCharacter darthVader = new DarthVader();
    SwCharacter obiWan = new ObiWanKenobi();

    printDetails(darthVader);
    printDetails(obiWan);
}

private static void printDetails(SwCharacter darthVader) {
    System.out.println("Name: " + darthVader.getName());
    System.out.println("LightSaber color: " +
        darthVader.getLightSaberColor());
    System.out.println("Birth place: " +
        darthVader.getBirthPlace());
}
```

These days, IDEs are perfectly capable of flagging duplicate code (for example, in IntelliJ IDEA, it's a built-in feature) and suggesting a small refactoring to extract the method. We will discuss how to get the most out of IDEs and other tools later in the book.

We'll now move on to long methods.

Long methods

This is a very typical code smell, very sneaky, and often underestimated. Even though it may seem like a trivial topic to address, I'd like to share some thoughts.

Code is read much more than it's written, so taking a little extra time to shorten a method can pay off big time. When you have to modify a long method, you have to read and comprehend every single line of code to make the change safely. In this case, we're burdened with loading all the work this method does into our brains just to understand what's happening, let alone have the ability to modify any part of it.

Long code is very likely doing more than one thing: according to the **Single Responsibility Principle**, a method should ideally focus on doing just one thing. It's almost impossible to achieve that when you have so many lines of code.

It would be useful to know when "long" becomes "too long." 10 lines? 20? 100? It's hard to establish a fixed rule. It's a bit like saying when a cake is too sweet or when pasta is too salty; we instinctively recognize the excesses, but we probably couldn't agree on the exact numbers.

My advice here is to follow your gut and, above all, reach a consensus within the team. For example, you can decide that 20 lines are the maximum limit or that it shouldn't exceed one screen height (of course, it depends on screen resolution, font size, etc.). Another cool thing would be to use standards for formatting, even through the use of automatic tools that take care of it; more on this later in the book. In short, it depends. It could also be the case that a method is long but only contains configurations, things that are very readable and don't require much effort to understand. In that case, you might even not care about it.

Furthermore, I want to bring up a heuristic tip from Martin Fowler's *Refactoring*: whenever you feel the need to insert a comment in the code to explain it, write a method instead. The method will contain the code you intended to comment on, but the name of the function itself will explain the intention behind the code, rather than its functionality.

The following are some small tricks that help in the case of long methods.

Replace temporary variables with query methods

Most of the time, extracting a method or a function from your long method should do the trick; look for parts of the function that go well together and create a fresh one. Sometimes you have a function with many parameters and temporary variables and they could become obstacles to the extraction process; extracting a function would lead to passing a lot of parameters to the extracted method, and that would be as unreadable as before. So, it could be useful to replace those temporary variables with a query function:

```
Double basePrice = this.getCostPerKm() *
    this.getDistanceInKm();
if (passengerIsChild()) {
    return basePrice * 0.5;
} else {
    return basePrice;
}
```

In this code snippet, the basePrice variable is used to store the result of a pricing operation and then again to calculate the final price, which is discounted by 50% for child passengers. It could be a good idea to remove the temporary variable and inline the calculation, writing a method (query function) called calculateBasePrice:

```
if(passengerIsChild()){
    return calculateBasePrice() * 0.5;
}else{
    return calculateBasePrice();
}
```

In the next section, we'll look at parameter objects.

Parameter object

It could also happen that you have functions or methods with a long or "repeated" signature, such as the `calculateFinalPrice` and `discountPrice` methods in the following code snippet:

```
public Double calculateFinalPrice(Double amount, String
    currency){ ... }

public Double discountPrice(Double amount, String
    currency){ ... }
```

You can see that we have a couple of methods with the same signature, repeated. It's also crucial to notice that in this case, the `amount` and `currency` parameters must always go together, as they represent a price. A cool solution is to pass to these methods a "parameter object" or a "request object" (I've heard it being called in many ways): that is, a complex object representing all the needed parameters that make sense together. Given that amount and currency represent a price, why don't we create a `Price` class? We do this in the following snippet:

```
public Double calculateFinalPrice(Price price){ ... }

public Double discountPrice(Price price){ ... }

class Price {
    private Double amount;
    private String currency;

}
```

In the next section, let's replace a function/method with a command.

Replace a function or method with a command

If you've tried to extract functions and create parameter objects but you're still left with an excessive number of temporary variables and parameters, another thing you can do is to replace the function with a command. Let's suppose you have the following method, which takes a lot of parameters and is very long:

```
public Double calculatePrice(Double basePrice, Integer
    adults, Integer children, Integer infants) {
    Double calculatedPrice = 0.0;
    // long body...
    return calculatedPrice;
}
```

If we implement a `PriceCalculator` object, everything becomes clearer; in this way, you have replaced a function with a command. All the parameters are passed at the beginning, of the constructor. You can reuse this component by passing all the parameters every time (and actually, this makes your component more reusable). The logic of the method is executed in the `calculatePrice()` method, which doesn't take any parameters; readability is also improved:

```
class PriceCalculator {
    private final Double basePrice;
    private final Integer adults;
    private final Integer children;
    private final Integer infants;

    public PriceCalculator(Double basePrice, Integer
        adults, Integer children, Integer infants) {
        this.basePrice = basePrice;
        this.adults = adults;
        this.children = children;
        this.infants = infants;
    }

    public Double calculatePrice() {
        Double calculatedPrice = 0.0;
        // long body...
        return calculatedPrice;
    }
}
```

When dealing with code extraction, which is to be put in a different method, it can be hard, sometimes, just to identify the code you want to separate. How can you spot the chunks of code to extract? A handy approach is to check for comments. They often indicate these types of meaningful sections. If you come across a block of code with a comment explaining its purpose, you can replace it with a method named after the comment (and then you can decide whether to keep the comments or not). Even a single line is worth extracting if it requires an explanation.

Decompose conditionals

There are also other indicators of code that need to be extracted; for instance, conditionals and loops also provide useful hints for extractions. If you have a conditional expression, such as the `if` in the following snippet, it can be handy to apply the "decompose conditional" technique:

```
if (1 <= rowNumber && rowNumber <= 30) {
    price = basePrice * plane.getFirstRowsCharge();
} else {
    price = basePrice * plane.getStandardCharge();
}
```

This code snippet calculates the price of a plane seat depending on the row numbers (it probably doesn't make any sense, but it's useful for this example!). If the seat is located in the first 30 lines, we have to pay a different fare. There is an `if`, which is quite simple here, but you have to imagine this in a real-world scenario, where conditions can be much more complex and involve many more parameters and objects. In the refactored snippet, we isolated some logic, including the condition, to improve readability and potentially reuse the code (and potentially, in the future, you could externalize the condition calculations, by doing requests to third-party systems or even rule engines):

```
if (firstRows()) {
    price = firstRowsPrice();
} else {
    price = standardPrice();
}
```

But conditions are not only *ifs*, but also *switches* (which are, in a way, *ifs* in disguise). If you encounter a lengthy switch statement, transform each case into a separate function call using the "extract function" approach, which we covered in the preceding section.

Split loops

Sometimes, loops can also become a problem; for instance, it is common to have a loop body that does more than one thing. In this case, you should create a distinct method for the loop itself and the code within it. If you struggle to find a suitable name for the extracted loop, it might be because it's performing two distinct tasks. In such cases, don't hesitate to use the following technique, called **split loop**, to separate the tasks into different parts:

```
Integer totalBaggageNumber = 0;
Double totalPrice = 0.0;

for (Passenger passenger : passengers) {
    totalBaggageNumber += passenger.getBaggageNumber();
    totalPrice += passenger.getPrice();
}
```

The previous snippet is made of a very basic `for` loop. Even in these two lines, a problem is hidden! In fact, you have two different things done in the same `for` loop. I can already hear you saying, "*Come on, it's just two lines!*" but – again – I'm simplifying things as much as possible here. Reality is often more complex, but the problem is the same. Refactoring the code by splitting the loop makes the code clearer and more reusable; should you move part of the logic elsewhere, now it should be simpler (we could also use Java streams, but we want to keep it as simple as possible):

```
for (Passenger passenger : passengers) {
    totalBaggageNumber += passenger.getBaggageNumber();
}
```

```
for (Passenger passenger : passengers) {
    totalPrice += passenger.getPrice();
}
```

Lots of programmers don't like this refactoring because it makes you run the loop twice. But please remember that we're separating refactoring from optimization. First, get your code nice and clean, then you can optimize it. If looping through a list is causing a slowdown, you can easily combine the loops again. But honestly, going through a big list is usually not the real issue, and splitting the loops can actually open up opportunities for better optimizations.

Large classes

This is another very common smell. How many times have you found yourself working on classes with thousands of lines? It's nobody's fault, it's just that classes start small and, very understandably, gradually end up incorporating more information and functionality. There's nothing wrong with that; the important thing is to realize it and refactor it.

A practical way to notice that a class is too big is when there are too many fields (instance variables). If there are too many fields in a class, it's likely doing too many things; besides having too many responsibilities, often in this case, code duplication becomes a problem.

You can create (extract) a new class to group several variables together. Pick the variables that naturally go hand in hand and put them in a component. For instance, if you see a bunch of parameters called something such as priceAmount and priceCurrency, they are probably meant to be part of the same component. In general, if you notice common prefixes or suffixes among a subset of variables in a class, it indicates the possibility of creating a component:

```
class Order {

    private String name;
    private String surname;
    private String streetName;
    private String streetType;
    private String streetDirection;
    private Double priceAmount;
    private String priceCurrency;

    //constructor and getter methods

}
```

The `Order` class contains numerous fields that each represent distinct properties of the order. However, if you look closer, it becomes evident that some of these fields can be logically "grouped" together, as they belong to specific aspects of an order property. For instance, the `name` and `surname` fields can be seen as representing the buyer's information (to simplify the concept). Similarly, the `streetName`, `streetType`, and `streetDirection` fields are related to the shipping address for the order, while `priceAmount` and `priceCurrency` provide information about the selling price.

Given these insights, it is possible to restructure the `Order` class by grouping certain fields to create new **entities**. These entities can (*should*) be reused effectively throughout the project, enhancing code organization and maintainability.

The restructured `Order` class should look something like this:

```
class Order {

    private User orderBuyer;
    private Address shippingAddress;
    private Price orderPrice;

    //constructor and getter methods

}
```

Of course, it should have all of the previous fields "distributed" among different classes:

```
class User {

    private String name;
    private String surname;

    //constructor and getter methods

}

class Address {

    private String streetName;
    private String streetType;
    private String streetDirection;

    //constructor and getter methods

}
```

```
class Price {

    private Double priceAmount;
    private String priceCurrency;

    //constructor and getter methods

}
```

If using inheritance makes sense for the component, you'll likely find that techniques such as extracting a superclass or replacing `type` with subclasses (also known as extracting a subclass) are often simpler to apply. The following is a very common situation; we have a class that takes a `type` parameter because, depending on its value, the class has to behave slightly differently:

```
public Transport createTransportation(String name, String
    type){
    return new Transport(name, type);
}
```

I bet some instances of `if` are hiding inside the `Transport` class! But object-oriented programming comes with inheritance, so why don't we use it? Take the following example:

```
public Transport createTransport(String name, TransportType
    type) {
    switch (type) {
        case PLANE -> {
            return new Plane(name);
        }
        case TRAIN -> {
            return new Train(name);
        }
        case BUS -> {
            return new Bus(name);
        }
    }
    return null;
}
```

In this refactored code snippet, we have two major improvements. We changed the class of `type` from `String` to an enum called `TransportType`; this allows us to perform the subsequent switch statement in a safer way because we'll be warned (by an IDE, likely) if we are not considering some of the possible values of type. Then, we created a specific class for each type of transport, avoiding mixing things up; of course, all of these classes will implement the same interface.

Aside from having a bunch of instance parameters, a class that is too large is generally not good; it's a breeding ground for duplicated code, unclear code, confusion, and despair. A simple, yet effective, approach to start with is to eliminate repetitions within the class itself. Simply put, you can look for code that makes sense to group together and write standalone methods for them. Shorten the methods within a very large class. Maybe the number of methods will increase, but you'll likely realize that you can move some of them to a separate class, if those methods make sense together and concern a single aspect. In very large classes, it's very common to have duplicated code or similar repetitions. At that point, from a 100-line method, we can extract two or three 10-line methods, with a few extra lines to invoke them. The most difficult part is probably understanding how to split the code. Here's a very simple tip that often works: the *clients* of such a class can often provide valuable hints for breaking it down. Take a closer look and perform some static analysis of the code (that is, open the code and go through it. There are also automatic tools for doing this; we'll meet them later) to see how clients utilize only a portion of the class's features. Each distinct subset of features can potentially become a separate class.

Switches

To put it simply, the `switch` statement itself is not problematic per se. In fact, we find it quite elegant and self-explanatory. Many programming languages even offer more advanced forms of `switch` statements that can use more complex code as their foundation. They can simplify code and replace ugly nested ifs. I must admit, we have a soft spot for the `switch` statement.

However, the issue arises when we encounter *repeated* switches in object-oriented programming. We consider this to be problematic for several reasons. The `switch` statements violate the **open-closed principle** because every time a developer needs to add a new type, they must insert a new `case` statement in each section. This leads to modifying existing code, which goes against the principle. Furthermore, switches can be challenging to maintain. As new requirements emerge, the `switch` statements can grow in complexity, making the code harder to manage. Another issue with switches is the potential for redundant code in certain cases.

The solution in this case is quite simple – use polymorphism:

```
public String printLightSaberColor(SwCharacter character){
    switch (character.getName()) {
        case "LUKE" -> {
            return "GREEN";
        }
        case "OBI-WAN" -> {
            return "BLUE";
        }
        case "DARTH VADER" -> {
            return "RED";
        }
```

```
        }
    }
```

I assume you're already familiar with these characters and you know what a *lightsaber* is. If not, I highly recommend Googling them and watching those movies right away. The previous piece of code could be refactored into the following classes/methods, in which we designed an abstract class, SwCharacter, that will be extended for each specific character. The printLightSaberColor method will take a "generic" SwCharacter and call the relative implementation of the getLightSaberColor method. In the following code, we're going to omit some boilerplate code, such as constructors or other getters, for simplicity:

```java
public String printLightSaberColor(SwCharacter character){
    return character.getLightSaberColor();
}


public abstract class SwCharacter {
    private final String name;
    protected SwCharacter(String name) {
        this.name = name;
    }
    public abstract String getLightSaberColor();

}

public class LukeSkywalker extends SwCharacter {

    protected LukeSkywalker() {
        super("Luke Skywalker");
    }

    @Override
    public String getLightSaberColor() {
        return "GREEN";
    }
}
public class ObiWanKenobi extends SwCharacter{

    public ObiWanKenobi() {
        super("Obi-Wan Kenobi");
    }

    @Override
    public String getLightSaberColor() {
```

```
            return "BLUE";
        }
    }
public class DarthVader extends SwCharacter{
    public DarthVader(String name) {
        super(name);
    }

    @Override
    public String getLightSaberColor() {
        return "RED";
    }
}
```

It is worth mentioning that in this particular case, we increased the number of code lines. However, in our opinion, this is highly acceptable as we improved readability. In the examples I've given you, I tried to keep things simple by using basic stuff such as int or String most of the time. But that's not always the best approach. It depends. Sometimes, relying too much on the language's primitive types can lead to a code smell called **Primitive Obsession**.

Primitive Obsession

To understand what Primitive Obsession is and how to deal with it, let's remember what primitive types are in a programming language. Primitive types are like the ready-made types that come with the language. You can think of them as straight from the manufacturer. Each language has its own set of primitive types, and since we're talking about Java here, let's focus on how it works in Java.

In Java, a **primitive type** is a type that is already defined in the language and has a special keyword associated with it. Primitive values are independent of each other, they don't share their state. Java supports eight primitive data types: byte, short, int, long, float, double, Boolean, and char. Along with these eight types, Java also provides special support for strings through the java.lang.String class. Although the String class is not technically a primitive data type, it's given special treatment in the language, so you might consider it as one.

Primitive Obsession is when the code becomes too dependent on basic data types. It means that a simple value takes charge of the class logic and lacks type safety. In simpler terms, it's a bad habit of using basic types to represent an object in a specific area of focus.

Let's take the example of representing a website's URL. Usually, we store it as a string. However, the problem arises because a URL has more details and distinct characteristics than just being a simple string. It includes elements such as the scheme, query parameters, and protocol. When we store it as a string, we lose the ability to directly access these URL-specific components (the essential parts of the URL) without writing additional code. We could use java.net.URL instead.

Strings are often breeding grounds for this kind of issue. Take a telephone number, for example. It's more than just a random assortment of characters. In many cases, a proper data type can provide consistent display logic when it needs to be shown in a user interface. Representing such types as strings creates a problem so common that they are sometimes referred to as *stringly typed* variables.

If you think about it, it is quite simple to solve the problem; it is necessary to replace the primitive(s) with objects. Take the following example:

```
String url = "https://www.packtpub.com/";
String protocol = extractProtocol(url);
String host = extractHost(url);
```

This can become the following:

```
URL url = new URL("https://www.packtpub.com/");
String protocol = url.getProtocol();
String host = url.getHost();
```

If you're curious about how the URL class works, look at its documentation (the `java.net.URL` class is included in the Standard Java Library).

If you have a group of primitives that can go together, you can group them by extracting a class, like in the address example we covered in the *Large classes* section.

Now that we've dealt with Primitive Obsession, let's tackle all those classes that have little desire to work and make others do all the work. This was just a playful way to say that we will talk about a smell called **middle man**.

Middle man

The middle man is a code smell that occurs when we have a class or, in general, an object that does only one thing, and that thing is... delegating the work to someone else. We are not suggesting that a class should have only one method to be considered a "middle man". Rather, each of its methods should only invoke others. So, the question arises spontaneously: why keep a class in our codebase that does nothing? In fact, there is (almost never) a reason. Let's delete this class or method and ensure that the client calls the "destination" directly. This way, we will eliminate unnecessary complexity and ensure that, when we modify or add features to the destination objects, we are not forced to also modify our middle man.

To give an example, suppose we have a class structured like this:

```
public class Person {
    private Address address;

    public City getCity() {
        return address.getCity();
```

```
    }

    public Address getAddress() {
        return address;
    }
}
```

A "client" method would use it in the following way:

```
Person person = getPerson();

var person = person.getCity();
```

You can easily notice that the getCity() method serves solely as a proxy to the other class. So why not use the other class directly? Our example would then become:

```
var city = person.getAddress().getCity();
```

And so, we can eliminate the middle man composed of the getCity() method in the Person class.

However, this refactoring can paradoxically lead to another code smell, the message chain!

Message chains

A **message chain** occurs when a client requests an object, which then requests another object, and so on. This makes all the objects dependent on the structure of the called objects, and a change in these objects would necessarily impact the entire chain of calls, at every point where they are made. Building upon the example from the previous section, we could have something like:

```
var cityName = person.getLocation().getAddress().getCity().getName();
```

The solution is to hide the "delegate", that is the method calling the other one(s). We could transform the previous example into this:

```
var cityName = person.getCityName();
```

Where the chain of calls is hidden in the getCityName() method.

Taken to the extreme, however, this refactoring can lead to the middle man smell! Have we ended up in a time loop like Christopher Nolan? The truth is, it depends. These refactorings must indeed be properly weighted, attempting to choose the lesser evil (also considering the possibility that perhaps the class modeling itself is flawed and might require changes in some way).

Opting for middle man instead of message chains offers the advantage of requiring fewer mocks during unit testing. Testing classes becomes challenging when you have to provide mocks not just for their immediate and indirect dependencies. Additionally, it aids in the separation of concerns. A code that possesses an *A* component and requires a *C* component should ideally remain unaware of the involvement of a *B* component. This contributes to better modularity. While the primary argument for message chains is the avoidance of writing boilerplate in the middle, and there might be cases where it makes sense, the general guideline should lean towards preferring the middle man.

Choosing middle man over message chains aligns with the principles of the Law of Demeter, often summarized as "only talk to your direct dependencies." This guideline encapsulates a design philosophy advocating for encapsulation and reduced coupling in object-oriented systems. We talked about the Law of Demeter in *Chapter 2*.

Feature envy methods

When we try to break down our code base into components that make sense based on our use case and domain, we're basically dividing the code into *zones*. One of the key things we need to be careful about is maximizing interactions within the zones and, conversely, minimizing interactions between different zones. **Feature envy** is like a warning sign in the code, describing when an object accesses another object's fields to perform an operation instead of simply instructing the object on what to do.

As a simple example, let's consider a method that calculates a price based on a payment request:

```
public Double calculatePrice(PaymentRequest paymentRequest);
```

Everything seems fine until we realize that we need the order and some user information to calculate the price. That's when we start writing its implementation and, for instance, we must retrieve the order related to the payment request; in the first lines of the method, we'll write something like the following:

```
Order order = orderRepository.findById
    (paymentRequest.getOrderId());
```

Very likely, a user will be needed too. So, after fetching the order, we'll probably add a line in which we also retrieve the user, because we need some information about them:

```
User user = userRepositoty.findById
    (paymentRequest.getUserId());
```

From these objects, we're going to take some specific properties that we need to complete the payment. For instance, we'll write something like the following:

```
order.getItems();
order.getOrderDate();
user.getLevel();
```

Once again, we're faced with a ton of finder/getter methods being called. It's very common to find methods invoking tons of getter methods of other objects to retrieve or calculate some value. In this case, it's also likely that your bean, your Java class, will have a lot of *collaborators*, that is, a lot of other classes injected in yours through the constructor.

In the most basic scenario, you can simply transfer the method you're using from one class to another (and modify its name, if necessary). If only a portion of the method requires access to another object's data, you can extract that specific part into a separate method. However, not all cases are straightforward; sometimes, a function relies on features from multiple modules, so it becomes a question of which module it should belong to. A rule of thumb (as suggested by Martin Fowler) is to determine the module that possesses most of the data and place the function there. This process is often facilitated by extracting methods to break down the function into smaller pieces that can be placed in different locations.

Sometimes, even when this guideline is not applicable, you have the option to use the Strategy or Visitor patterns described in the book by the *Gang of Four*. However, providing a detailed explanation of these patterns is beyond our scope. For more in-depth explanations, you can refer to the *Further reading* section. The fundamental principle remains unchanged: grouping elements that undergo changes together. Typically, data and the corresponding behavior that relies on that data tend to change simultaneously, though exceptions exist. In such scenarios, relocating the behavior ensures that changes are consolidated in a single location. Strategies and Visitors offer a practical means of modifying behavior by isolating specific portions that require overriding, even though this approach introduces some additional indirection.

Divergent change

As software engineers, we know our work product is soft and flexible. Once, a professor at university told us, *"We're the only engineers who are asked to change the project many times, even when it's done. Imagine doing that with a bridge. This is our strength and our curse."*

As we know from the Agile philosophy, *change is good*, but it needs to be controlled and managed. Going back to code smells, we have divergent changes when we need to modify a certain class often, even though we're touching seemingly unrelated aspects. Think of a class that handles the results of a search for transportation options like for a travel booking website (those where you put when you want to leave, when you want to return, where you want to go and they give you a bazillion options to choose from – planes, trains, buses and so on). At some point, we need to change the database the application relies on. Consequently, we modify class X. Then, we need to integrate a new type of transportation, and we must modify class X again. New payment method? Again, class X needs modification.

All these aspects are unrelated, but class X is always in the middle! Divergent change happens when a module (or a class, or a project) is frequently modified for various reasons, resulting in a mixing of different contexts in a single location. To enhance our programming experience, we can improve it by segregating these contexts into separate modules.

The most likely reason is that the **Single Responsibility Principle** has been violated. In general, we either have a flawed programming structure or we've gone overboard with copy and paste. Thus, it becomes necessary to create appropriate modules and move the methods accordingly. Sometimes it may be necessary to extract ad hoc methods (and perhaps relocate them) or even extract entire classes.

Sometimes, we come across a special situation where two aspects, mistakenly tangled up in a single class, naturally form a sequence. A classic example is when we fetch data from the database, process it, and then feed it to a function that uses it. In cases like these, we can use a refactoring technique called **split phase**. In this refactoring process, we break down a complex computation into two phases (or more). During the first phase, we calculate a result, and then we pass this result, along with some intermediate data structure, to the second phase for further processing.

For example, take the following code snippet: it retrieves some flight data array from a database, parses an element of that array to a double, then takes some of the output and uses it to perform further calculation... the point is that it does a lot of different things one after the other:

```
String[] flightData =
    getFlightDataFromDatabase(flightId).split("-");
double basePrice = parseDouble(flightData[3]);
double totalPrice = basePrice * parseDouble(flightData[0])
    + basePrice * parseDouble(flightData[1]) + basePrice *
        parseDouble(flightData[2]);
```

It would be nice to refactor this code and make it a bit more readable and somehow modular, even if this term could be inappropriate when talking about a small set of code lines. Anyway, we're going to split this code into phases, almost like it was a workflow: we'll call getFlightDataFromDatabase (without splitting the result immediately; that is something that will be needed only in the next code line). The flightData string, of course, is not very handy (we're assuming we cannot change the return type because we're using a third-party library) so we're going to use parseFlightData into a FlightInfo object, which handles the flight information in a very handy way. At the end, we're going to finally implement calculateTotalPrice, using the flightInfo object. See how this code – even a four-line piece of code – can become much more readable:

```
String flightData = getFlightDataFromDatabase(flightId);
FlightInfo flightInfo = parseFlightData(flightData);
double totalPrice = calculateTotalPrice(flightInfo);
...
double calculateTotalPrice(FlightInfo flightInfo) {
    var basePrice = flightInfo.getBasePrice();
    return basePrice * flightInfo.getAdultsCount() +
        basePrice * flightInfo.getChildrenCount() +
            basePrice * flightInfo.getInfantsCount();
}
```

When the change you need is not in a single class you have to change often, but spread across the project, you're forced to modify the code in a lot of different points. That's when you have the code smell known as *Shotgun Surgery*.

Shotgun Surgery

Although it might seem a bit violent at first, to me, the term seems also funny, to be honest; that's why I really like it. Sometimes, I've heard it referred to as *shooting a fly with a bazooka*. It is, basically, the opposite of divergent change.

When you're dealing with Shotgun Surgery, it means you must make a bunch of changes in your code base just to tackle seemingly simple tasks. Frequently, you'll find yourself altering code that appears quite similar, either directly copy-pasted or with a similar purpose. The term refers to the work of a surgeon, which is done very precisely, with a scalpel, in the least invasive way possible. Now replace the image of the scalpel with a shotgun and... well, you get the idea.

There can be several examples or reasons that lead to Shotgun Surgery; let's quickly go through some of them, so we can prevent the problem:

- **Copy and paste**: This is the first example that comes to mind; you've done some good old copy and pasting of code! This means, of course, that making changes to some of the copied code requires you to make those same changes to each and every copy. It's pretty straightforward, really.

- **Excessive layering**: Sometimes, our application tends to be too layered. For example, imagine a basic CRUD app that goes all out with multiple layers, including data transfer objects, data access objects, and domain objects. Every time you want to add a table to the database, you not only have to add stuff to all four layers but also deal with all the property bag objects within those layers. It's another case of Shotgun Surgery. (But the world isn't all black or white; there are many shades of gray. Sometimes, an application with well-defined layers helps to isolate concepts and responsibilities. So, be careful; I'm not saying that designing multiple layers in an architecture is inherently bad. You always have to find the right balance, just like in life!)

- **Limited layering**: Just as sometimes there are too many layers in the design of an application, there are also times when responsibilities are excessively separated: one class for constants, another for static variables, and so on. Then, when you need to make a change, you find yourself having to touch them all! Has it ever happened to you? It happens to me quite often. And there you are again, using a shotgun in the operating room.

You should care about these problems because changes become more time-consuming since you have to edit your code base in more places. *Merge conflicts* become more likely, as more people are touching the code in different locations, making collaborative projects more difficult. You're also more likely to introduce bugs due to the cognitive load of remembering to change the code in multiple places. Additionally, you end up with more code because of knowledge duplication and the need for additional constructs to connect the different pieces. Lastly, the learning curve is higher for new team members as development becomes like a treasure hunt in navigating through the code base.

When you have your logic spread all over the code base, you could simply move your method(s) or your field(s) into the same class or module. By doing so, you make sure that related software elements are clustered together, making it easier to locate and comprehend the connections between them. All the relevant context would be consolidated in one place, enhancing encapsulation and enabling other parts of the software to be less reliant on the specifics of this module.

Another intriguing approach to tackle Shotgun Surgery is to employ inlining refactorings. In other words, it can be beneficial to merge methods or classes in order to consolidate poorly separated logic. This may result in a long method or a large class; I know we just said that this would be bad, but this would only be a temporary (but very useful) situation so that you can subsequently use extractions to break it down into more coherent pieces. Of course, we typically prefer small functions and classes in our code but don't hesitate to create something large as an intermediate step toward reorganization.

Inlining a method means, basically, doing the opposite of extracting a method. Suppose we have the following:

```
public Double calculatePrice(Integer passenger, Double
    baseFare){
    var basePrice = passenger * baseFare;
    var basePriceWithVAT = VATCalculator.addVat(basePrice);
    return basePriceWithVAT;
}

class VATCalculator {
    public static Double addVat(double basePrice) {
        return basePrice * (1 + DefaultValues.DEFAULT_VAT);
    }
}

class DefaultValues {
    public static final Double DEFAULT_VAT = 0.22;
}
```

You have created a separate class, with a static method, just to implement the VAT addition. Supposing that this method is used only once, this seems a bit too much; the suggestion here is simply to inline the content of the static method, avoiding creating a separate class, which would make the code a bit more difficult to read. You could simply do the following:

```
public Double calculatePrice(Integer passenger, Double
    baseFare){
    var basePrice = passenger * baseFare;
    return basePrice * (1 + 0.22);
}
```

Anyway, the real deal is to always keep Shotgun Surgery on your radar as you work. Keep asking yourself whether future maintenance programmers (which could also be your future self) will need a shotgun or a scalpel to make the anticipated changes. If the answer leans toward *shotgun*… then it's high time you rethink your approach.

God object

Of all the anti-patterns mentioned in this chapter (there are many more; I encourage you to delve into the *Further reading* section), perhaps the one called **god object** (or **god class**) is the one I most frequently come across. As the name suggests (I must say, in the world of refactoring and clean code, the level of naming is remarkable!), a god class is a negative coding practice characterized by a class that assumes an excessively considerable number of responsibilities. It manifests as a class that consolidates and oversees numerous objects, performing all tasks within the application. This anti-pattern violates the principle of keeping classes focused and modular, leading to poor maintainability and hindered code readability.

You may think that this may be a good pattern; also, the name can suggest something positive. Well, this is not the case, and we are about to see why.

God objects violate SOLID, especially the Single Responsibility Principle. God classes go completely against the Single Responsibility Principle by assuming an excessive number of responsibilities and lacking focus. As a result, engineers end up reinventing the wheel, duplicating code, and accumulating technical debt.

Because of god objects, your code will be more fragile. Due to the overwhelming responsibilities of a god class, it requires frequent updates, which significantly raises the chances of introducing breaking changes. Understanding the impact of modifications to a god class on the rest of the application can be challenging, if not impossible.

God objects are hardly testable. A class is easily testable, in general, when it is small, focused, and independent of other types. On the contrary, a god class operates in the opposite manner. Being a large, all-encompassing entity that controls and manages numerous other objects, it becomes tightly coupled to those types. Consequently, testing the god class becomes a daunting task due to its intricate setup and the necessity to stub or mock numerous dependencies just to instantiate it for testing purposes. You can often become aware you are writing a god object when it has too many *collaborators*, that is, too many other objects needed for the class itself to work.

Finally, the main pain point. We always end up with this. A god object makes your code harder to read and understand. It is no wonder that the code within these classes becomes complex, considering their extensive responsibilities and interactions with several types. I am not (only) talking about cyclomatic complexity here; for example, relying on external dependencies that cause side effects and mutability. The cumulative effect of these complexities contributes to the overall cognitive complexity of the code, creating obstacles in understanding and reducing engineers' productivity and performance.

The solution here is not unique, but the approach can be. It is quite easy to create a god object (especially in object-oriented programming) but it can be extremely hard to undo them. So, use the good old *divide et impera* technique (again, the Single Responsibility Principle) and split the class into smaller pieces; be guided by your domain; and group the common methods and properties in a class while keeping the classes loosely coupled. If classes or methods have a lot of code or functionality in them, break them into simple, manageable, testable classes and methods. Finally, delete or deprecate the god object.

Summary

In this chapter, we learned how to spot some – not all – code smells. We covered the ones that I think are the most common. Some of them you'll pick up instinctively and avoid them as you write code. We tackled duplicated code, long methods, large classes, and repeated switches. We also learned to avoid our obsession with primitive types (using string for everything is a strong temptation!) and looked at feature envy methods. Finally, we talked about divergent change and its opposite, Shotgun Surgery. Oh, and let's not forget about the god object. This is just a partial selection of all the existing code smells out there, but I believe it's a good starting point to steer clear of them.

A crucial condition to perform any kind of refactoring, especially god object refactoring, is good test coverage. In the next chapter, we are going to tackle this extremely important matter.

Further reading

- **Primitive Data Types**: `https://docs.oracle.com/javase/tutorial/java/nutsandbolts/datatypes.html`

- **Strategy**: `https://refactoring.guru/design-patterns/strategy`

- **Visitor**: `https://refactoring.guru/design-patterns/visitor`

- Erich Gamma, Richard Helm, Ralph Johnson, and John Vlissides (1994). *Design Patterns: Elements of Reusable Object-Oriented Software*. Addison-Wesley Professional.

- **Code Smells**: `https://refactoring.guru/refactoring/smells`

4

Testing

When we talk about refactoring, as we have already mentioned, we essentially mean rewriting the code in a better way (where "better" can have various meanings) without changing its behavior. This last point is crucial, and we have not yet delved deep enough into it. To ensure that the behavior does not change and, in general, to approach every refactoring with a high level of confidence, it is necessary to be covered by an adequate set of tests.

It may sound obvious, but a test is nothing more than a way to verify the functionality of certain software (whether it is a piece of code, a module, or an entire architecture) against a set of requirements. In practice, we're saying: *"Check that my code, given a certain input X, produces a certain output Y."* It can be much more complex than that, but for now, let's settle with this explanation.

There can be various types of tests, as well as different approaches to writing them, as we will see during the course of this chapter. But before discussing the "how," we will look at why testing is essential, especially when it comes to refactoring. Within the context of refactoring, I would say testing is a fundamental condition.

Fortunately, there are methodologies and tools that can assist us, such as the famous **JUnit framework**. In terms of methodologies, it is certainly worth mentioning **Test-Driven Development (TDD)**, which *serves* refactoring and simultaneously *uses* refactoring – you will see what I mean by this somewhat cryptic statement. But to be truly safe, it is also necessary to ensure that most of the implemented functionalities have been rigorously tested; also, for this, we have tools that can save us quite a bit of headaches.

In this chapter, we'll cover the following topics:

- Why you should test, and why you should do it often
- Unit testing
- Integration testing
- Contract testing
- Be safe – checking and improving your test coverage
- Test-driven development

Before anything else, however, as a famous book by Simon Sinek suggests, let's start with "why."

Why you should test (often)

As already mentioned, testing is a fundamental part of the work of a software engineer. It is a statement that we can all agree on – I would say it is almost intuitive – but let's try to dig a little deeper and truly understand why it is essential to test our code (and our code interacting with other code and systems). The reasons I am about to present are not necessarily listed in order of importance, and they may not be the only ones. I am sharing what, in my experience, has been significant.

Identifying and fixing defects

Let's start with the most obvious motivation. Testing your software allows you to identify defects (bugs), errors, and faults. In this regard, we have included an article in the *Further reading* section that explains the differences between these terms, which are often used interchangeably. These issues can manifest in various forms, such as functional flaws, performance bottlenecks, security vulnerabilities, or usability problems. When left unresolved, these problems can have severe consequences, leading to system failures, data breaches, dissatisfied users, and costly rework.

By conducting comprehensive testing throughout the development cycle, developers can detect and address these issues early on. This proactive approach to testing allows them to pinpoint and rectify potential problems before they escalate into more significant issues, thereby minimizing the risk of critical defects in the final product.

One of the primary benefits of early bug identification and resolution is the prevention of downstream complications. As the development progresses, the complexity of the software typically increases, making it more challenging to identify and fix defects. Bugs that go unnoticed in the initial stages can compound as new features are added, resulting in a cascade of interconnected problems that are difficult and time-consuming to resolve.

Moreover, addressing bugs at later stages of development – or, worse, after the software is released – can significantly impact the project's timeline and budget. The cost of fixing defects in the production phase is usually much higher than resolving them during the development phase. Additionally, urgent bug fixes might necessitate disrupting regular development activities, leading to delays in delivering new features or updates (I can already see you nodding and sighing).

In brief, the more you test and the earlier you do so (that is, test small chunks of software while you're writing it – we'll see in a moment how we can be helped in such an activity), the better it is. Thinking a bit more laterally, anticipating potential issues brings both financial benefits (cost-effectiveness) and risk mitigation, especially in the case of software where even small defects can lead to significant damages (consider, for example, sectors such as healthcare, finance, or the aerospace industry).

Ensuring quality and reliability

Testing is a critical aspect of the software development process that goes beyond simply identifying bugs and defects. It involves a systematic and comprehensive examination of the software to ensure that it meets the required quality standards and performs as expected. This process is essential to deliver a reliable, stable, and high-quality product that meets the needs and expectations of its users.

When software undergoes thorough testing, it is placed under rigorous scrutiny across various dimensions. **Functional testing** verifies that the software's features and functionalities behave correctly and in accordance with the specified requirements. **Non-functional testing**, on the other hand, evaluates aspects such as performance, security, usability, and compatibility to ensure that the software meets the expected levels in these areas.

By subjecting the software to a suite of tests, developers can have confidence that the application will operate smoothly under normal conditions and handle challenging scenarios without unexpected crashes or malfunctions. This is especially crucial in mission-critical systems where any unforeseen issues could have severe consequences.

When talking about quality and reliability, it is worth defining some terms that I often hear being used – and I sometimes use myself – incorrectly. Let's define what performance tests, load tests, and stress tests are:

- **Performance tests**: These are tests designed to assess the speed, responsiveness, and overall efficiency of a system or software under specific conditions. They aim to evaluate how well the system performs in normal situations.

- **Load tests**: Load tests are conducted to evaluate how well a system can handle a specific amount of load or user activity. The objective is to determine the system's capacity and identify any performance bottlenecks under anticipated loads. They are a subset of performance tests.

- **Stress tests**: Stress tests involve pushing the system or software beyond its normal operating limits. The purpose is to check how the system behaves under extreme conditions, such as high user traffic, excessive data volumes, or limited resources. The goal is to identify potential weaknesses or failures in the system's stability and resilience. Stress tests are also used for sizing environments (e.g., you need to set up a new tier, and you know in advance how many resources you will need) or simply to know what the limit is, so you know in advance if and when to scale.

There is a very common tool, used for performance testing, which you probably know, called **JMeter**. We're mentioning it just because it's one of the most famous, but it's not necessarily the best – it heavily depends on your needs. It's likely very widespread because it is open source and free to use and there is a lot of knowledge and documentation around it. **Apache JMeter** is a Java application explicitly crafted for conducting load testing while measuring application performance and response times. JMeter boasts numerous sophisticated features. It operates as a thick client Java application and offers the capability to conduct performance testing across various technologies, employing a diverse range of protocols, including Java objects, web HTTP/HTTPS, SOAP and REST services,

FTP, and databases with JDBC. Additionally, it provides a user-friendly IDE for recording, building, and debugging performance tests effectively. Starting from **JMeter 3.1**, **Groovy** is set as the default programming language, because it's easy to use, flexible, and constantly being developed. In addition, Groovy can be fully integrated with Java, which provides many scripting capabilities via an expressive, concise, and readable syntax. As one of the most popular load-testing tools, JMeter allows users to configure and assess the performance of mobile apps. Moreover, with `jmeter-java-dsl`, you have the option to write your performance tests in Java, taking advantage of IDEs' autocompletion and inline documentation. To get started, you can find a good resource in the *Further reading* section.

While JMeter remains one of the popular load-testing tools, scaling it for a large, distributed test can be somewhat challenging, particularly when dealing with multiple machines that require intricate configurations to communicate effectively. Additionally, executing large JMeter tests may lead to a range of orchestrating issues.

Customer satisfaction

Customer satisfaction is the level of contentment customers feel after using a product or service, based on their perceptions and expectations. It's a critical indicator of business success, impacting loyalty and reputation. There are many ways to measure it; jump to the *Further reading* section if you'd like to learn more.

High-quality software that undergoes rigorous testing not only ensures its reliability but also increases the likelihood of meeting the needs and expectations of its users. When customers find the software to be efficient, stable, and bug-free, they are more likely to be satisfied with their experience.

Satisfied customers tend to build a sense of trust and loyalty toward the product and the company behind it. They are more inclined to continue using the software for extended periods, fostering long-term engagement and loyalty. Moreover, happy customers often become advocates for the product, enthusiastically recommending it to their peers, friends, and colleagues.

Word-of-mouth referrals from satisfied users can be a powerful driver for the software's success. Positive recommendations can significantly expand the software's user base, leading to increased adoption rates and potential revenue growth for the company.

Compliance and standards

In certain industries, such as healthcare, finance, and aerospace, the software used plays a critical role in the safety, security, and well-being of individuals and organizations. Due to the high stakes involved, these industries are subject to strict regulations and standards that software must adhere to.

In healthcare, for example, software for medical devices and health management must meet strict regulations set by authorities such as the FDA and EMA to ensure patient safety. The financial industry relies on software to handle critical tasks, and compliance with SEC and FCA standards is vital to protect consumers from fraud and data breaches. Similarly, aerospace software must adhere to FAA and EASA standards to ensure passenger safety and avoid accidents or operational disruptions. Non-compliance can have severe consequences for all these sectors.

Testing helps identify and address potential issues, vulnerabilities, and defects that could compromise the software's performance, security, or compliance. By conducting deep testing, organizations can avoid legal and financial consequences that may arise from non-compliance with industry regulations.

Security

In today's digital landscape, where cyber threats and attacks are becoming increasingly sophisticated, it is imperative to fortify software systems against potential security breaches.

During the testing process, security experts and testers employ various methodologies and tools to simulate real-world attack scenarios, attempting to exploit weaknesses in the software's defenses. This includes techniques such as penetration testing, where testers try to gain unauthorized access to the system, and vulnerability assessments, which identify potential areas of weakness.

By conducting such tests, developers can proactively identify and address security flaws before the software is deployed to the production environment. This proactive approach significantly reduces the risk of potential security breaches that could lead to data breaches, unauthorized access, or service disruptions.

Here are some suggestions to effectively integrate security testing into the **Software Development Life Cycle (SDLC)**; these are just a few ideas, based on what we have encountered in experience, and we suggest you look deeper into each point if it piques your interest:

- **Create security requirements specific to your application**: Ensure these requirements align with industry standards and compliance regulations.

- **Training and awareness**: Train developers and the development team on secure coding practices, fostering a security-aware culture within your organization.

- **Dependency scanning**: Regularly scan third-party dependencies for known vulnerabilities. Implement or use automated tools that can alert you when a dependency has a security issue.

- **Penetration testing**: Conduct penetration testing to simulate real-world attacks. Test the application from an attacker's perspective to identify vulnerabilities that automated tools might miss.

These are just some of the measures we've seen implemented in companies, usually large companies that have dedicated teams. These activities are not only time-consuming but also very complex and require specific skills.

Integration and compatibility

Testing plays a crucial role in verifying the seamless integration and compatibility of software with other components or systems. In today's complex technological landscape, software rarely operates in isolation; it often interacts with various hardware, software modules, databases, APIs, and external systems. Ensuring that all these pieces work harmoniously together is essential for the overall success and efficiency of the application.

One of the primary testing methodologies used to assess integration and compatibility is **integration testing**. This type of testing focuses on evaluating how different modules or components of the software interact and exchange data with each other. We'll deep dive into this topic in a dedicated section.

Compatibility testing is another vital aspect of the testing process. With the wide variety of devices, operating systems, web browsers, and configurations available, it is essential to validate that the software functions correctly across different environments. Compatibility testing involves testing the software on various platforms to ensure that it behaves consistently and uniformly across all of them.

By conducting compatibility testing, developers can identify platform-specific issues and make necessary adjustments to the software. This not only improves the user experience but also expands the potential user base, as a broader range of users can access and use the software without encountering compatibility-related problems.

Integration and compatibility issues can arise at different stages of software development, from the initial design to the final implementation. By incorporating testing throughout the development process, developers can proactively address these challenges, reducing the likelihood of integration bottlenecks (that is, a point in a system where the flow of data or functionality between different components is restricted, causing delays or inefficiencies) or compatibility conflicts in the later stages of the project.

Confidence and peace of mind

It might sound strange, but rigorous testing of our software allows us to sleep more peacefully, and that is not a trivial matter. Let me explain further. If every time we release a new version of our software, we know that it has been well tested and we are confident in its proper functioning, this increases the team's self-confidence and, ultimately, we work better, which is undoubtedly a benefit for everyone. When we work better, we become more productive and produce something of higher quality.

Furthermore, I must add that many developers don't enjoy working on bugs, especially when they are complex to identify and resolve. Bug-fixing is time-consuming and often difficult to predict. As already mentioned, it takes time away from the team's core activities.

That's why it's essential for developers to care about testing; it's not only crucial in itself but also affects people's well-being in some way. The primary goal (before clean code and refactoring – which cannot be safely done without a proper battery of tests) of developers must be that their software is adequately and automatically tested every time a change is made. The first and most immediate way to perform automatic tests is to write so-called "unit tests"; in Java, the most widely used framework for this is undoubtedly JUnit.

Unit testing

Unit testing is a type of software testing where individual units or components of a software application are tested in isolation to ensure they function correctly. A *unit* typically refers to the smallest testable part of the software, such as a function, method, or class. The main goal of unit testing is to validate that each unit of the software works as expected and produces the correct output for a given input. By testing units independently, developers can identify and fix bugs or issues in the early stages of development, making it easier to maintain and improve (hence, to refactor) the code base.

There are several benefits to adopting unit testing, some of which are as follows:

- **Velocity**: Unit tests are fast! They focus on testing small, isolated units of code, typically individual functions or methods, in isolation from the rest of the system. This isolation allows unit tests to execute quickly because they don't rely on external dependencies or perform complex setup and teardown processes. This helps developers to run them often and get quick feedback.

- **Isolation**: Each unit test is designed to run independently of the rest of the application. This isolation ensures that if a test fails, the cause is likely within the specific unit being tested, making it easier to pinpoint and fix the issue.

- **Automation**: Unit tests are usually automated, meaning they can be run automatically and regularly as part of the development process. This automation helps ensure that new code changes don't introduce regressions or break existing functionality.

- **Early detection of issues**: Unit testing facilitates the early detection of defects, which can significantly reduce the cost and effort required for debugging and maintenance later in the development cycle.

- **Documentation**: Unit tests serve as living documentation, providing examples of how units are expected to behave. Developers can refer to these tests to understand the intended functionality of a unit and its possible edge cases. This is crucial; a well-written unit test can be better than 10 pages of documentation.

- **Refactoring support**: Of course, that's why we're talking about tests in this book! When refactoring code, unit tests act as a safety net. If the refactored code breaks any functionality, the unit tests will catch it, helping ensure the changes do not introduce bugs.

In practice, in a unit test, nothing else is done except executing a certain portion of code (for example, a method) and verifying that, starting from a specific input, the same output is always produced. Easy, right? Well, not always, and soon we'll see why.

To test our unit, we will write – in fact – a Java class with several methods (each of which is a unit test) that will test the various functionalities. It is always advisable to be organized even in the design of test classes; by convention, to test, for example, the `com.acme.demo.MyClass` class, we will create a class called `com.acme.demo.MyClassTest`. The former will be placed under the `main` folder, while the latter will be under the `test` folder. Inside each unit test, it is advisable to follow a fairly established pattern, called **AAA**, or the three As:

- **Arrange**: This phase involves preparing the objects that will be subjected to testing. During this phase, you establish the desired condition of the system under test and set up its dependencies. This can involve directly creating instances of the necessary objects or getting them ready by creating their test counterparts. This may include initializing resources (collaborators) needed for the class under test, and so on.

- **Act**: This is where you interact with the system under test. In this phase, you invoke one of its methods, providing any required dependencies, and capturing any resulting output values if applicable.

- **Assert**: This is where you check Boolean expressions (assertions) that must be true if the test is successful; that is, the observed output data and/or post-conditions are different from the expected ones. Sometimes, it is not only the output that is evaluated, but it is also possible to verify the method's execution flow by making assertions regarding whether a certain component – present *inside* the class under test – has been called, how many times, and with what input.

Let's go through a trivial example. Let's suppose we have a `Calculator` class, which has a method that takes two integers and returns their sum (I said it was trivial!):

```
public class Calculator {
    public int add(int a, int b) {
        return a + b;
    }
}
```

Let's now write a test class for `Calculator`:

```
public class CalculatorTest {

    public static void main(String[] args) {
        testAddition();
    }

    public static void testAddition() {
        // Arrange
        Calculator calculator = new Calculator();

        // Act
        int result = calculator.add(5, 3);

        // Assert
        int expected = 8;
```

```
        if (result == expected) {
            System.out.println("testAddition PASSED");
        } else {
            System.out.println("testAddition FAILED");
        }
    }
}
```

In this example, we have created a test method called testAddition. The test method creates an instance of the Calculator class, calls testAddition with a specific input, and then compares the result with the expected output. When you run the CalculatorTest class, it will output whether the test has passed or failed based on the comparison of the actual results and expected results.

Keep in mind that this is just a basic example to demonstrate how unit tests can be written without using a testing framework such as JUnit. In real-world scenarios, using a testing framework such as JUnit provides many additional features and benefits, such as easier test organization, assertions, test reporting, and integration with build tools and CI/CD pipelines.

JUnit framework

JUnit is a popular testing framework for Java that is primarily used to perform unit testing of Java applications. It provides a set of annotations, assertions, and test runners that make writing and executing tests easier and more organized. JUnit is widely used in the Java development community and has become a standard for writing unit tests.

Here are some key features and concepts of JUnit:

- **Annotations**: JUnit uses annotations to define test methods, setup, and teardown methods. Some commonly used annotations in JUnit are @Test, @Before, @After, @BeforeClass, and @AfterClass.

- **Test methods**: Test methods are annotated with @Test and are responsible for verifying specific functionality in the code being tested. Each test method should be independent and focus on testing a specific part of the code base.

- **Setup and teardown**: The @Before and @After annotations are used to mark methods that will be executed before and after each test method. They are used for setting up the test environment (e.g., initializing objects) and cleaning up resources after each test.

- **Test runners**: JUnit provides various test runners that determine how tests are executed. A widely used test runner is BlockJUnit4ClassRunner, but **JUnit 5** has introduced a more flexible and extensible model based on org.junit.platform.runner.JUnitPlatform.

- **Assertions**: JUnit provides a set of static methods (e.g., assertEquals, assertTrue, assertFalse, etc.) to perform various types of assertions to check the expected outcomes of the tests.

- **Test suites**: JUnit allows you to group related test classes into test suites using the @RunWith and @Suite annotations.

- **Parameterized tests**: **JUnit 4** introduced the concept of parameterized tests, allowing you to run the same test with multiple sets of data.

JUnit 5 is the next major version of JUnit and introduced several new features and improvements over JUnit 4. It offers a more modular and extensible architecture, better support for **Java 8** and above, and various new annotations, such as @BeforeEach, @AfterEach, and @DisplayName.

If we wanted to rewrite the CalculatorTest class using JUnit, the result would be as follows. The example is straightforward, but it helps us understand how the framework works:

```
@Test
@DisplayName("Tests the Addition method of the Calculator")
void testAddition() {
    Calculator calculator = new Calculator();
    int result = calculator.add(5, 3);
    int expected = 8;

    Assertions.assertEquals(result, expected);

}
```

You can notice the @Test annotation, which allows the framework to "understand" that that is a unit test. @DisplayName is utilized to specify a personalized name for the annotated test class or test method; these display names are commonly employed for test reporting within IDEs and build tools, and they have the flexibility to include spaces, special characters, and emojis.

This is how the IntelliJ IDE represents the execution of a successful JUnit test:

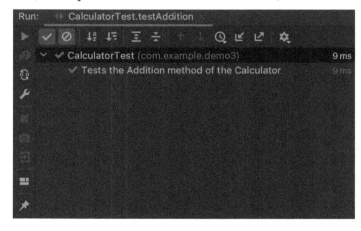

Figure 4.1 – Execution of a successful JUnit test in the IntelliJ IDE

Now, it is quite intuitive, I believe, to understand how an automated test suite can be integrated into the code development process; frameworks such as JUnit help developers test their code, find bugs, and potentially improve performance. JUnit (and unit testing in general) reaches its full potential when integrated through tools such as **Maven** or **Gradle** (which allow code build management and automated test execution) and **Jenkins** or **GitHub**, which handle **Continuous Integration** (**CI**), a practice that involves automatically and regularly integrating code changes into a shared repository and running automated tests to detect integration issues early. CI is a very broad topic, so I refer you to the *Further reading* section, where there is a related Wikipedia entry. Unfortunately, it is challenging to find *agnostic*, meaning not tied to specific products, material online that explains the concepts. I hope this can serve as a starting point and stimulate your curiosity.

Writing unit tests is hard and complicated, much more than it may seem from these few simple examples. It is also a crucial task, essential both for a smooth production release and to be able to perform any desired refactoring. One of the most challenging aspects is imagining all possible test cases (i.e., all potential behaviors of the application, all the "flows" it can follow – think of all the if statements and polymorphism you have used in your code); fortunately, we don't have to imagine, as we can use tools designed for this purpose.

Integration testing

Integration testing involves checking how various pieces, modules, or parts of a software application work together, even if different programmers coded them.

The goal of integration testing is to examine the connections between these modules and uncover any issues that might pop up when these components come together and have to work together.

It is usually performed downstream of unit tests; assuming that individual software modules (be they projects, classes, or entire applications) are tested individually, we begin to test the interactions they have with other modules with which they collaborate, as shown in *Figure 4.2*:

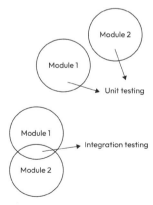

Figure 4.2 – Unit tests concern each module individually, while integration tests concern interactions

To carry out integration testing, testers use test drivers and *stubs*, that is, placeholder programs that step in for any absent modules and mimic data exchange between modules for testing. There are several frameworks that can help you along the way; you don't have to do all the work by yourself! The most famous framework used to perform integration testing (at least on a basic and widespread level) is JUnit (which we just saw) in combination with Mockito.

Mockito

Mockito is a widely used Java-based open source framework for creating and configuring mock objects in both unit testing and integration testing. In the context of Java software development, Mockito is favored for its ability to facilitate testing by creating mock objects that mimic the behavior of real components. These mock objects are especially valuable in integration testing for several reasons:

- Firstly, Mockito aids in isolating specific parts of an application. It allows developers to create mock objects that simulate the behavior of real components, thereby enabling them to test particular modules, components, or services in isolation. This isolation is crucial when you want to verify the behavior of a specific part of your application without involving the entire system or interacting with real dependencies, such as databases, web services, or external APIs. In the following code snippet, we can get an idea of how Mockito works:

```
import static org.mockito.Mockito.*;
// Create a mock HTTP client
HttpClient httpClientMock = mock(HttpClient.class);

// Create an instance of your service and inject the
  mock
MyService myService = new MyService(httpClientMock);

// Define the behavior of the mock
when(httpClientMock.get(anyString())).thenReturn
  ("Mocked response");

// Perform a test using MyService
String result = myService.getDataFromExternalService
  ("https://example.com/api");
```

- Secondly, Mockito provides control and verification capabilities. Developers can define the behavior of mock objects, specify what methods should return, and record interactions with these objects during the test. This level of control and verification ensures that the component under test correctly interacts with its dependencies. To verify something, you just have to write something such as the following:

```
// Verify interactions with the mock
verify(httpClientMock).get("https://example.com/api");
```

Additionally, Mockito contributes to the efficiency and speed of integration tests. Using real external dependencies in integration tests can be slow and complex to set up, and may result in undesirable side effects. In contrast, Mockito's mock objects are lightweight and do not rely on external resources, making integration tests faster, more efficient, and less prone to side effects.

* Lastly, Mockito offers test flexibility. Developers can create customizable mock objects that allow them to specify different behaviors for various test cases. This flexibility simplifies the simulation of various scenarios in integration tests.

We have left some material in the *Further Readings* section to deep dive into the magic of Mockito.

Contract testing

We have seen that integration tests are also used to test external services, services that are probably not in our code base and that may not even be maintained by us. You then create a stub, or mock, that returns a "fake" answer, based on documentation or, often, on the real answers exchanged at runtime between the two services. But what happens if something changes, if one of the two changes the contract? How do you make sure that the mock we've created is really a representation of the outside service? Contract testing helps us.

Contract testing aims to ensure compatibility and agreement between different services or components within a distributed system. It is particularly useful in scenarios such as microservices architectures where different services need to communicate seamlessly. In contract testing, services communicate with each other based on well-defined interfaces or contracts. These contracts outline how data is exchanged, specify available methods or endpoints, and describe expected responses.

There are two primary roles in contract testing: consumers and providers. Consumers are the services or components that utilize data or functionality from another service, known as the provider. Contracts define what the consumer expects from the provider; that is why it is said that contract tests are consumer-driven.

The process starts with the definition of contracts, which can take various forms, such as API specifications or interface documentation. Contract testing primarily focuses on the consumer's perspective. Consumer tests are written to ensure that the provider's behavior aligns with the contract. These tests are typically managed by the consumer's team. Provider tests, on the other hand, are written by the provider's team. They verify that the provider complies with the contract specifications. Automated contract tests run continuously as part of the build and deployment process. They help detect compatibility issues early whenever changes occur in either the consumer or provider service. Here is a diagram to help understand contract testing:

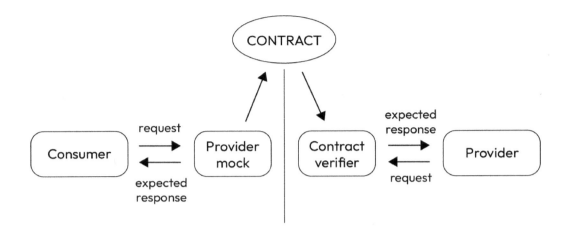

Figure 4.3 – Contract testing

Various tools and libraries support contract testing, depending on the project's technology stack and requirements. Some popular options include Pact, Spring Cloud Contract, and Pacto.

Be safe – checking and improving your test coverage

Testing is important, but we need to make sure we test our code thoroughly, not just a part of it; covering all the code doesn't only mean all the classes, but also all possible execution paths. We might think it's easy to keep all possible cases in mind, and perhaps this is true for very small projects; but as the project grows and inevitably becomes more complex (for example, the number of features increases or the possible execution paths multiply), it becomes difficult to understand the efficiency of our tests for keeping us safe. This is why we introduce the concept of test coverage and a tool to measure it.

What is test coverage?

Test coverage, also known as **code coverage**, is a metric used to measure the extent to which the source code of a program is executed by a set of test cases. It is a quantitative measure that helps developers and testers understand how much of the code is being exercised during testing.

Test coverage is usually expressed as a percentage, representing the proportion of code lines, branches, statements, or methods that have been executed by the test suite compared to the total number of such elements in the code base.

There are different types of coverage metrics:

- **Line coverage**: This measures the percentage of lines of code that have been executed at least once during testing.

- **Branch coverage**: Branch coverage measures the percentage of branches (i.e., decision points – basically, and simplifying, the `if` instances in your code) that have been taken or not taken during testing. It ensures that both true and false branches of conditional statements are tested.

- **Statement coverage**: This measures the percentage of executable statements that have been executed during testing.

- **Method coverage**: Method coverage measures the percentage of methods or functions that have been called during testing.

Test coverage is not a definitive measure of software quality but provides valuable insights into the thoroughness of testing efforts. High coverage indicates that a significant portion of the code has been tested, increasing confidence in the correctness of the application. However, even 100% coverage does not guarantee a bug-free application, as it is possible to have untested edge cases or incorrect assumptions in the test cases.

By improving test coverage, developers can mitigate the risk of undiscovered defects and make their code more robust and maintainable. We use code coverage tools to generate coverage reports, which can be analyzed to identify areas of the code that need more testing.

A Java code coverage tool – JaCoCo

JaCoCo (short for **Java Code Coverage**) is a widely used open source code coverage library for Java projects. It provides a comprehensive and detailed analysis of code coverage, allowing developers to understand how much of their Java code is exercised by their tests.

JaCoCo offers various types of code coverage analysis, including line coverage, branch coverage, and method coverage. It instruments the Java bytecode during the build process to collect execution data, which is then used to generate coverage reports.

JaCoCo primarily provides three significant metrics:

1. **Line coverage** indicates the extent of code that has been executed based on the number of Java bytecode instructions called by the tests

2. **Branches coverage** shows the percentage of exercised branches in the code, usually associated with `if/else` and `switch` statements

3. **Cyclomatic complexity** reflects the code's complexity by quantifying the number of paths required to cover all the possible code paths through a linear combination

To illustrate with a simple example, if the code contains no `if` or `switch` statements, the cyclomatic complexity will be 1, as only one execution path is needed to cover the entire code. In general, the cyclomatic complexity represents the number of test cases required to achieve full code coverage.

To illustrate how JaCoCo works, let's start with a very simple example. It is not my intention to create a tutorial on this tool here – there are already plenty of them online – but I would like to show you its main features so that you can get a rough idea of how it works.

Let's suppose we have a project consisting of only one class named `Calculator`, defined as follows:

```
public class Calculator {

    public Integer sum(Integer a, Integer b) {
        return a + b;
    }

    public Integer subtract(Integer a, Integer b) {
        return a - b;
    }

    public Integer multiply(Integer a, Integer b) {
        return a * b;
    }

}
```

As you can see, the `Calculator` class exposes three very simple methods that take two integers as input and return, respectively, their sum, difference, and product. Let's proceed to write the corresponding test class, which we will define as follows:

```
class CalculatorTest {
    private final Calculator calculator = new Calculator();

    @Test
    void sum() {
        var sum = calculator.sum(1, 4);
        assertEquals(5, sum);
    }

    @Test
    void subtract() {
        var sum = calculator.subtract(10, 4);
        assertEquals(6, sum);
    }

}
```

The test class creates an instance of `Calculator` and then performs two unit tests, one for the sum and the other for the difference. Using the JUnit framework, we verify that the expected result matches the actual result.

There are many ways to use a tool like JaCoCo, but in my opinion, the best approach is to integrate it into the development cycle. Assuming we are using Maven, we will configure our `pom.xml` file so that the plugin is executed and reports are generated:

```
<plugin>
    <groupId>org.jacoco</groupId>
    <artifactId>jacoco-maven-plugin</artifactId>
    <version>0.8.10</version>
    <executions>
        <execution>
            <goals>
                <goal>prepare-agent</goal>
            </goals>
        </execution>
        <execution>
            <id>report</id>
            <phase>prepare-package</phase>
            <goals>
                <goal>report</goal>
            </goals>
        </execution>
    </executions>
</plugin>
```

The execution of JaCoCo's Maven plugin will create a report inside the `target/site` folder, which can be easily viewed through any web browser.

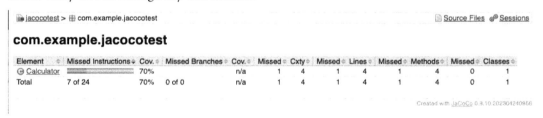

Figure 4.4 – The mini-website created by JaCoCo shows the test coverage for each class

In this table, we find the only class in our project. We can see from the report that the `Calculator` class has **70%** test coverage. This is because we haven't performed any tests on the `multiply` method. Let's add a third unit test to our test class:

```
@Test
void multiply() {
    var sum = calculator.multiply(6, 5);
    assertEquals(30, sum);
}
```

Then, let's run the JaCoCo Maven plugin again. The report will now look like this:

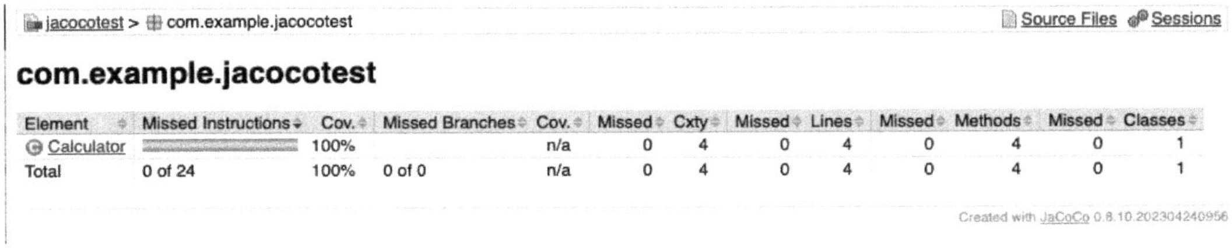

Element	Missed Instructions	Cov.	Missed Branches	Cov.	Missed	Cxty	Missed	Lines	Missed	Methods	Missed	Classes
Calculator		100%		n/a	0	4	0	4	0	4	0	1
Total	0 of 24	100%	0 of 0	n/a	0	4	0	4	0	4	0	1

Created with JaCoCo 0.8.10.202304240956

Figure 4.5 – After adding a test case, coverage is now 100%

All the methods of Calculator have been tested. The coverage is **100%**.

What happens if we make changes? Let's say, for example, we decide not to support negative results in the subtraction operation by adding a check that throws an exception when the subtrahend (the number that is subtracted from another number) is greater than the minuend (the number from which another number is subtracted):

```
public Integer subtract(Integer minuend, Integer
    subtrahend) {
    if (subtrahend > minuend) {
        throw new IllegalArgumentException("Minuend must be
            greater than the subtrahend");
    }
    return minuend - subtrahend;
}
```

If we run JaCoCo again, we can notice something very interesting:

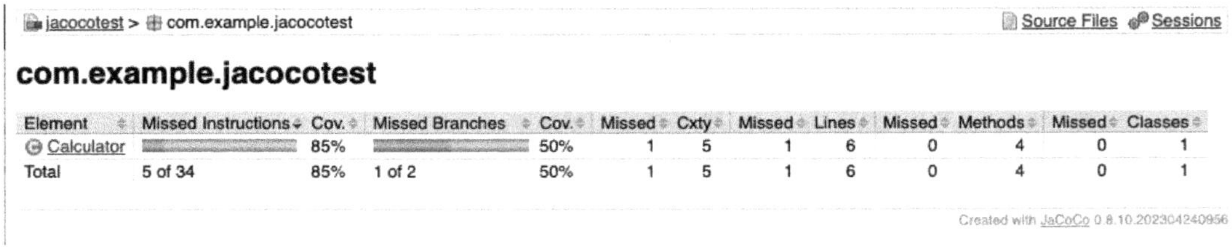

Element	Missed Instructions	Cov.	Missed Branches	Cov.	Missed	Cxty	Missed	Lines	Missed	Methods	Missed	Classes
Calculator		85%		50%	1	5	1	6	0	4	0	1
Total	5 of 34	85%	1 of 2	50%	1	5	1	6	0	4	0	1

Created with JaCoCo 0.8.10.202304240956

Figure 4.6 – By adding a new feature without adding the relative test, the coverage decreases

The coverage has decreased, and specifically, the **Missed Branches** column has been populated. In the context of JaCoCo, a *branch* refers to a specific path or decision point in the code where the program flow can take different routes. Branches are typically associated with conditional statements, such as if-else statements and switch-case statements.

We can see which method is affected by clicking on `Calculator`:

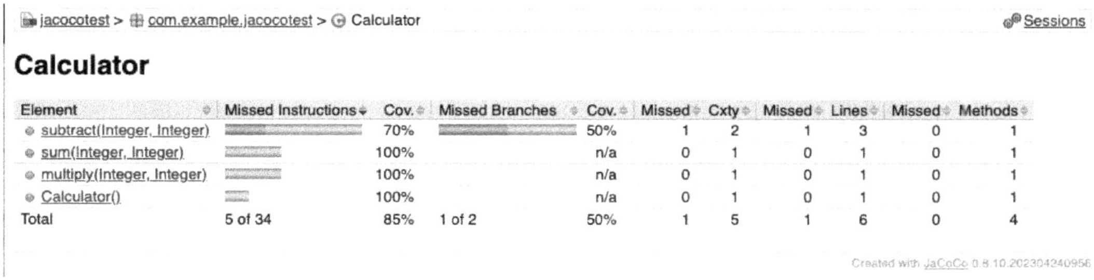

jacocotest > com.example.jacocotest > Calculator   Sessions

Calculator

Element	Missed Instructions	Cov.	Missed Branches	Cov.	Missed	Cxty	Missed	Lines	Missed	Methods
subtract(Integer, Integer)		70%		50%	1	2	1	3	0	1
sum(Integer, Integer)		100%		n/a	0	1	0	1	0	1
multiply(Integer, Integer)		100%		n/a	0	1	0	1	0	1
Calculator()		100%		n/a	0	1	0	1	0	1
Total	5 of 34	85%	1 of 2	50%	1	5	1	6	0	4

Created with JaCoCo 0.8.10.202304240956

Figure 4.7 – By clicking on the Calculator entry, it is clearer which of its methods is not fully covered

We can even click on the method to see which part of the code is not covered:

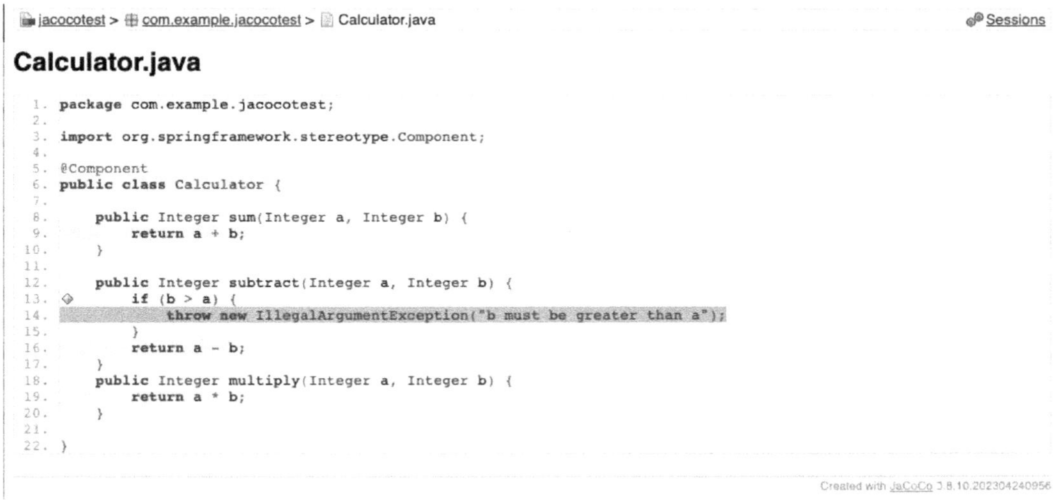

jacocotest > com.example.jacocotest > Calculator.java   Sessions

Calculator.java

```
1.  package com.example.jacocotest;
2.
3.  import org.springframework.stereotype.Component;
4.
5.  @Component
6.  public class Calculator {
7.
8.      public Integer sum(Integer a, Integer b) {
9.          return a + b;
10.     }
11.
12.     public Integer subtract(Integer a, Integer b) {
13.         if (b > a) {
14.             throw new IllegalArgumentException("b must be greater than a");
15.         }
16.         return a - b;
17.     }
18.     public Integer multiply(Integer a, Integer b) {
19.         return a * b;
20.     }
21.
22. }
```

Created with JaCoCo 0.8.10.202304240956

Figure 4.8 – Clicking on the single method entry, it's possible to see where the test coverage is missing

Since we have added an `if` statement, we have created a branch. Whenever a branch is created, which represents a new possible execution flow, we must cover it with tests. Let's do this:

```
@Test
void subtractWithIllegalArgument() {
    assertThrows(IllegalArgumentException.class, () ->
        calculator.subtract(10, 21));
}
```

Let's regenerate the report to see the changes:

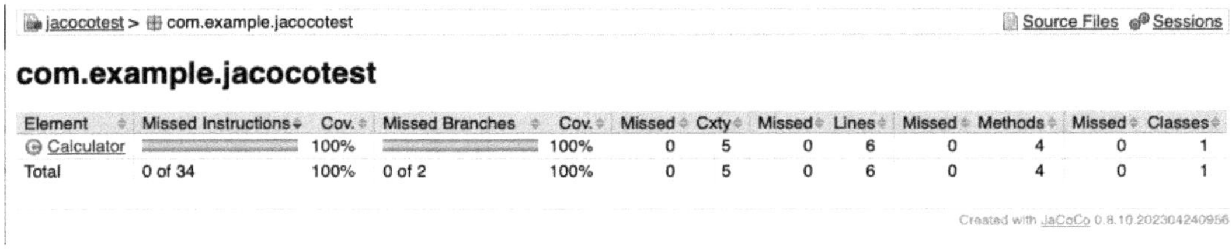

jacocotest > com.example.jacocotest Source Files Sessions

com.example.jacocotest

Element	Missed Instructions	Cov.	Missed Branches	Cov.	Missed	Cxty	Missed	Lines	Missed	Methods	Missed	Classes
Calculator		100%		100%	0	5	0	6	0	4	0	1
Total	0 of 34	100%	0 of 2	100%	0	5	0	6	0	4	0	1

Created with JaCoCo 0.8.10.202304240956

Figure 4.9 – Again, full coverage

The coverage is now back to **100%**.

This is just the tip of the iceberg. JaCoCo is highly configurable (for example, you can configure branches and missed instructions) and can be used to completely block the build when a minimum coverage threshold is not met. You can exclude individual classes, class patterns, packages, and more. I strongly encourage you to explore this tool further.

Now that we have roughly seen how JaCoCo works and, above all, what test coverage is, let's delve further into our reasoning and try to understand why it is convenient, sensible, and extremely advantageous, when developing, not only to write tests but also to... start with them!

Test-driven development

As the name suggests, **test-driven development**, abbreviated as **TDD**, is a widely used software development practice in Agile methodologies, especially in **Extreme Programming**. It is widely regarded as a fundamental technique for achieving higher-quality software.

As the name itself suggests, development is driven by tests, not the other way around. The classic development cycle involves the following:

DESIGN ⟶ CODE ⟶ TEST

Figure 4.10 – The classic development cycle involves designing, coding, and then testing

This is flipped around. We start with the tests to arrive at defining the design; of course, writing the code in between:

TEST ⟶ CODE ⟶ DESIGN

Figure 4.11 – The TDD cycle starts with the tests

Attention is given to the functional aspects of the code, specifically the method signatures, before the actual implementation of the code. To start with the tests, you need to take the perspective of the "client" of your code and primarily consider the public methods:

1. The methodology involves immediately writing a test; by executing this test (which requires defining an input, invoking a method, and asserting the result), the outcome will inevitably be a failure since the implementation does not exist yet. This phase is called **Red** (the color that commonly indicates a failure of a unit test in many IDEs).

2. The next step is to implement the missing functionality by writing the bare minimum to make the test pass as quickly as possible. When the test passes, you are in the so-called **Green** phase. Don't worry if the code you wrote is not perfect or if you think it could be improved; that will be addressed in the next phase.

3. The third and final phase of TDD is **Refactor**, which allows you to transform your code by adapting, simplifying, streamlining, and removing duplicates. In this phase, you do not add new features, as it is purely a refactoring process. If you want to add new features, you must go back to the Red phase and start again from there.

Here is a diagram of the TDD process:

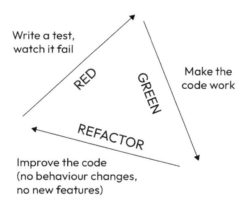

Figure 4.12 – The TDD cycle

I think that by this point, you will have understood how cool this technique is; however, as with all things, there are not just advantages. Let's take a closer look at the pros and cons of this methodology so that you can form your own opinion. As usual, don't expect an exhaustive list; even though I tried to refer to the existing literature on the subject, much of it is influenced by my personal experience.

Advantages of TDD

Here are some advantages of TDD:

- **You only write code that's needed**: According to the principles, it's important to avoid writing production code right after all your tests pass. Instead, when your project requires a new feature, you should create a test first to guide the implementation process. The code you write should be the most straightforward and minimal necessary to fulfill the feature's requirements. In this way, only the essential code to implement the features will end up in the final product.

- **Fast failing**: The distinctive aspect of TDD is its ability to facilitate rapid failure. This shortens the feedback loop, allowing the development team to quickly determine whether the code is correct. Developers can conduct self-assessments and manual acceptance tests, while also engaging in peer-to-peer reviews. The outcome is a reduced turnaround time, leading to minimal defects during testing.

- **Continuous change**: As usual, most developers collaborate on the same code base. Whenever an individual developer starts working, CI tools detect the changes and promptly execute the unit tests, assessing the code within a few minutes. If any failures occur, they are promptly reported to the developers, who resolve the issues before proceeding to manual or integrated testing, ensuring that end users do not encounter these problems.

- **Easier to maintain and refactor the code base**: Decoupling and clear interfaces make code more manageable. You can replace microfeature implementations without affecting other modules and rewrite the entire application with preserved tests. Thorough testing for each feature eliminates the fear of making changes. A complete test suite allows confident code improvements without breaking the application.

- **Clear documentation**: TDD uses unit tests, which act as effective documentation, sparing the need for time-consuming and difficult-to-maintain written documentation. This aspect is a key characteristic of good test coverage overall. TDD significantly contributes to achieving comprehensive test coverage.

- **Nudge to refactoring**: There is a dedicated Refactor step as part of the Red-Green-Refactor cycle, ensuring that developers think about improvements in the design for every single line of code that they write.

Development speed – a note

Especially at the beginning, the feeling is that of progressing very slowly. TDD is more focused on delivering quality code rather than delivering code quickly. People might also write too many tests that are similar or redundant, or perhaps write tests that are too simple or test trivial parts of the code. Until the mindset is well integrated within the team, it may take some time to proceed at a decent pace.

Anyway, when developers delay the creation of tests, it may initially appear to expedite the development process. However, this approach frequently results in tightly coupled code, rendering certain portions untestable. In the event of discovering bugs, the debugging phase can become a time-consuming and unpredictable task. Consequently, choosing to replace the uncertain and variable debugging process with a more predictable and structured testing procedure is often a better idea.

To summarize, TDD is a software development methodology in which developers create automated tests before writing the actual code. This process involves three main steps: writing a failing test that defines the desired functionality, writing the minimum code required to pass the test, and then refining the code while ensuring all tests continue to pass. It can be implemented over unit tests and also other kind of tests, such as integration tests. TDD encourages iterative development, improves code quality, and helps catch bugs early in the development process.

Summary

I hope I have conveyed to you the importance of testing, not only as a necessary condition for refactoring but also as a cornerstone of quality code. In this chapter, we have understood why testing is crucial and why it is beneficial to do it frequently, allowing us to fail as early as possible – this may appear like a paradox, but it isn't.

We have various types of tests at our disposal, but we focused particularly on unit testing, for which a framework such as JUnit is of great help.

Since testing is essential, it is crucial to have as much of our code base covered by tests as possible. For this purpose, we have the assistance of another tool, JaCoCo.

Furthermore, we introduced the fundamental methodology TDD, reversing the traditional development flow to start with tests and then proceeding to write the code.

Now that we have covered all the fundamentals, we can move on to the next chapter, where we will finally analyze some refactoring techniques, delving deeper into topics that we only briefly touched upon in the chapter on code smells – *Chapter 3*.

Further reading

- **The Confusion: Error vs. Fault vs. Bug vs. Defect vs. Failure**: https://farhan-labib.medium.com/the-confusion-error-vs-fault-vs-bug-vs-defect-vs-failure-c557af04726b

- Getting started with Apache JMeter: https://jmeter.apache.org/usermanual/get-started.html

- Customer satisfaction: https://www.linkedin.com/advice/1/what-key-performance-indicators-measuring-customer

- Continuous integration: `https://en.wikipedia.org/wiki/Continuous_integration`
- *Continuous Delivery: Reliable Software Releases through Build, Test, and Deployment Automation* by Jez Humble and David Farley (Addison-Weasley, 2010)
- The JUnit framework's official website: `https://junit.org/junit5/`
- Getting started with Mockito: `https://www.baeldung.com/mockito-series`
- JaCoCo website: `https://www.jacoco.org/jacoco/`

5
Refactoring Techniques

We're now getting into the meat of the subject: how to do refactoring. It would be a bit silly to think we can cram all the refactoring techniques ever known into one chapter. So, we've decided to focus on the most common and more interesting ones. Our main source of wisdom comes from Martin Fowler's fantastic work in his book, *Refactoring: Improving the Design of Existing Code*. He teamed up with Kent Beck to explain, step by step, how to do refactoring, from the simplest to the trickiest cases. For each one, they provide a kind of *how-to* guide so that you won't mess things up. Here, we're offering a selection of the most important refactoring techniques, an importance that we consider based largely on our own experience.

> Tip
>
> For those who don't know, Martin Fowler and Kent Beck are influential figures in software development. Martin Fowler is known for his contributions to software design, refactoring, and agile methodologies, while Kent Beck is the creator of **Extreme Programming** (**XP**) and the JUnit testing framework. Both have had a significant impact on shaping agile practices and improving software development processes.

We've tried to simplify even more what Fowler wrote and sprinkle in a bit of our own work background. If you haven't already, we suggest you read the chapter on code smells (*Chapter 3*) before you dive into this.

In this chapter, we'll cover the following:

- Techniques for making well-structured methods
- Moving features from one object to another
- Making your data more organized
- Simplifying those tricky `if-else` blocks
- Cleaning up your method calls
- Some tips on using generalization
- A nudge to use enums when they make sense

But let's cut to the chase, starting with the basics: composing methods.

Writing better methods

Composing methods is a fundamental skill that should be a part of every developer's refactoring toolkit. To put it simply, almost bluntly, it's about breaking your code into smaller pieces, each of which does just one thing in a very readable way, in a very procedural manner; you could almost think of it as a recipe (please forgive me; I'm Italian, so I always bring everything back to food). The details are hidden in the methods beneath the composed method; this allows us to read our logic, our code, at a high level – I dare say, almost "in prose."

When refactoring your code, the process typically involves extracting code from the original method. If you find it challenging to come up with meaningful names for the extracted methods, it's a clear sign that the code chunk you were about to extract may be too extensive. Another case I've come across is when someone (sometimes myself) suggested naming a method that contained the conjunctions "and" or "or"... also in this situation, it's clear that the method we are working on has too many responsibilities and is doing too many things. In such cases, try to identify a smaller, more focused portion for extraction. Often, in longer methods, you may notice that certain sections are already marked with comments; these labeled sections can frequently be refactored into new methods.

You might find yourself, after applying this refactoring technique, having many short methods within the same class; this, in itself, is already an improvement. However, at this point, it might be desirable to further shorten the class by extracting a dedicated one.

Here are some guidelines you can follow when you have to compose methods:

- **The shorter, the better**: Lean toward brevity and conciseness in your code. Smaller functions and code blocks are generally preferred, as they enhance readability and maintainability.

- **Minimize redundancy**: When employing the composing method pattern, pay close attention to eliminating duplicate code fragments. This practice not only trims down your code base but also prevents inconsistencies and simplifies future updates.

- **Show your purpose**: To foster code clarity and adopt a naming convention that leaves no room for ambiguity. Every variable, method, and parameter should be named in a way that succinctly conveys its role and function.

- **Strive for simplification**: Simplification is a guiding principle in code improvement. It entails the removal of unnecessary complexities, streamlining logic, and adhering to best practices. Simplified code is not only more elegant but also more maintainable.

- **Maintain consistent detail levels**: When applying the composing method pattern, it's essential to harmonize the complexity level of the methods you call. Avoid mixing simple, straightforward getters with functions that perform resource-intensive computations. Consistency in detail levels fosters code cohesion and comprehension.

There are many ways to achieve these goals; next, we will see some of them.

Extract Method

We have already seen something about it in the previous chapters, but I would like to delve a bit deeper. In my opinion, this is the refactoring that we do (or should do) most often. It is quite simply taking a very long method – too long – and breaking it down into smaller methods. How long can a method be at most? Obviously, there is no general rule; it depends on your sensitivity and that of the team. Let's say that I have to scroll with the mouse to read it all; this is already a small indicator of excessive length. I like to follow what Martin Fowler has taught us once again and try to limit the lines of my methods as much as possible; it sometimes happens that I have methods that are only two or three lines long. In addition to the code length for which I perform method extraction, sometimes I also consider the reusability of the code I am extracting, as it's important to avoid copy-paste. However, I agree with Fowler (and of course I do!) in saying that methods should be written with their *intent* in mind; that is *what* those methods are supposed to do, and not *how* they're gonna do it: isolate all the code needed to do a certain thing in a single method, no matter how small. The method's name should then be based on "what" the method does and not "how" it does it.

Let's illustrate these concepts with a very simple example. Suppose we have the following method:

```
public void calculate(int num1, int num2) {
    int sum = num1 + num2;
    System.out.println("Sum: " + sum);
    int difference = num1 - num2;
    System.out.println("Difference: " + difference);
}
```

As you can see, the method is very simple: it is a method that calculates the sum and difference of two numbers and prints them. Of course, the reality is much more complex than that, but the principles do not change. We refactor the code like this:

```
public void calculate(int num1, int num2) {
    int sum = addNumbers(num1, num2);
    printResult("Sum", sum);
    int difference = subtractNumbers(num1, num2);
    printResult("Difference", difference);
}

private static void printResult(String operationName, int result) {
    System.out.printf("Result of %s: %d%n", operationName, result);
}

public static int addNumbers(int a, int b) {
    return a + b;
```

```
    }

    public static int subtractNumbers(int a, int b) {
        return a - b;
    }
```

We have extracted three methods: one that sums up the numbers, a second that makes the difference, and a third that prints the result on the screen to avoid repetition. Don't be fooled by the length of this specific piece of code; again, it's just one example to illustrate the concept – in reality, you have to think of sum and difference operations as longer methods that implement perhaps more complex logic. Another reflection we can make here is that extracting methods promotes code reuse because the logic thus extracted can be invoked in many different points.

Inline Method

This is exactly the opposite of extracting methods. It may seem strange, after having insisted so much on the extraction of methods, on short methods, to suggest that sometimes it is appropriate, instead, to inline the method. This little refactoring can be very useful when you have a very short method (typically a line of code or two) that is never reused and that already expresses very well what it does; in this case, isolation in a method with the sole purpose of "explaining," through the name of the method itself, what the method does may be excessive.

I'll provide you with a very trivial example of what method inlining is. Let's suppose we have the following three methods in a class:

```
    public int add(int a, int b) {
        return a + b;
    }

    public int multiply(int a, int b) {
        return a * b;
    }

    public int calculate(int x, int y) {
        int sum = add(x, y);
        int result = multiply(sum, 2);
        return result;
    }
```

As you can easily see, we have a `calculate` method that takes two integers as input and performs a series of operations on them. The operations are represented by the `add` and `multiply` methods, which, of course, make the sum and the product of the two integers they take as input. These methods are used only once and are very simple: in fact, only one line. So, let's take the opportunity to perform method inlining and make the code shorter and more readable:

```
public int calculate(int x, int y) {
    int sum = x + y;
    int result = sum * 2;
    return result;
}
```

The `add` and `multiply` methods disappeared, and their implementation, consisting of a single line of code, replaced them where they were invoked. We could further refactor the code by returning directly the result of the last operation, avoiding the `result` variable:

```
public int calculate(int x, int y) {
    int sum = x + y;
    return sum * 2;
}
```

This example may seem contradictory to what we wrote in the previous chapter (in fact, we are now inlining something that before we isolated), but it's just for the sake of providing a very simple example.

To sum up, what you have to do to perform an "Inline Method" refactoring is this:

1. Check that the method hasn't been changed in subclasses. If it has been modified, avoid using this technique.

2. Hunt down all the places where the method is called, then replace those calls with the actual code from the method.

3. Go ahead and delete the method.

Of course, since we are talking about refactoring, the behavior must never change; to be sure, there's no other way than to include testing in the little recipe written previously. Be sure to always carry out a test before eliminating a method that you have inlined. We'll get to that later in the book, but most modern **integrated development environments** (IDEs) offer tools to do this refactoring with a simple click of the mouse.

Use Inline Method refactoring in the following cases:

- **When the method's implementation is straightforward**: If the method's logic is simple and direct, as demonstrated in the preceding example, consider employing this refactoring technique to eliminate it.

- **When you want to eliminate unnecessary delegation**: At times, you may transfer the method's implementation to another method or class, introducing unnecessary indirection in the code. To streamline the code and remove this extra layer of delegation, use the Inline Method technique.

- **As a foundation for subsequent refactorings**: The process of refactoring is not always a linear one, and there are various ways to refactor the same code. For instance, you can employ extract method refactoring to isolate different code segments. However, if the refactoring path you initially chose does not yield improved code, you can use the inline method to reintegrate previously extracted code back into its original method and then explore alternative refactoring approaches.

Extract and inline variables

We summarize these two refactoring techniques in a single section since – in our humble opinion – they are very similar to the Extract Method and Inline Method techniques but applied to a single variable.

The main motivation – perhaps the only one – to introduce (extract) a variable instead of an expression is when the latter could be difficult to understand (not so much and not only on a technical level; we talk here about the motivation behind the expression itself). Let's try to explain ourselves better with an example:

```
if (transport.getEquipment().toUpperCase().equals("PLN") || transport.
getEquipment().toUpperCase().equals("TRN")) {
    //do something
} else {
    //do something else
}
```

In this code snippet, we analyze a field of a generic `transport` object that represents a means of transport; among its various fields, the object also has an `equipment` object that tells us what means of transport it is. Unfortunately, this field is a string (see *Chapter 3, Primitive Obsession*), and we are forced to write an `if` statement to understand what type it is, whether plane or train. The code snippet is a bit clearer if we insert the result of `equals` within a couple of variables with a self-explanatory name:

```
boolean isPlane = transport.getEquipment().toUpperCase().
equals("PLN");
boolean isTrain = transport.getEquipment().toUpperCase().
equals("TRN");
if (isPlane || isTrain) {
    //do something
} else {
    //do something else
}
```

Someone would be tempted to simply insert a comment to explain what those cryptic strings `"PLN"` and `"TRN"` refer to, but personally, we find this kind of approach more effective. You could also use enums instead of plain strings so that a possible typo would be caught by the compiler. By introducing these "intermediate parts" formed by the variables, the code is made more understandable. The drawback is... that your code contains more variables. As always in life, it is a problem of balance! The choice is yours.

The technique of "inline variable," on the other hand, is so similar to that of the *inline method* that it is worth explaining it directly through an example that is practically the same as the one seen in the relative section:

```
int sum = num1 + num2;
printResult("Sum", sum);
```

In this case, assigning to the sum variable the result of the addition – and then never using it again after printing it – does not add much to the understanding of the code compared to the expression itself. It is therefore better to inline the variable directly in the only point where it is used, eliminating the first line of the snippet:

```
printResult("Sum", num1 + num2);
```

Combining a function into a class

As the last notable example of refactoring that reorganizes code by "recomposing" methods, we propose one that combines several methods within a single class. This technique is used when we have several methods that have in common one (or more) input parameters; that is, that – in practice – go to act on the same classes. Again, let's go directly to show an example that should better clarify the concept. Suppose we have this set of methods:

```
String getLocalizedName(Location location) { ... }

Collection<Location> getAdjacentLocations(Location location) { ... }

Coordinates getCoordinates(Location location) { ... }
```

All of these methods take a single parameter of the Location type. It would be better to enclose all the logic concerning the Location parameter in a single point. For this, we create a class that contains all the logic:

```
public class LocationHandler {

    private final Location location;

    public LocationHandler(Location location) {
        this.location = location;
    }

    String getLocalizedName() { ...}

    Collection<Location> getAdjacentLocations() { ...}
```

```
        Coordinates getCoordinates() { ...}

    }
```

A `Location` instance is passed only once, in the constructor. From the signatures of the methods we then removed the parameter; now, you no longer need to pass it. Of course, consider carefully whether to refactor this way; if your `Location` instance changes often, such as for each method call, using such a pattern might not be the best idea, because you should instantiate a `LocationHandler` for each call.

Moving features between objects

As we have already mentioned several times, and as those who have been in this profession for more than a few years know organizing our code is perhaps one of the most challenging parts. Personally, I believe I have never managed to get the design of a software project right on the first try. But, once again, the software is fortunately (or unfortunately!) malleable, so with the right limits and a good amount of refactoring, we can move methods and fields from one class to another without too much difficulty. We can decide to extract a class or remove one and inline it. Above all, we can eliminate the so-called dead code. But let's start showing something.

Moving a method or field

This refactoring is quite basic (Martin Fowler calls it the "bread and butter" of refactorings), but it is one of the most frequently performed ones. This is because, as we have already mentioned, it is good practice to maintain a certain modularity in your software project so that classes, packages, and so on are grouped coherently based on the context in which they operate. For example, in one package, we may place all classes responsible for managing user information, while in another, we may gather all clients for external services. There is no single criterion, but rather, often, a certain subjectivity. This is why it can often happen that methods or individual fields are moved from one class to another. This movement, guided by the principle of keeping related things together and separating things that should be separate, simplifies the code.

This is one of those cases where doing something is simpler and more intuitive than explaining it, but I'll try to give you Martin Fowler's "recipe" for it, perhaps simplifying it a bit.

Transferring a method from the source class to the target class involves several steps that must be followed to ensure a successful refactoring process:

1. Examine the dependencies and other class members that the method utilizes. Determine if it's necessary to relocate them to the new class as well.

2. Check whether the method is referenced by a superclass or subclass. If it's being used by these classes, it may not be feasible to move the method.

3. Establish the method in the target class and replicate existing code into it. If the relocated method relies on an instance of the original class, you can pass it as a method parameter.

4. Delete the code within the old method and direct the call to the new method. (This is optional; you could also use a **feature toggle**.)

5. Optionally, make a decision about whether to eliminate the old method entirely and directly invoke the new method.

Feature toggle

Feature toggles, also known as **feature flags**, are a technique that allows us to activate or deactivate specific functionalities without directly modifying the source code. This approach brings benefits such as continuous deployment, simplified testing in real-world conditions, efficient issue management, gradual feature rollouts for risk management, and the ability to compare feature variants for informed decision-making.

In the most abstract sense, a feature toggle would work like this in a Java method:

```
public void applyLogic() {
    if (newFeatureEnabled) {
        applyNewLogic();
    } else {
        applyCurrentLogic();
    }
}
```

In the end, it is advisable to execute your test suite. It's essential to bear in mind, even though it should be implicit when discussing refactoring.

With a single field, the process is very similar. We have a field that is used by another class more than the class in which it is defined. The context is not respected; therefore, we move the field to that other class, subsequently changing all points where that field is used.

Fields are often moved around when applying the **Extract Class** technique, and deciding which class should keep a particular field can be a bit tricky. Here's a practical rule of thumb: put the field in the same class as the methods that use it the most, or in the class where you find most of these methods. This rule can also prove beneficial in scenarios where a field is clearly situated in an inappropriate location.

Once again, let's present the methodology as described by Fowler:

1. When dealing with a public field, refactoring becomes significantly more manageable by converting it into a private field and providing public access methods (you can utilize the **Encapsulate Field** technique for this purpose, as explained in the *Field encapsulation* section).

2. Establish the same field within the receiving class along with its corresponding access methods.

3. Determine how you will access the receiving class. You may already possess a field or method that yields the required object. If not, you'll need to create a new method or field to store the object associated with the receiving class.

4. Substitute all occurrences where the old field is referenced with appropriate method calls in the receiving class. If the field is not private, address this in both the superclass and any subclasses as necessary.

5. Eliminate the field from the original class.

Moving statements into/from methods

Repeated code is one of the most common problems in our code base; the temptation to copy and paste is sometimes too strong. This can be seen before calling a certain method, a certain line of code; it can also happen that the same line of code is repeated before each call to that method. At this point, you will have understood that the best alternative is to take that statement and move it directly inside that method.

On the contrary, there may be a statement within the code that doesn't fit well with the context of the method; perhaps it makes sense in one execution flow but not in another. In this case, make the opposite move to the previous one and move the statement outside of the method, to the point where it's truly needed.

I consider this technique very common but quite straightforward. For a deeper exploration of the "mechanics" of how it works, I refer you to the *Further reading* section.

Hiding delegates

This refactoring technique is applied when a class (referred to as the client) obtains an object of type *B* (referred to as the delegate) through another class of type *A* (referred to as the server). When client code calls a method defined on an object within a server object's field, it establishes a direct dependency on that delegate object. Consequently, if the delegate object's interface undergoes changes, all clients of the server relying on that delegate are affected. To eliminate this dependency, one can introduce a straightforward delegation method within the server, effectively hiding the delegate. Any subsequent modifications made to the delegate's interface will then only impact the server itself, shielding clients from these changes.

An example will clarify a bit what we just said. Let's suppose to have two classes:

```
public class Itinerary {

    private final String departureAirport;
    private final String arrivalAirport;
```

```
    //constructor, getters...
}

public class Flight {

    private final Itinerary itinerary;
//constructor, getter...
}
```

If we want to get `departureAirport`, but we have an instance of `Flight`, our code will be something like this:

```
var departureAirport = flight.getItinerary().getDepartureAirport();
```

This is OK, of course, except for the fact that now we must also be aware of the `Itinerary` class; that is actually useless since we need just `departureAirport`. We don't want to change our code if the `Itinerary` class changes. So, we will write something like this:

```
public class Flight {

    private final Itinerary itinerary;

    public String getDepartureAirport(){
        return itinerary.getDepartureAirport();
    }

    //constructor, getter...
}
```

So, we just call a method of the `Flight` class to get the field we need. Of course, we will also have to change the client code:

```
var departureAirport = flight.getDepartureAirport();
```

The delegate is now hidden. We have less code and fewer relations between objects.

But as a recipe, as Martin Fowler does, here are the steps to perform this refactoring:

1. For every method in the delegate class that the client class calls, generate a corresponding method in the server class that forwards the call to the delegate class.

2. Modify the client code to invoke the methods in the server class instead of directly calling the delegate class.

3. If your modifications successfully eliminate the client's dependency on the delegate class, you can safely remove the access method to the delegate class within the server class (the method originally used to obtain the delegate class).

One downside is that if you have to generate an excessive number of delegate methods, the server class may end up being an unnecessary intermediary, resulting in an abundance of middlemen.

Removing dead code

Ah, here's one of the things that satisfies me the most: deleting unnecessary code! Dead code refers to parts of the source code that are no longer executed or reachable during the program's execution.

Dead code can occur for various reasons, such as the following:

1. **Code removal or refactoring**: When developers modify a program, they may delete or comment out certain sections of code that are no longer needed. These leftover code snippets become dead code.

2. **Conditional branches**: In some cases, code may be written within branches of conditional statements that are never true during execution, making the code within those branches effectively dead.

3. **Unused variables or functions**: If variables or functions are defined but not used anywhere in the program, they are considered dead code.

You don't want dead code in your project: it makes it harder to understand, increases maintenance costs, and potentially introduces bugs.

So, please, if you are aware of dead code in your project – and modern IDEs now are perfectly capable of doing that – please just remove it. No – don't comment it out! Get rid of it; if you just want to recover it, I bet you're using a versioning control system (such as Git or Subversion) that will do the trick.

Watch out also for so-called **dead comments**. As we mentioned before, our view on comments is that there should be as few as possible and focused on explaining *why* something is done. In an ideal and fantastic world, the code itself should be able to explain without needing extra comments. What often – very often – happens is that comments don't get updated along with the code, becoming not only irrelevant but also harmful, sometimes misleading. Even if you're taught to add lots of comments to code in school (at least, I was), please try to keep it to a minimum.

What we've said about dead code can of course be applied also to modules, services, or even individual features. It's quite common to see the proliferation of modules and services deployed in production that are no longer actually used, and their only effect is to consume precious (read: expensive) resources. Typically, everyone forgets about them until it's time to update them (for example, due to a discovered vulnerability among their dependencies) or when someone realizes they're costing a lot of money in hardware resources! In the case of features, it's similar: why keep unused features that make the code more complex without any real benefit? Get rid of them at the first opportunity, and you won't regret it!

We've seen a very important part of code refactoring, and we've learned some techniques for moving pieces of code without too much disruption. In addition to being in the right place, features must be well structured and organized. Let's see some suggestions about this.

Organizing data

How data is organized is one of the most important aspects of our profession; coherently aggregating information forms the foundation for building a solid, maintainable, and extensible software project. Various types of refactoring assist us in this regard, and once again, Fowler helps us navigate them in great detail. In the upcoming sections, we will present a selection of those we consider to be the most common or potentially misleading.

Field encapsulation

We will group together in a single section techniques that we believe are very similar to each other and ultimately concerned with not revealing the internal structure of a class to its users. This principle is known as **encapsulation** and is one of the fundamental concepts of **object-oriented programming (OOP)**; hiding the internal structure of a class and providing access methods to its fields is beneficial because it simplifies the use of the class, protects data, improves maintainability, encapsulates behavior, and allows access control. Data is not separated from the associated behaviors, the modularity of program sections is not compromised, and maintenance is simplified. To achieve encapsulation starting from a public field, it is sufficient to make the field private and expose so-called *getter* and *setter* methods. For example, take a look at the following code:

```
class Flight {
    public Airport departureAirport;
}
```

This would become the following:

```
class Flight {
    private Airport departureAirport;

    public Airport getDepartureAirport() {
        return departureAirport;
    }

    public void setDepartureAirport(Airport departureAirport) {
        this.departureAirport = departureAirport;
    }
}
```

The departureAirport field has been made private, and we expose two methods that respectively read and write the field itself. If you want to make the class immutable – something we highly recommend in general – you would just need to make departureAirport final, add it to the constructor, and eliminate the *setter* method.

Someone might argue that this way, we still expose the class's structure, and... they would be right! However, keep in mind that this is a very simple case: for example, it's not necessary for getters and setters to exist for all fields or that they must exclusively perform read or write operations on the fields – they could also involve some logic (but be cautious about performance in this case!).

Another important note: starting from Java 14, the `Record` keyword was introduced – a construct that allows you to define a class such as `Flight` in a single line, with less boilerplate. You can refer to the *Further reading* section for more details.

We can also encapsulate the field within the class itself. Let's extend our `Flight` class a bit, assuming that we also need to access the `departureAirport` field internally:

```
class Flight {
    private Airport departureAirport;

    // getter and setter

    public String getDepartureAirportCode(){
        return this.departureAirport.getAirportCode();
    }
}
```

At times, directly accessing a private field within a class may lack the desired flexibility. You have the option to execute intricate operations when data within the field is set or received – tasks such as *lazy initialization* and validation of field values can be effortlessly incorporated within the field's getters and setters. Other than that, you'd have the ability to override getters and setters in subclasses.

So, the `Flight` class would look like this (please observe the `getDepartureAirportCode` method):

```
class Flight {
    private Airport departureAirport;

    // setter

    public Airport getDepartureAirport() {
        return departureAirport;
    }

    public String getDepartureAirportCode(){
        return this.getDepartureAirport().getAirportCode();
    }
}
```

Someone could argue that we gained in flexibility but lost a bit in readability because of the need to read the getDepartureAirport method; someone else could say that this is untrue, as long as the methods are named well and represent just a getter; we're also promoting loose coupling. It's up to you to choose which path to follow.

The final case of encapsulation that we want to present concerns collections, and I have indeed seen this problem many times. In this case, the class contains a field of the Collection type, and its getters and setters operate on the entire collection, making it more challenging to interact with it. Modifying the previous examples slightly, let's suppose we have a Flight class that contains a Collection field of airports, one for each stopover:

```
class Flight {
    private List<Airport> itineraryAirports;

    public List<Airport> getItineraryAirports() {
        return itineraryAirports;
    }

    public void setItineraryAirports(List<Airport> itineraryAirports)
{
        this.itineraryAirports = itineraryAirports;
    }
}
```

The protocol for utilizing these collections differs slightly from that employed by other data types. It is important to note that the getter method should not return the actual collection object itself. Doing so would permit clients to manipulate the contents of the collection without the owner class's awareness. Moreover, this would reveal an excessive amount of the object's internal data structure to clients. Instead, the method for retrieving collection elements should provide a value that prevents any modifications to the collection and avoids revealing too much information about its structure. There should be no method for directly assigning a value to a collection. Instead, the protocol should provide operations for adding and deleting elements. This approach empowers the owner object to exercise control over the addition and removal of elements within the collection:

```
class Flight {
    private List<Airport> itineraryAirports;

    public List<Airport> getItineraryAirports() {
        return Collections.unmodifiableList(itineraryAirports);
    }
    public void addAirport(Airport itineraryAirport) {
        this.itineraryAirports.add(itineraryAirport);
    }
    public void removeAirport(Airport itineraryAirport) {
```

```
        this.itineraryAirports.remove(itineraryAirport);
    }
}
```

We have removed the setter method and added two methods for adding and removing elements from the list. When we return the list through the getter, we instantiate a new immutable list using Java 17's `Collections::unmodifiableList` methods (but we could have used Guava, Apache Commons, or whatever).

> **A couple of disclaimers**
>
> We are modifying objects, which goes against the concept of immutability that we have advocated for on these pages, so please be cautious. Also, remember that the type of the collection for which you are performing add and remove operations (in this case, `Airport`) must override the `equals` and `hashCode` methods.

Replacing primitives with objects

This refactoring comes to our rescue when dealing with the code smell called **Primitive Obsession**, which we encountered in *Chapter 3*. This happens when we use integer, double, string types, and so on, instead of more complex types; these primitives are fine if we only need to print this information without any special logic. But often, we discover that things are more complicated than that. Going on with our `Flight` class, this time, let's assume that a field containing the service level, also known as "cabin class," is defined, as follows:

```
class Flight {
    private String cabinClass;

    public Flight(String cabinClass) {
        this.cabinClass = cabinClass;
    }

    //getter and toString

}
```

If we wanted to filter from a list of flights only the most expensive ones, we would have to do something like this:

```
var expensiveFlights = flightList.stream().filter(f ->
f.getCabinClass().equals("Business") || f.getCabinClass().
equals("First Class")).collect(Collectors.toList());
```

It's not ideal. I need to know what all the possible values for the cabin class are, and I must know exactly which one is more expensive than the other. In these cases, it's better to use a class to replace the primitive type, allowing not only wrapping but also the implementation of custom logic:

```
var expensiveFlights = flightList.stream().filter(f ->
f.getCabinClass().higherThan(new CabinClass("Economy"))).
collect(Collectors.toList());
```

As you can see, the higherThan method allows us to implement a logic that compares our cabin class to another, without worrying about managing and maintaining the logic itself.

I think it is worth taking a look at the CabinClass class:

```
public class CabinClass {

    private final String name;
    private final int value;

    public CabinClass(String name) {
        this.name = name;
        switch (name) {
            case "Economy":
                value = 1;
                break;
            case "Premium":
                value = 2;
                break;
            case "Business":
                value = 3;
                break;
            case "First":
                value = 4;
                break;
            default:
                throw new IllegalArgumentException();
        }
    }

    //getters

    public boolean higherThan(CabinClass other){
        return this.getValue() > other.getValue();
    }

}
```

It has a name and a value; the latter is used to determine the position in the "value scale" of the cabin classes, and it is assigned to the class constructor. We still have a lot of strings around, but I think we can do better. Let's go ahead.

Replacing type code with subclasses

Let's start with the previous example, that of the cabin class. You may have noticed that defining the "type" of the cabin class by passing a string in the constructor is not ideal. In a simple scenario, we could make a typo while writing the type; in reality, the real issue is that we are delegating to the caller knowledge that should be internal to the `CabinClass` class. When we have a situation such as this, a situation in which our class has a "type," and the behavior of the class itself can depend on this type, a useful refactoring is to create subclasses. Our `CabinClass` class would then become the following:

```
public class CabinClass {

    protected final String name;
    protected final int value;

    protected CabinClass(String name, int value) {
        this.name = name;
        this.value = value;
    }

    //getters, toString, and higherThan
}
```

But we would also have a series of subclasses defined as follows:

```
public class Economy extends CabinClass{
    public Economy() {
        super("Economy", 1);
    }
}

public class Premium extends CabinClass{
    public Premium() {
        super("Premium", 2);
    }
}

public class Business extends CabinClass{
    public Business() {
        super("Business", 3);
    }
```

```
    }

public class First extends CabinClass{
    public First() {
        super("First", 4);
    }
}
```

Notice how the parameters are defined within the constructor, and how it is impossible for the caller to modify them. In this way, among other things, we leverage all the advantages of OOP, and code readability is also improved as a result. For completeness, here is a snippet that filters expensive flights, modified accordingly:

```
var economyClass = new Economy();

var expensiveFlights = flightList.stream().filter(f ->
f.getCabinClass().higherThan(economyClass)).toList();
```

Notice that we simply instantiate an Economy class to be used into the higherThan method.

Organizing data well means, at the end of the day, simplifying things – or at least making them more readable. One thing that can make code very complicated to read is conditional logic. Let's see how you can simplify it a bit.

Simplifying conditional logic

For this section, we will also rely on Martin Fowler and try to explain some of the refactorings to what we consider to be the most common problems. The selection is arbitrary and based solely on our experience. For further details, we refer you to the *Further reading* section.

Returning a special case instead of null

Do not return null. This is a mantra that everyone – even engineers with years of experience – sometimes forgets. There are cases where a method should return a result but cannot: some error in the execution flow; some exceptional cases. Java and many other languages allow returning null, but it's preferable not to do so for obvious reasons – among them, avoiding a NullPointerException in the caller or forcing it to check every time that the method's result is not null.

> **Tip**
> Tony Hoare introduced Null references in **ALGOL W** back in 1965 "simply because it was so easy to implement," according to him. Reflecting on that decision, he refers to it as his "billion-dollar mistake". More on this in the *Further reading* section.

There are various ways to avoid null references, but one of the most common is to return a so-called **Special Case** object, which is a default object with predefined values.

Take, for example, the following code snippet:

```
CustomerAddress customerAddress = addressRepository.
findByCustomerId(customer.getId());
if (customerAddress == null) {
    customerStreet = "Unknown";
    customerCity = "Unknown";
} else {
    customerStreet = customerAddress.getStreet();
    customerCity = customerAddress.getCity();
}
```

We can notice how we need to differentiate the logic by checking if the object returned by the repository is null. In this case, it wouldn't even be very useful if the repository method returned an Optional because we would still need to write an if statement; in our opinion, however, it would be better because it would at least make the caller aware that the call may not return the desired result. One solution, though, is to introduce a Special Case object. Here is a possible implementation in Java:

```
interface CustomerAddress {
    String getStreet();
    String getCity();
}
```

We introduce an interface that allows us to implement the special case, and then we implement it in two classes:

```
class UnknownCustomerAddress implements CustomerAddress {

    @Override
    public String getStreet() {
        return "unknown";
    }

    @Override
    public String getCity() {
        return "unknown";
    }
}

class ActualCustomerAddress implements CustomerAddress {

    String street;
```

```
      String city;

   //constructor and getters

}
```

Notice how the ActualCustomerAddress class is the actual "real" one, while the other is a kind of "dummy object" used to allow the caller to not change the execution flow when calling the method. Of course, we have the (small?) disadvantage of creating more classes than there were before; the cleanliness of the code greatly benefits from this.

In theory, we could also craft a specific exception for our situation and throw that instead of giving back a fake object. But, honestly, we don't see that happening a lot (and we're not big fans of it!). Still, it is worth acknowledging this for the sake of completeness.

Using polymorphism instead of conditions

Let's revisit a code smell discussed in *Chapter 3*: repeated switches. When there is a lot of conditional logic, it's better to introduce some structure. When a switch statement is repeated many times in the code, especially around a variable named type, it's highly likely that refactoring is a better approach:

```java
public Long calculateDistance(Itinerary itinerary) {
    Long distance;
    switch (itinerary.getType()) {
        case "TRAIN": {
            var departureLocation = getDepartureStation(itinerary);
            var arrivalLocation = getArrivalStation(itinerary);
            distance = calculateItineraryDistance(departureLocation,
arrivalLocation);
            break;
        }
        case "FLIGHT": {
            var departureLocation = getDepartureAirport(itinerary);
            var arrivalLocation = getArrivalAirport(itinerary);
            distance = calculateItineraryDistance(departureLocation,
arrivalLocation);
            break;
        }
        default:
            throw new IllegalArgumentException("Unknown type");
    }
    return distance;
}
```

In this method, which calculates the distance traveled in a travel itinerary – whether it's by plane or by train – we encounter several issues. The caller must be aware of the possible values that `type` can take, implementing different logic at each point in the code where it's needed. Furthermore, we anticipate that there will be other points in the code where it needs to behave differently based on the type of itinerary.

Instead, we can simply utilize polymorphism:

```
abstract class Itinerary {
    public abstract Long calculateItineraryDistance();
}

final class FlightItinerary extends Itinerary {
    @Override
    public Long calculateItineraryDistance() {
        //calculations for a flight...
    }
}

final class TrainItinerary extends Itinerary {
    @Override
    public Long calculateItineraryDistance() {
        //calculations for a train...
    }
}
```

Polymorphism in the previous code allows us to treat different types of itineraries (`FlightItinerary` and `TrainItinerary`) as instances of a common base class (`Itinerary`). This enables you to call the `calculateItineraryDistance` method on them without knowing their specific types, promoting code flexibility and reuse, and creating two classes that extend the same abstract class. At this point, the caller will no longer have to worry about anything:

```
public Long calculateDistance(Itinerary itinerary) {
    Long distance = itinerary.calculateItineraryDistance();
    return distance;
}
```

Removing duplicated conditions

It can sometimes happen that identical code is duplicated within the two branches of an `if-else` block in a conditional statement. Why this happens, I honestly couldn't say; however, I can testify that I've seen it more often when methods are very long or as a result of refactoring. In my humble opinion, it's usually a simple oversight, but it's an oversight that happens more often than you might think. For example, in the previous example, we can observe precisely that calculateItineraryDistance(departureLocation, arrivalLocation); is called in two different cases within the switch statement. In general, when we are in a condition in which the same call is repeated, we can do as follows:

```
var result = doCalculations(x, y);
if (doCalculations(x, y) > 5) {
    //do something
    printResult(result);
} else {
    //do something else
    printResult(result);
}
```

The advice is simply to take the duplicate call out of the if statement, like so:

```
var result = doCalculations(x, y);
if (doCalculations(x, y) > 5) {
    //do something
} else {
    //do something else
}
printResult(result);
```

Keep in mind that maybe the method in question does not exist yet; however, there is repeated code that you can put together using the **Extract Method** technique.

Guard clauses

The last piece of advice I give you is on simplifying conditional logic concerns' nested if statements; I must admit that I suffer a lot when I find them, with the code moving further and further to the right of the screen, almost forming mandalas that need a really large monitor to be appreciated! A slope toward the abyss.

Here is an example of a method that, in addition to being very trivial, has many nested if statements. It takes three parameters as input and finds the largest, but none of them must be negative:

```
public void printLargestPositive(int x, int y, int z) {
    if (x > 0) {
        if (y > 0) {
            if (z > 0) {
                if (x > y && x > z) {
                    print("x is the largest.");
                } else if (y > x && y > z) {
                    print("y is the largest.");
                } else {
```

```
                print("z is the largest.");
            }
        } else {
            print("z is not positive.");
        }
    } else {
        print("y is not positive.");
    }
} else {
    print("x is not positive.");
}

}
```

Understanding the purpose and functionality of each conditional is challenging due to the lack of clarity in a typical code execution flow. These conditionals suggest a disorganized development process, with each condition added as a temporary solution without considering the optimization of the overall structure.

To simplify the situation, separate exceptional cases into distinct conditions that promptly terminate execution and return a null value if the guard clauses are evaluated as true. Essentially, your goal here is to streamline the code structure and make it more linear, like this:

```
public void printLargestPositiveRefactored(int x, int y, int z){
    if (x <= 0) {
        print("x is not positive.");
        return;
    }

    if (y <= 0) {
        print("y is not positive.");
        return;
    }

    if (z <= 0) {
        print("z is not positive.");
        return;
    }

    if (x > y && x > z) {
        print("x is the largest.");
    } else if (y > x && y > z) {
        print("y is the largest.");
    } else {
        print("z is the largest.");
```

```
        }
    }
```

We know this code could be even more rewritten, but it's just for explaining the concept. Some might argue that this method has too many returns within it and that it would be better to have only one. I can't say, honestly, if there are too many, but it's a good point to observe. I agree, however, with what Steve McConnell says in his book, *Code Complete*: use a `return` statement when it makes your code easier to understand. In some functions, as soon as you have the answer, just give it back to the calling function right away. If the function doesn't need any extra cleanup after finding an error, not returning immediately would mean having to write more code.

Also, if the code is mainly focused on performance, stopping after the most usual condition can skip some extra checks. This can be really helpful, especially if one or two situations make up the majority, like 80 or 90% of the time it runs.

Simplifying method calls

Method calls are essential in OOP, as they enable objects to perform specific tasks or actions. There are many techniques intended to simplify the way objects interact with each other; we're going to see some of the most interesting ones.

Avoiding side effects

We already discussed the side effects and mutability of objects in *Chapter 3*, explaining why they are not ideal in a software project. A typical way to cause side effects is when you mix a query, which is a part of the code that simply retrieves information, and a modifier, which is code that performs an action on some data or system, thereby changing its state. Here's an example of this:

```
public Price getTotalItineraryPrice(User user, Itinerary itinerary){
    Price totalPrice = calculateTotalPrice(itinerary);
    emailService.sendPriceRecap(user);
    return totalPrice;
}
```

In this example, the method calculates the total price for a specific travel itinerary and simultaneously sends a summary email to the customer. We have several issues here. First (but this is the least of them), the name is misleading because it is not consistent with the actual behavior of the method. Furthermore, the method does more than one thing; particularly, it returns information (a `Price` instance) on one hand, but on the other hand, it changes the state of things by notifying the user. It's better to separate these concerns, like so:

```
public Price getTotalItineraryPrice(Itinerary itinerary) {
    return calculateTotalPrice(itinerary);
```

```
    }

    public void sendEmailRecap(User user) {
        emailService.sendPriceRecap(user);
    }
```

We now have two distinct methods, one that requests information and another that somehow modifies the system's state. It's worth noting that a query method can be called as many times as desired without affecting the system's state. The code is cleaner, and we have also removed a parameter from the getTotalItineraryPrice method.

Removing setter methods

Actually, this section should almost be a continuation of the previous one. Removing so-called *setter* methods, which allow you to set the value of an object's field, makes them immutable, removing undesirable side effects.

We've already discussed this in this chapter, but we'd like to go into a bit more detail. Let's consider a very simple class representing a person; let's include only two fields for simplicity:

```
class Person {

    private String taxCode;
    private String name;
    public String getTaxCode() {
        return taxCode;
    }

    public void setTaxCode(String taxCode) {
        this.taxCode = taxCode;
    }

    public String getName() {
        return name;
    }

    public void setName(String name) {
        this.name = name;
    }

}
```

The Person class is represented with taxCode and name. taxCode is unique and represents the identifier for a person. As we see, you can instantiate this class and set its fields, like this:

```
Person p = new Person();
p.setTaxCode("4598308JKFLD3424243");
p.setName("John Doe");
```

If we returned this instance to a calling method, no one would guarantee that its fields would not be modified. The refactoring in question simply aims to remove setter methods, adding its parameter inside the constructor, like this:

```
Person p = new Person("4598308JKFLD3424243");
p.setName("John Doe");
```

Notice how taxCode is passed inside the constructor. In the Person class, the taxCode field can then become final.

True immutability – the builder pattern

To make an object truly immutable in each of its fields, we recommend using the **builder pattern**.

The builder pattern is a design pattern used to construct complex objects step by step. It separates the construction of an object from its representation, allowing you to create different representations of the same object.

Here's how the builder pattern typically works:

- **Create a builder class**: First, you create a separate builder class for constructing an object. This builder class has methods for setting the various attributes of the object you want to create.

- **Set attributes**: You use the methods in the builder class to set the attributes of the object. Each method typically returns the builder object itself, allowing you to chain method calls (this is known as **method chaining**).

- **Build**: When you've set all the desired attributes, you call a build method on the builder object, which constructs and returns the final object with the specified configuration.

A builder class for the Person class would look like this:

```
public final class PersonBuilder {
    private String name;
    private final String taxCode;

    private PersonBuilder(String taxCode) {
        this.taxCode = taxCode;
    }

    public static PersonBuilder builder(String taxCode) {
        return new PersonBuilder(taxCode);
    }
```

```
public PersonBuilder name(String name) {
    this.name = name;
    return this;
}

public Person build() {
    Person person = new Person(taxCode);
    person.setName(name);
    return person;
}
}
```

You can clearly see a static `builder` method that instantiates the builder itself, taking `taxCode` as its only parameter, which is mandatory. The `name` method is just a setter of the `name` attribute; you can have one setter for each field of your class. At the end, the `build` method creates and populates an instance of `Person`. Using the builder pattern on a type is meaningful as long as you do not provide any other method to instantiate that type; for example, you can keep the constructor of the `Person` type private and create `builder` as an inner class.

The usage of `PersonBuilder` is quite straightforward:

```
Person p = PersonBuilder.builder("4598308JKFLD3424243")
        .name("John Doe")
        .build();
```

Once the object has been built (instantiated), you cannot modify its fields. In this example, the `builder` method (in this instance, the builder, in fact, and not the `Person` class) takes as a parameter `taxCode`, which is mandatory.

There are tools to automate the creation of builder classes, which we will discuss later in the book.

Using generalization

Generalization is one of the most powerful features of OOP, and it must be used wisely (*with great power comes great responsibility*). I'll report here just some of the most interesting refactorings in this area, going fast with the most basic and delving a little bit deeper with the others.

Pull up field

This technique consists of moving a field (or variable) from a subclass to a superclass. This is typically done when multiple subclasses share the same field or when you want to establish a common interface or behavior in the superclass. Here's an example:

```
public class Triangle {
    private Integer sidesNumber;

}

public class Square {
    private Integer sidesNumber;
}
```

Triangle and Square have a field in common; just extract an interface or an abstract class to do the trick:

```
public abstract class Polygon {
    private Integer sidesNumber;
}

public class Square extends Polygon {
}

public class Triangle extends Polygon{
}
```

Push down field

This is the opposite of a pull down field, and it's used when you have a field (or attribute) defined in a superclass, but it's only relevant to a specific subclass or a subset of subclasses. You just have to move the field from the superclass to the subclass where it's actually used.

For example, let's take a Vehicle class containing a single field called engine. We have two subclasses extending from it:

```
public class Vehicle {
    protected EngineType engine;
}

public class Car extends Vehicle{
}

public class Bicycle extends Vehicle{
}
```

While it makes sense for a Car to have an engine, of course, it doesn't for a Bicycle. Let's move the engine field into the only class it needs to be in:

```
public class Vehicle {

}

public class Car extends Vehicle{
    protected EngineType engine;
}

public class Bicycle extends Vehicle{
}
```

Pull up method

This consists of moving a method from a subclass to a superclass. This is typically done when multiple subclasses share a common behavior, and you want to establish that behavior in the superclass to promote code reuse. Here's an example:

```
public class Triangle extends Polygon{
    public Long calculatePerimeter(){
        //calculations...
    }
}

public class Square extends Polygon {
    public Long calculatePerimeter(){
        //calculations...
    }
}
```

It's worth pulling the calculatePerimeter method up in the superclass and removing the method from Triangle and Square:

```
public abstract class Polygon {
    private Integer sidesNumber;
    public Long calculatePerimeter(){
        //calculations...
    }

}
```

```
public class Triangle extends Polygon{
}

public class Square extends Polygon {
}
```

Push down method

This is the opposite of the pull up method, and it is used when you have a method defined in a superclass, but its behavior is relevant only to a specific subclass or a subset of subclasses. You just have to move the method from the superclass to the subclass where it's actually used.

For example, let's take again a `Vehicle` class containing a single method called `fillTank`. We also have two subclasses extending from it:

```
public class Vehicle {
    protected void fillTank() {
        //method implementation
    }
}

public class Car extends Vehicle{
}

public class Bycicle extends Vehicle{
}
```

As you can easily guess, having a `fillTank` method doesn't make any sense for a class representing a bicycle, but only for a class representing a car. So, what we're gonna do is just push the method down onto the `Car` subclass:

```
public class Vehicle {
}

public class Car extends Vehicle{
    protected void fillTank() {
        //method implementation
    }
}

public class Bycicle extends Vehicle{
}
```

Template method

It often happens, when we program, that we have algorithms or processes of some kind to apply to objects in a way that is almost entirely similar but not exactly the same. A certain logic may apply generally to an entire category of objects, but these objects may have some specific characteristics that make them different. In the previous examples, we used the classic example of polygons. We can say that for a polygon, the calculation of the perimeter always involves summing the lengths of its respective sides. However, between a triangle and a square, for example, the number of sides changes. Therefore, it could be useful to have a method in the superclass that is implemented in the subclasses and represents their specific characteristics. I believe it's easier to explain this with an example:

```java
public class Triangle extends Polygon {
    private final Long aLength; //length of side a
    private final Long bLength; //length of side b
    private final Long cLength; //length of side c

    public Triangle(Long aLength, Long bLength, Long cLength) {
        this.aLength = aLength;
        this.bLength = bLength;
        this.cLength = cLength;
    }

    public Long getPerimeter() {
        return aLength + bLength + cLength;
    }
}

public class Square extends Polygon {
    private final Long sideLength;

    public Square(Long sideLength) {
        this.sideLength = sideLength;
    }

    public Long getPerimeter() {
        return sideLength * 4;
    }
}

public abstract class Polygon {
}
```

Both `Triangle` and `Square` have a `getPerimeter` method that basically sums up the length of their sides; we could not just pull up the method, because the implementation is different – one has three potentially different sides, and the other has four equal sides. What we're going to do is implement a template method, in which we will call another method defined in the subclasses, which just returns a `Collection` field of side lengths:

```
public class Triangle extends Polygon {
    private final Long aLength; //length of side a
    private final Long bLength; //length of side b
    private final Long cLength; //length of side c

    public Triangle(Long aLength, Long bLength, Long cLength) {
        this.aLength = aLength;
        this.bLength = bLength;
        this.cLength = cLength;
    }
    @Override
    protected Collection<Long> getSideLengths() {
        return List.of(aLength, bLength, cLength);
    }
}


public class Square extends Polygon {
    private final Long sideLength;

    public Square(Long sideLength) {
        this.sideLength = sideLength;
    }


    @Override
    protected Collection<Long> getSideLengths() {
        return List.of(sideLength, sideLength, sideLength,
sideLength);
    }
}

public abstract class Polygon {
    public Long getPerimeter() {
        Collection<Long> sideLengths = getSideLengths();
        Long perimeter = 0L;

        for (Long length : sideLengths) {
            perimeter += length;
        }
```

```
        return perimeter;
    }


    protected abstract Collection<Long> getSideLengths();
}
```

We have created a `getSideLengths` template method that reduces redundancy by consolidating common algorithmic steps in a superclass while allowing distinctions to remain in the subclasses. This is a vibrant example of the **Open/Closed Principle (OCP)** in practice. If a new version of the algorithm is introduced, you can simply create a new subclass without needing to modify the existing code.

Using enums instead of constants

At this point, we have seen some of the main refactoring techniques discussed in the literature. Now, we move on to a final section where we allow ourselves to give you a couple of tips on how to better organize your code design. These may seem trivial, but they often lead to considerable annoyance. The first tip, as the title of this section suggests, concerns the excessive use of constants (a thorough study based solely on my perception and experience undoubtedly shows that these constants will be strings 99% of the time).

Let's suppose we have the following class:

```
public class Itinerary {

    private String transportType;
    private String cabinClass;

    //getters and setters
}
```

In another class, we defined the following constants:

```
private static final String FLIGHT = "FLIGHT";
private static final String TRAIN = "TRAIN";

private static final String ECONOMY = "ECONOMY";
private static final String FIRSTCLASS = "FIRSTCLASS";
```

In one method, let's instantiate our `Itinerary` class:

```
Itinerary itinerary = new Itinerary();
itinerary.setCabinClass(FLIGHT);
itinerary.setTransportType(ECONOMY);
```

Do you see anything weird? We accidentally swapped `cabinClass` with `transportType`! We didn't even realize it because everything compiles when we're just dealing with strings. If we don't really need to create custom types to represent these concepts, such as the transport type and the cabin class, our suggestion is to use enums.

In fact, let's introduce enums:

```
enum TransportType {FLIGHT, TRAIN}
enum CabinClass {ECONOMY, FIRSTCLASS}
```

We can then rewrite the code like this:

```
public class Itinerary {

    private TransportType transportType;
    private CabinClass cabinClass;

    public Enums.TransportType getTransportType() {
        return transportType;
    }

    public void setTransportType(Enums.TransportType transportType) {
        this.transportType = transportType;
    }

    public Enums.CabinClass getCabinClass() {
        return cabinClass;
    }

    public void setCabinClass(Enums.CabinClass cabinClass) {
        this.cabinClass = cabinClass;
    }
}
```

This will then be used without the possibility of error:

```
Itinerary itinerary = new Itinerary();
itinerary.setCabinClass(CabinClass.ECONOMY);
itinerary.setTransportType(TransportType.FLIGHT);
```

Using enums is generally better than constants in Java because they offer the following:

- **Type safety**: Enums are types themselves, meaning they allow you to define a set of distinct values that are of the same type. This prevents you from accidentally using incorrect values in your code, reducing runtime errors.

- **Readability**: Enums provide meaningful names for each of their values, making the code self-documenting. This improves code readability and comprehension because you can understand the purpose of each value just by looking at its name.

- **IDE support**: IDEs offer features such as code completion and error checking specific to enums. When you use constants, you may not get the same level of support, and you might need to remember or look up valid values.

- **Refactoring ease**: When you need to change or add a value, enums make it easier. IDEs can automatically update all references to the enum value throughout your code, reducing the chances of errors during maintenance.

- **Additional behaviors**: Enums can have methods and fields associated with them, allowing you to encapsulate behavior related to each enum value. For example, you can define a method that calculates a specific value or behavior for each enum, improving code organization and maintainability.

- **Enum-specific collections**: Java provides specialized data structures such as `EnumSet` and `EnumMap` that are highly efficient when working with enums. These collections are tailored to work specifically with enum values, making your code more concise and performant.

- **Compile-time checking**: Errors related to incorrect constant values may only surface at runtime, potentially causing unexpected issues. In contrast, issues with enums, such as missing values or incorrect references, are caught by the compiler, ensuring that your code is correct before it's executed.

- **Serialization support**: Enums have built-in support for serialization and deserialization, which simplifies tasks such as saving enum values to a file or transmitting them over a network.

Basically, when you use enums in Java, you get a bunch of benefits compared to plain constants. These perks include making your code safer, easier to read, and simpler to maintain. Enums also play well with your development tools, making your life easier. But that's not to say constants don't have their uses – they do, especially in specific situations. However, for most cases where you have a fixed set of values with some extra behavior, enums are the way to go.

Summary

Here we are, at the end of this journey through refactoring techniques. We hope we've given you some ideas on how to craft methods better, making them clear and readable. We've explored how it can sometimes be helpful to shuffle features between objects and better organize your data. We've simplified conditional logic (you know – those `if` statements and switches that help us solve problems quickly but can make our code unreadable!). We've simplified method calls, used a bit of good old generalization, and talked briefly about the immutability of objects. In the next chapter, we'll dive into how to use automated tools to (hopefully!) make our code even better.

Further reading

- For other examples and use cases: Martin Fowler, *Refactoring*, Addison-Wesley

- *Null references: The Billion Dollar mistake*: `https://www.infoq.com/presentations/Null-References-The-Billion-Dollar-Mistake-Tony-Hoare/`

6

Metaprogramming

In a book about refactoring, it may seem a bit strange to talk about metaprogramming. More than refactoring per se, in our opinion, talking about metaprogramming and tools that use it can be useful concerning clean code, and writing clean code means "preventing" the refactoring, which is indeed still relevant to our goal.

As we will see shortly, metaprogramming involves writing programs that work on programs. In our context, we will endorse the usage of frameworks written by others (the first virtue of a good software engineer: laziness) that help us write less code (told you!).

Writing less code (or rather, having it written by tools) is a good thing: it means less code to maintain, trivially, and it means that those portions of code are in charge of dedicated tools that will then write that code in the best possible way.

In this chapter, we're going to cover the following main topics:

- What is metaprogramming?
- Exploring compile-time and runtime metaprogramming tools
- Lombok and MapStruct
- Weighing the pros and cons of metaprogramming

What is metaprogramming?

When we encounter software designed to create, manipulate, or interact with other software in various ways, we are engaging in **metaprogramming**. This technique allows computer programs to treat other programs as their data. In my opinion, it represents a very powerful instrument in the hands of wise people; as with everything in life, it also has some drawbacks that we'll analyze later.

Metaprogramming means writing software (or, as we'll see in a moment, using software) that can be set up to do things such as read, create, analyze, or change other programs. It can even tweak its own code while it's running. This cool trick allows developers to write solutions with less code, saving time. Plus, it makes programs more flexible so that they can handle new situations without needing a full rewrite.

Just as with any programming language, grasping the fundamentals of metaprogramming and adopting sound software development practices is crucial for enhancing the overall quality of applications, including those that incorporate metaprogramming techniques.

First and foremost, metaprogramming promotes **code reusability**. It accomplishes this by allowing developers to create code generators and templates that eliminate redundancy in their code bases. This not only reduces the likelihood of errors but also streamlines maintenance efforts. When code is generated automatically, developers can make changes in one place, and those changes will propagate throughout the code base. This results in more maintainable, cleaner, and less error-prone code.

One of the most compelling aspects of metaprogramming is its capacity to enable dynamic behavior in programs. This dynamic behavior empowers software systems to adapt to changing conditions at runtime. In practical terms, this means that the behavior of a program can be adjusted or configured without the need for extensive code modifications and recompilation. As a result, metaprogramming is particularly valuable in scenarios where a program's behavior must be flexible, configurable, or subject to frequent changes.

Furthermore, metaprogramming has a direct impact on developer productivity. By automating repetitive coding tasks, it allows developers to focus on higher-level design and problem-solving. This, in turn, leads to faster development cycles and more efficient code bases. The time and effort saved through metaprogramming can be channeled into improving the overall quality of the software.

Metaprogramming is not limited to making code more efficient; it also promotes the creation of **domain-specific languages (DSLs)**. These DSLs are tailored to specific problem domains, enabling developers to express complex ideas more naturally and concisely. DSLs abstract away the intricacies of general-purpose programming languages and allow developers to communicate directly with the domain's concepts, significantly improving communication between technical and non-technical stakeholders. To illustrate this concept, imagine you are working on a financial application, and you need to calculate the interest on a loan. In Java, using a general-purpose language, it might look like this:

```
double principal = 10000;
double rate = 0.05;
int years = 3;

double interest = principal * rate * years;
```

In this Java code, you are dealing with low-level details such as variable types, operators, and calculations.

Now, let's see how a DSL could make this more domain-specific:

```
LoanDSL loan = LoanDSL.builder()
        .principal(10000.0)
        .interestRate(0.05)
        .term(3)
        .build();
```

```
double interest = loan.calculateInterest();
```

In this example, `LoanDSL` is a DSL that's designed to work with financial calculations. It abstracts away the low-level details and provides a higher-level interface that directly communicates with the financial domain's concepts, making it easier to understand and work with. This can greatly improve communication between developers and domain experts in finance.

Lastly, metaprogramming helps in building efficient abstractions. These abstractions hide the underlying implementation details, making the code more understandable and maintainable. By encapsulating complexity and exposing only essential information, metaprogramming enhances the code base's overall clarity and comprehensibility. Metaprogramming can be split into two main categories: compile-time and runtime. Let's taste a bit of each of them.

Exploring compile-time metaprogramming tools

Compile-time metaprogramming involves code transformations and generation that occur during the compilation phase. In other words, operations, transformations, or code generation are performed on a program during the compilation process – that is, before the program is executed. Macros, code generators, and annotation processors are common tools for compile-time metaprogramming in Java. Given the subject of this book, compile-time metaprogramming will be our main focus since we think that the instruments and frameworks that fall under this definition are the best ways to keep your code clean. In particular, we'll focus on code generator tools: programming languages and tools that provide facilities for generating code based on certain specifications or models (in the following section, we will focus specifically on Lombok and MapStruct). The code generated by these tools can be customized according to the specific requirements of the program.

Lombok

Project Lombok (born in 2009) is a popular Java library that simplifies Java development by reducing boilerplate code and making the code cleaner and more concise.

In Java (at least until version 14 with the introduction of the `record` keyword), there is often a significant amount of boilerplate code that needs to be written for basic tasks such as defining getter and setter methods, constructors, and the `toString()`, `equals()`, and `hashCode()` methods. This boilerplate code can be time-consuming to write and maintain, making the code base longer and harder to read.

Lombok addresses this issue by providing annotations that automatically generate this boilerplate code during compilation. This means developers don't have to write these repetitive code elements themselves, reducing the likelihood of errors and making the code base more concise.

Lombok functions as an annotation processor that enhances your classes by introducing additional code during the compilation phase. Annotation processing was introduced to the Java compiler in version 5. The concept involves users placing annotation processors, whether self-authored or obtained from third-party dependencies such as Lombok, in the build classpath. During the compilation process, as the compiler encounters an annotation, it effectively inquires, "Is anyone in the classpath concerned with this @Annotation?" For those processors answering yes, the compiler delegates control to them, along with the compilation context, allowing them to perform their respective tasks.

Lombok's annotation processing involves making adjustments to the compiler's data structures that represent the code, specifically the **abstract syntax tree** (**AST**). Think of the AST as a roadmap for the computer program. It shows all the necessary steps that must be taken to create the final program. In Java, it is created before the actual program code (**bytecode**) is made. The cool thing is that you can change and work with this AST in Java. Through these modifications to the compiler's AST, Lombok indirectly influences the generation of the final bytecode. To achieve this functionality, Lombok is required to intercept and manage calls that are made to the Java compiler for handling the generation of intermediate code. This interception process is facilitated using plugins, which can be configured within your **integrated development environment** (**IDE**), such as IntelliJ, VS Code, or Eclipse, or integrated into your build automation tools, such as Maven, Gradle, or Make. It's important to note that if your IDE or build management system lacks compatibility with Lombok, it may result in compilation issues for your code; anyway, that simply will not happen with modern versions of the most used IDEs (they support Lombok out of the box).

As we already said, Lombok works with a bunch of very simple annotations. Let's see some examples of its magic. We'll provide you with the basics. However, there's much more to discover in the Lombok official documentation, which you can find in the *Further reading* section.

Getting started with Lombok with an example

Let's start with the most basic form of a Java class: a **POJO**. The acronym, born more by habit than by a standard, stands for **Plain Old Java Object**, and it usually describes a simple Java type that does not adhere to any particular framework or contain any business logic; just a bunch of fields with their accessor methods, one or more constructors, maybe a toString() method, an often equals() and hashcode() to complete the picture. It's faster to write one than to describe it (the following code is intentionally long):

```
class Person {

    private String name;
    private String surname;
    private Date birthDate;

    public Person() {
    }
```

```java
    public Person(String name, String surname, Date birthDate) {
        this.name = name;
        this.surname = surname;
        this.birthDate = birthDate;
    }

    public Person(Person anotherPerson) {

        if (anotherPerson == null) {
            throw new NullPointerException("AnotherPerson cannot be
null");
        }

        this.name = anotherPerson.getName();
        this.surname = anotherPerson.getSurname();
        this.birthDate = anotherPerson.getBirthDate();
    }

    public String getName() {
        return name;
    }

    public void setName(String name) {
        this.name = name;
    }

    public String getSurname() {
        return surname;
    }

    public void setSurname(String surname) {
        this.surname = surname;
    }

    public Date getBirthDate() {
        return birthDate;
    }

    public void setBirthDate(Date birthDate) {
        this.birthDate = birthDate;
    }

    @Override
    public boolean equals(Object o) {
```

```
        if (this == o) return true;
        if (o == null || getClass() != o.getClass()) return false;
        Person person = (Person) o;
        return Objects.equals(name, person.name) && Objects.
equals(surname, person.surname) && Objects.equals(birthDate, person.
birthDate);
    }

    @Override
    public int hashCode() {
        return Objects.hash(name, surname, birthDate);
    }

    @Override
    public String toString() {
        return "Person{" +
            "name='" + name + '\'' +
            ", surname='" + surname + '\'' +
            ", birthDate=" + birthDate +
            '}';
    }
}
```

It should be simple to understand what this class does: nothing! It has three fields, all of which are `private`, three constructors (the default one with no argument and one with all the fields – one that takes another instance of the same object), one getter and one setter for each of the fields, `equals` and `hashcode` methods that involve all of the fields, and finally a `toString` method. All of this code has been generated from my IDE; this class just represents a piece of information. It is what is called a **data class** in other languages. And just for this, we have more than 70 lines of code! Let's see how Lombok can rescue us.

First things first, add Project Lombok to your classpath. If you are using Maven, you just have to add the dependency to your `pom.xml` file (we're going to use the latest version at the time of writing):

```
<dependency>
    <groupId>org.projectlombok</groupId>
    <artifactId>lombok</artifactId>
    <version>1.18.30</version>
</dependency>
```

One funny thing is that if you just start typing Lombok's annotations into your code, some IDEs, such as IntelliJ IDEA, will suggest that you include Lombok in your classpath. It is that smooth.

As we said, Lombok works by adding annotations to the source code, which implement some behaviors considered *boilerplate*. For example, in the *copy constructor* of the object, we can see an if statement that checks for the possible nullity of the parameter that's passed in as input:

```
public Person(Person anotherPerson) {

    if (anotherPerson == null) {
        throw new NullPointerException("AnotherPerson cannot be
null");
    }

    this.name = anotherPerson.getName();
    this.surname = anotherPerson.getSurname();
    this.birthDate = anotherPerson.getBirthDate();
}
```

This if statement can be replaced with the @NonNull annotation next to the parameter in the constructor: the null check takes the form of an if statement, if (param == null) throw new NullPointerException("param is marked non-null but is null"), and will be placed at the beginning of your method. In the case of constructors, the null check will be inserted right after any explicit this() or super() calls:

```
public Person(@NonNull Person anotherPerson) {
    this.name = anotherPerson.getName();
    this.surname = anotherPerson.getSurname();
    this.birthDate = anotherPerson.getBirthDate();
}
```

Now, let's look at the default constructor:

```
public Person() {
}
```

With the @NoArgsConstructor annotation, we can get rid of the default constructor. A constructor with no parameters will be automatically generated. However, if this isn't feasible due to the presence of final fields, a compiler error will occur. This will happen unless you explicitly annotate with @NoArgsConstructor(force = true), in which case all final fields will be initialized with default values (0 for numeric types, false for Boolean, and null for reference types).

The second constructor we can get rid of is the **all-arguments** constructor:

```
public Person(String name, String surname, Date birthDate) {
    this.name = name;
    this.surname = surname;
    this.birthDate = birthDate;
}
```

We can replace these lines of code with the @AllArgsConstructor annotation, which produces a constructor that accepts one parameter for each field within your class.

Should any of the arguments be final, this means that only some of the fields are required:

```
private final String name;
private String surname;
private Date birthDate;
```

In this case, we can use @RequiredArgsConstructor, which generates a constructor with one parameter for each field that necessitates specific treatment. This includes all non-initialized final fields, as well as any fields annotated with @NonNull that haven't been initialized where they are declared. For the fields marked with @NonNull, an explicit null check is also created. If any of the parameters intended for @NonNull fields contain null, the constructor will throw a NullPointerException error. The parameter order corresponds to the order in which the fields are defined in your class.

The next features of Lombok are the **accessor methods** – that is, the getters and the setters. You have the option to apply the @Getter and/or @Setter annotations to any field, allowing Lombok to automatically generate default getter and setter methods:

```
@Getter @Setter private String name;
@Getter @Setter private String surname;
@Getter @Setter private Date birthDate;
```

A default getter method essentially retrieves the field's value and follows the getName naming convention if the field is named name (or isName if the field is of the Boolean type). Meanwhile, a default setter method named setName is used if the field is named name, returns void, and accepts a single parameter of the same type as the field. This setter method simply assigns the field the provided value.

It's also possible to apply the @Getter and/or @Setter annotation to a class itself. In such cases, it's as though you've annotated all non-static fields within that class with the same annotation. So, the previous code snippet can be also written in the following manner:

```
@Getter
@Setter
class Person {

    private String name;
    private String surname;
    private Date birthDate;

    //other code here...

}
```

By default, the generated getter and setter methods are public, unless you explicitly specify `AccessLevel`. The access levels that you can use are `PUBLIC`, `PROTECTED`, `PACKAGE`, and `PRIVATE`. For example, you could write the following:

```
@Setter(AccessLevel.PROTECTED) private String name;
```

The `equals` and `hashcode` methods can be generated by adding the `@EqualsAndHashCode` annotation: this allows Lombok to automatically generate implementations for the `equals(Object other)` and `hashCode()` methods. By default, it includes all non-static, non-transient fields. However, you have the flexibility to customize which fields are included (and even specify that the results of certain methods should be considered) by annotating type members with `@EqualsAndHashCode.Include` or `@EqualsAndHashCode.Exclude`.

Alternatively, you can precisely specify the fields or methods you want to include by annotating them with `@EqualsAndHashCode.Include` and using `@EqualsAndHashCode(onlyExplicitlyIncluded = true)`.

Last but not least, you have the chance to make Lombok generate a `toString` method simply by adding the `@ToString` annotation. Configuration options are used to determine whether field names should be included. Otherwise, the format follows a fixed structure, which is the class name followed by parentheses containing fields separated by commas – as an example, it appears as `Person(name=charlie, surname=brown)`. To enhance the clarity (although it may increase the length) of the `toString()` method's output, you can set the `includeFieldNames` parameter to `true`. By default, all non-static fields are printed. If you wish to exclude certain fields, you can annotate them with `@ToString.Exclude`. Alternatively, you can precisely specify which fields to include by using `@ToString(onlyExplicitlyIncluded = true)` and then marking each field you want to include with `@ToString.Include`.

In the end, our 70-lines-long code is reduced to the following:

```
@NoArgsConstructor
@AllArgsConstructor
@Getter
@Setter
@EqualsAndHashCode
@ToString
class Person {

    private String name;
    private String surname;
    private Date birthDate;

    public Person(@NonNull Person anotherPerson) {
        this.name = anotherPerson.getName();
        this.surname = anotherPerson.getSurname();
```

```
            this.birthDate = anotherPerson.getBirthDate();
    }
}
```

Still not satisfied? You can use @Data, a convenient shortcut annotation that bundles the features of @ToString, @EqualsAndHashCode, @Getter / @Setter, and @RequiredArgsConstructor together:

```
@AllArgsConstructor
@NoArgsConstructor
@Data
class Person {

    private String name;
    private String surname;
    private Date birthDate;

    public Person(@NonNull Person anotherPerson) {
        this.name = anotherPerson.getName();
        this.surname = anotherPerson.getSurname();
        this.birthDate = anotherPerson.getBirthDate();
    }
}
```

If you want to preserve immutability (and you definitively should!), you can use the @Value annotation, which is the immutable variant of @Data. In this case, all fields are automatically set as private and final by default, and no setters are generated. Additionally, the class itself is made final by default because enforcing immutability on a subclass is not feasible. Similar to the @Data annotation, it includes helpful toString(), equals(), and hashCode() methods generation. Each field is equipped with a getter method, and a constructor is generated to encompass all arguments (excluding final fields, which are initialized in the field declaration).

This is just a general overview of Lombok's annotations. Using their properties (and also some other configurations that can be added to the project through a file called lombok.config (the link for the official documentation can be found in the *Further reading* section)), it is possible to make the behavior of Lombok much more granular, acting at the level of a single field, a single method, or customizing the implementation generated by this powerful library. This was just the proverbial tip of the iceberg.

Lombok's builder

In *Chapter 5*, we saw what the builder pattern is: a design pattern that helps construct complex objects by separating their construction from their representation, making it easier to create objects with various configurations.

The @Builder annotation lets you create a *builder* class for your type with basically no effort. If we take the Person class we wrote at the end of the previous section and add the @Builder annotation on top of it, Lombok will generate some code that we can use to instantiate a Person instance in the following manner:

```
Person p = Person.builder()
        .name("Luke")
        .surname("Skywalker")
        .birthDate(parseDate("1951-09-25"))
        .build();
```

In this example, you're creating an instance of Person using a fluent and readable builder pattern. You set the values of the fields using the generated builder's methods and then call .build() to create the final instance.

The @Builder annotation can also handle optional fields and default values, making it a convenient way to create objects with a variable number of properties.

Lombok's @Builder annotation is especially useful in scenarios where you need to construct complex objects with many optional parameters or when you want to create immutable objects. It eliminates the need to write repetitive, verbose, and error-prone boilerplate code for building objects, making your code more concise and maintainable.

The @Builder annotation can generate "singular" methods for collection parameters/fields, which accept a single element rather than an entire list, and add that element to the collection. Let's look at the following example:

```
@Builder
class Team {
    private String name;

    @Singular
    private List<String> members;
}
```

Notice the @Singular annotation that was put on a collection field. When you annotate a parameter in a method or constructor with the @Singular annotation or a field in a class with the @Singular annotation, Lombok treats that builder node as a collection. As a result, Lombok generates two **adder** methods instead of a **setter** method. The first adder method allows you to add a single element to the collection, while the second adder method allows you to add all elements from another collection to the existing collection. Lombok does not generate a setter method that replaces the entire collection. Additionally, Lombok generates a **clear** method for the collection.

For example, you could write the following code for the previously shown Team class:

```
Team myTeam = Team.builder()
        .member("John")
        .member("Susan")
        .member("Chris")
        .build();
```

Alternatively, you could also write the following:

```
var members = List.of("John", "Susan", "Chris");
Team myTeam = Team.builder()
        .members(members)
        .build();
```

You will get the same result.

If a particular field or parameter is not explicitly set during the object construction process, it will default to values such as 0, null, or false, depending on its type. When you use the @Builder annotation in a class (rather than a method or constructor), you can define a default value directly on the field and annotate it with @Builder.Default. Look at the following code as an example:

```
@Builder
class Team {
    private String name;
    @Builder.Default private Long created = System.
currentTimeMillis();

    @Singular
    private List<String> members;
}
```

In this example, if the created field is not set during object construction, it will default to the result of System.currentTimeMillis(), ensuring that it always has a valid timestamp value.

When used in a sentence, Lombok's builder feature is particularly useful because it simplifies the creation of complex objects with a fluent and concise syntax, reducing the need for manual builder pattern implementation in Java. However, there are also some drawbacks to using this library, which we will investigate in the following section.

Some final considerations about Lombok's pros and cons

By reducing the boilerplate code, Lombok helps improve code cleanliness and readability. Developers can focus on writing the essential business logic of their classes, making the code base more understandable and maintainable. It also reduces the chances of introducing bugs in the manually written boilerplate code.

With Lombok, maintaining the code becomes more straightforward. When you need to add or remove fields from a class, you don't have to update all the related methods manually. Lombok's annotations take care of these changes automatically during compilation.

Most modern IDEs support Lombok out of the box. They can recognize Lombok annotations and provide code completion, navigation, and refactoring assistance as if the code were written manually. This ensures a seamless development experience for developers.

In our humble opinion, Project Lombok is a valuable tool in the Java ecosystem that simplifies code development by automating the generation of common code elements, reducing boilerplate, and improving code readability. It allows developers to focus on the core functionality of their classes and reduces the chances of introducing errors in repetitive code. This makes Java code cleaner, more concise, and easier to maintain.

However, to give a complete and honest overview, we have to highlight some common criticisms about Lombok. Let's start with the most subjective (almost a "gut feeling" some people have) criticism: Lombok's unique and sometimes forceful way of doing things (in particular, modifying the bytecode) has often made people see it as a bit of a workaround. We see it as a clever, technically sound, and innovative solution rather than a negative hack. However, some developers still see it as a workaround and avoid using Lombok for that reason. That's a valid perspective, but in our experience, Lombok's advantages in terms of productivity are more significant than any worries about its approach. We've been using it happily in real-life projects for many years.

It is useless to deny that, since Lombok intervenes as a sort of "extra step" at the time of compilation, the time to carry out this practice increases. As the code base increases, of course, the times increase proportionally. As high as the efficiency is and the Lombok team actively working on further improvements, it is undeniable that projects compile faster without Lombok.

There could also be problems related to compatibility between different versions of Java. With each version change, Java could change the way your AST is generated and/or interpreted. Consequently, it is not certain that Lombok can generate the code correctly or that it succeeds at all. The code may stop compiling. Unfortunately, we would only notice this after upgrading Java, but it is also true that new versions of the library are released before the final versions of Java. However, there is still one possibility to be considered.

This eventuality leads us to another problematic aspect, namely the fact that Lombok makes the code we write non-standard; since we need the Lombok plugin to compile, it is undeniable that the code we are writing, in a sense, is not valid. We will always depend on tools that are "external" to Java.

The last possible flaw that comes to mind is not a defect in my opinion, but something I have often heard. It's true that Lombok greatly reduces the number of lines of code, eliminating the so-called boilerplate, but it is also true that all IDEs can generate that boilerplate in a couple of clicks. This is a pseudo-criticism of Lombok. While it is certainly true that getters, setters, equals, builders, and more are generated in a moment by any IDE worthy of the name, it is also true that all of this code must then be maintained. How many times have we added a field to a class and forgotten to update the `equals` method? How many times have we had to change the getters and setters of a field because we changed its name or type? With Lombok, the chances of all these errors occurring simply do not exist.

I hope I've given you some interesting ideas to think about so far. Unfortunately, I don't have a one-size-fits-all solution for all these considerations. As always, we recommend evaluating each situation individually and trying to reach a team agreement.

In the next section, we will tell you about another library that can save you from a lot of manual work, especially when it comes to converting one type into another, which is something that unfortunately needs to be done in practically every project. MapStruct will free you from this burden or at least make it easier.

MapStruct

While it's not great to say, part of our job as software engineers is shipping information from one place to another. Sometimes, this shipping becomes a mere translation of a model into another model. Sad, but true.

Object mapping (sometimes referred to as **object adapting**) refers to the process of transforming data between different data models, such as from objects in an object-oriented programming language to database tables and vice versa. This process also includes objects belonging to different subdomains or even different layers of the application. Another notable example of mapping that is done frequently is when you have to call an external service (for example, via an HTTP/REST call) and you have to map the response you get from that service into your objects or your model. This situation is represented in the following diagram:

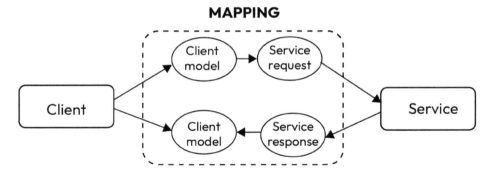

Figure 6.1 – Mapping between client and service request models and back to the client model

Writing mapping code can be very boring, and it's prone to mistakes. But what if there was a tool that could do all this grunt work with minimal effort? Luckily for us, there are quite a few such tools out there, and our top pick is MapStruct.

MapStruct is an open source Java-based code generation library that simplifies the process of mapping between Java beans (POJOs). It is specifically designed for generating mapping codes between objects, eliminating the need to write this code manually, which can be time-consuming and error-prone. MapStruct's primary purpose is to provide a straightforward and efficient way to convert data between different Java bean classes.

MapStruct serves as an annotation processor that's seamlessly integrated into the Java compiler, making it compatible with command-line build tools such as Maven and Gradle, and equally suitable for use within your favorite IDE. While MapStruct provides sensible defaults for mapping, it also allows you to configure and implement specific behaviors when needed, giving you flexibility without imposing rigid constraints.

Let's see how MapStruct works. Suppose you have the following two classes:

```
public class Person {

    private String name;
    private String surname;
    private Integer age;

    // getters and setters...

}
public class PersonDTO {

    private String name;
    private String lastName;
    private LocalDate birthDate;

    // getters and setters...

}
```

We need to transfer the data from an instance of `PersonDTO` to an instance of `Person`. To do it in plain Java, we would need to write the following:

```
public Person from(PersonDTO personDTO) {
    if (personDTO == null) {
        return null;
    }

    Person person = new Person();
    person.setName(personDTO.getName());
    person.setSurname(personDTO.getLastName());
    person.setAge(calculateCurrentAge(personDTO.getBirthDate()));
```

```
        return person;
    }


    private Integer calculateCurrentAge(LocalDate birthDate) {
        return Period.between(birthDate, LocalDate.now()).getYears();
    }
```

That is quite a lot of code for only three fields; it's boring, time-consuming, and error-prone.

Using MapStruct, we could just write an interface and let it do the magic:

```
@Mapper
public interface PersonMapper {
    PersonMapper INSTANCE = Mappers.getMapper(PersonMapper.class);
    @Mapping(source="lastName", target="surname")
    Person personDtoToPerson(PersonDTO personDto);


}
```

The presence of the @Mapper annotation designates the interface as a mapping interface and triggers the MapStruct processor to engage during the compilation process. In the mapping method itself, you can freely select its name, and it should accept the source object as a parameter while returning the target object.

To handle attributes with distinct names in the source and target objects, you can employ the @Mapping annotation to specify the desired configuration. When necessary and feasible, type conversions will be carried out for attributes with differing types in the source and target objects. For instance, an enumeration type may be transformed into a string.

It's worth noting that a single interface can host multiple mapping methods, each of which will have an implementation auto-generated by MapStruct. You can obtain an instance of the interface's implementation through the Mappers class. As a convention, the interface typically includes a member called INSTANCE, offering clients a means to access the mapper implementation.

MapStruct will generate all the needed code for you.

You might have noticed that we're missing the mapping from birthdate to age; this cannot be done automatically by MapStruct since a little bit of logic is involved (to calculate the current age from the birth date). In this case – and in any case, we should need it – we can implement specific mappings; also, in this case, the method names are not important since MapStruct will choose the right one based on the parameter and return types:

```
@Mapper
public interface PersonMapper {
    PersonMapper INSTANCE = Mappers.getMapper(PersonMapper.class);
    @Mapping(source="lastName", target="surname")
```

```
@Mapping(source="birthDate", target="age")
Person personDtoToPerson(PersonDTO personDto);

default Integer calculateCurrentAge(LocalDate birthDate) {
    return Period.between(birthDate, LocalDate.now()).getYears();
}
}
```

In the auto-generated implementation of the method, MapStruct will choose the `calculateCurrentAge` method just because it takes a `LocalDate` parameter and returns an `Integer` value. It is also possible to specify Java expressions and other stuff in the `@Mapping` annotation, but I recommend reading the documentation to dig a little bit deeper.

With that, we've seen how MapStruct works and how it can make our lives easier by handling time-consuming tasks. As I mentioned, these were static metaprogramming tools – they work directly on the code. Now, let's look at runtime metaprogramming tools, which work on the running program instead.

Exploring runtime metaprogramming tools

Runtime metaprogramming operates while the program is being executed. It enables the program to inspect and modify its own code and data structures during runtime, often using techniques such as reflection, dynamic code generation, and dynamic proxy. Learning about runtime metaprogramming tools can empower you to manipulate and adapt the behavior of a running program dynamically, enhancing flexibility and customization within your software.

Now, let's talk about reflection since it is the most used feature in runtime metaprogramming.

Reflection

Reflection is a feature in programming languages such as Java that allows a program to examine or *reflect* upon its structure, data, and behavior during runtime. In Java, reflection is primarily used to inspect and manipulate classes, objects, methods, fields, and other elements of the program at runtime.

Reflection allows you to perform the following tasks in Java:

1. **Inspect classes**: You can obtain information about classes, including their name, superclass, implemented interfaces, constructors, methods, and fields

2. **Inspect objects**: You can examine the properties and fields of objects, even if their types are not known at compile time

3. **Invoke methods**: You can invoke methods on objects, even if you don't know the method's name until runtime

4. **Access fields**: You can read or modify the values of fields within an object, even if you don't know the field's name until runtime

For example, let's add the following method to the `Person` class (see the *MapStruct* section):

```
public void greet(){
    System.out.printf("Hello I'm %s%n", name);
}
```

Now, let's create another class that operates on it using reflection:

```
public class ReflectionExample {
    public static void main(String[] args) throws Exception {
        // Obtain the class object
        Class<?> personClass = Class.forName("com.example.demo3.
mapstruct.Person");

        // Create an instance of the Person class
        Object personInstance = personClass.getConstructor(String.
class, String.class, Integer.class)
                .newInstance("Alice", "Smith", 30);

        // Access and modify fields using reflection
        Field nameField = personClass.getDeclaredField("name");
        nameField.setAccessible(true); // Bypass private access
                                       // modifier
        String nameValue = (String) nameField.get(personInstance);
        System.out.println("Original Name: " + nameValue);
        nameField.set(personInstance, "Bob");

        // Access and invoke methods using reflection
        Method greetMethod = personClass.getDeclaredMethod("greet");
        greetMethod.invoke(personInstance);

        // Verify the modified name
        String modifiedName = (String) nameField.get(personInstance);
        System.out.println("Modified Name: " + modifiedName);
    }
}
```

In this example, we do the following:

- We obtain the `Class` object representing the `Person` class using `Class.forName("com.example.demo3.mapstruct.Person")`

- We create an instance of the `Person` class dynamically using its constructor

- We access the private name field, bypassing the access modifier and modifying its value

- We invoke the `greet` method of the `Person` instance using reflection
- We verify that the name field has been modified successfully

Please note that while this example demonstrates the use of reflection, it is essential to exercise caution when using reflection in practice. Reflection should be used judiciously, and you should be aware of the potential risks and performance implications associated with it.

For example, there could be security risks because reflection can bypass Java's access controls, allowing you to access and modify private members of classes. While this flexibility can be beneficial, it can also introduce security vulnerabilities if it's not used with due care. Unauthorized access to sensitive data or the manipulation of internal program states can occur, which is why it's crucial to employ security measures to prevent abuse.

Another very common problem is type safety: reflection operates at a low level and doesn't provide the same level of type safety as traditional Java code. This can lead to unexpected type errors at runtime. For instance, you might call a method with the wrong parameters, and the error won't be discovered until your code is running. This lack of compile-time checks can result in hard-to-debug runtime exceptions. It is also true that most of the modern IDEs warn the developer about this risk at the moment of writing code.

There are also some other challenges, concerning reflection in association with the clean code, that we will expand on in the following section.

Reflection and clean code

In a chapter about metaprogramming, we felt we had the duty to tell you something about runtime metaprogramming and its most (in)famous declination, which is reflection. But let's think a bit about what reflection involves in terms of keeping your code base clean.

Reflection and **clean code** can sometimes be at odds with each other as reflection introduces complexities and potential code readability issues. However, when used carefully and thoughtfully, reflection can be employed in a clean and maintainable way. Let's explore how reflection can impact clean code principles and how to strike a balance between them:

- **Readability**: Clean code promotes readability. Reflection can make code less readable as it often involves working with class names and method names as strings, which are error-prone and can lead to code that is challenging to understand. To mitigate this, document your use of reflection thoroughly and provide clear comments explaining your intentions.

- **Maintainability**: Reflection can make code harder to maintain because it bypasses some of the compile-time checks that the Java compiler provides. If you're using reflection to access private members or perform operations that wouldn't be allowed through normal means, it can lead to unexpected behavior or maintenance challenges. You should consider alternatives, such as making the necessary changes to the code structure, whenever possible.

- **Simplicity**: Clean code encourages simplicity. Reflection, being a complex feature, can introduce unnecessary complexity. It's essential to ensure that your use of reflection is justified and that you are not introducing complexity where it's not needed.

- **Consistency**: Clean code aims for consistency and a uniform style. Reflection can lead to inconsistent code because different parts of your program might access and manipulate elements in a variety of ways. To maintain consistency, consider establishing conventions and patterns for your use of reflection.

- **Testing**: Clean code emphasizes testability. Reflection can make it challenging to write unit tests since it allows you to bypass encapsulation. You might need to rely on integration tests or mock objects, which can be less ideal for isolated unit testing. Whenever possible, prefer to design your code for easy unit testing without relying heavily on reflection.

- **Performance**: Clean code should be efficient. Reflection can introduce performance overhead due to its dynamic nature. Before using reflection, profile your code and ensure that the performance impact is acceptable. In performance-critical applications, you might need to explore alternative approaches.

- **Documentation**: Clean code aims to have no technical documentation at all since the code is so clear that it explains itself. However, since reflection decreases readability (we just said that a few words ago), the need for clear documentation or comments becomes essential. When using reflection, think about providing comprehensive documentation explaining the purpose, expected behavior, and potential risks associated with your reflective code.

So, reflection is a powerful but potentially dangerous feature in Java, and it should be used sparingly and with caution. It's essential to weigh the benefits of using reflection against the added complexity and potential drawbacks it introduces to your code base. If you decide to use reflection, do so thoughtfully and document your code thoroughly to maintain clarity and transparency. Clean code principles should remain a top priority, even when you're using reflection, to ensure your code base remains maintainable, readable, and efficient (nevertheless, it is worth noticing that reflection is often used "under the hood" in many metaprogramming frameworks).

Now that we've learned what metaprogramming is, both in its static and runtime flavor, let's add some considerations about the pros and cons of these very powerful tools.

Weighing the pros and cons of metaprogramming

Metaprogramming and clean code are two essential concepts in software development, and while they can sometimes appear to be at odds, they can also work in harmony when used effectively.

Metaprogramming, in essence, involves dynamically manipulating or generating code during compilation or runtime. It offers the ability to automate repetitive tasks, create abstractions, and introduce flexibility into software development. Clean code, on the other hand, is a coding philosophy that emphasizes writing code that is easily readable, understandable, and maintainable. It promotes principles such as meaningful naming, eliminating redundancy, small and focused functions, and adhering to established coding conventions.

Metaprogramming can aid in generating clean code by automating the creation of repetitive code structures and reducing clutter in source code files (for example, eliminating some boilerplate code, as we saw in the case of Lombok).

Moreover, it can facilitate the development of abstractions that hide implementation details, leading to cleaner and more maintainable code.

However, not all that glitters is gold; you must ensure that the generated code is clean and adheres to clean code principles. Automation should not result in messy or cryptic code. In this sense, using well-known and well-tested frameworks with a solid community and a lot of documentation is probably the way to go. We don't endorse reinventing the wheel, never; it's very unlikely that you will find yourself in a situation where metaprogramming from scratch is what you need unless it's for very small and limited use cases.

You also have to balance the advantages of automation with code readability and understandability since metaprogramming can introduce complexity. I once found myself in front of a Java method that returned a string containing an HTML web page! Without getting to sadness peaks like that, be sure that your teammates (and don't forget your future self) can expand or modify your software with only a reasonable amount of headaches. We invite you to discuss every metaprogramming choice with the team. Avoid excessive "magic" in your code as it can obscure the understanding of the underlying processes. This obscurity may result in the emergence of bugs or unpredictable performance issues.

If you just have to go for metaprogramming, document complex metaprogramming solutions thoroughly, providing clear explanations to assist future developers. Provide examples and write comments; in a single word, be merciful.

Having said that, we think that clean code's advantages in terms of testing and debugging are notable, especially when dealing with compile-time metaprogramming tools such as Lombok and MapStruct. The essence of that advantage is that not only do you have cleaner code (because, for instance, the usage of Lombok facilitates object immutability) but you have less code. Having as little code as possible should be one of your top priorities.

Metaprogramming and clean code can coexist harmoniously. Combining the advantages of automation and flexibility with a commitment to writing clean and maintainable code ensures that software projects remain both efficient and sustainable in the long run.

While talking about metaprogramming's pros and cons, it is worth mentioning the so-called **Not-Invented-Here** (**NIH**) syndrome. NIH syndrome refers to the tendency of some development teams or individuals to prefer creating their own solutions or tools rather than adopting existing, external solutions. This can happen even when existing solutions are well-established, proven, and readily available.

NIH syndrome can lead to several issues, including increased development time, reinvention of the wheel, and missed opportunities to leverage the expertise and contributions of the broader development community. It's often considered a counterproductive behavior, and many software development communities encourage a more open-minded approach to adopting existing solutions when appropriate.

Teams and developers are encouraged to weigh the pros and cons of building something in-house versus using external libraries or frameworks while considering factors such as time, expertise, maintenance, and the availability of well-established solutions in the open source community.

Summary

In this chapter, we talked about metaprogramming: what it is, how it works, and how it can or cannot be useful concerning clean code and refactoring. In particular, we looked at two very popular libraries that involve metaprogramming, especially code auto-generation: Lombok and MapStruct.

We also warned you about the potential risks of using reflection and, in general, spoke about the pros and cons of using metaprogramming tools.

In the next chapter, we will dive into static analysis, a method of code inspection that checks for issues without executing the code, and dynamic analysis, which involves evaluating code during its execution to identify problems.

Further reading

- Lombok's official documentation: `https://projectlombok.org/features/`
- *Lombok: The Good, The Bad, and The Controversial*, by Felix Coutinho `https://www.linkedin.com/pulse/lombok-good-bad-controversial-felix-coutinho/`
- MapStruct's official website: `https://mapstruct.org/`

7

Static and Dynamic Analysis

On our way to clean, robust, and maintainable code, we'll often need to "take a look" at how our software works and how it's written. After identifying the code smells and doing some refactoring steps (in fact, we should never stop doing this!), it can be useful to scan our code for design flaws, security vulnerabilities, and more.

This analysis can be carried out directly on the code – that is, static analysis – or on the running program – that is, (without involving too much imagination) dynamic analysis.

Static and dynamic analysis tools scrutinize code to identify issues and inefficiencies. Their insights provide the foundation for improvements, and this is where refactoring comes into play.

In this chapter, we're going to talk about the following topics:

- What is static analysis?
- Why do we need static analysis?
- Some static analysis tools
- What is dynamic analysis?
- Some dynamic analysis techniques

What is static analysis?

As the name may suggest, **static analysis** in the context of Java (or any programming language, actually) refers to the process of analyzing source code without running it. It is a technique that's used to find issues, potential bugs, security vulnerabilities, and other issues in the code before it is run or compiled. Static analysis tools are used for this purpose (we'll jump into that shortly).

There are lots of reasons to perform static analysis; let's see some of them.

Code errors or bad practices

The first one we will show you may seem trivial, but it is the main reason we scan our code in search of problems – that is, problems in the code! Which problems? We'll put them under the generic term of coding errors – that is, mistakes made by programmers when writing code (yes, it turns out that even programmers make mistakes – no matter how much experience they have, programmers still make mistakes. But, as they gain more experience, they're more likely to own up to their errors!). These errors can lead to a variety of problems, including crashes, unexpected behavior, and security vulnerabilities:

- You could have **null pointer dereferences** when a program tries to access a memory location that has not been initialized, as shown here. This can lead to crashes and other unexpected behavior:

```
String text = null;
int length = text.length();
```

In this example, we have a null reference (`text`) to a string, and attempting to access its `length()` method leads to a `NullPointerException`.

- **Unreachable code** is code that can never be executed. This can happen when there is a mistake in a conditional statement, such as an infinite loop or an `if` statement that is always false. Unreachable code is not harmful, but it can make code more difficult to read and maintain. In general, it is useless, and we do not like useless code (unless your pay increases with the number of code lines you write, but we don't believe that's the case). Here's an example of the same:

```
public void unreachableCodeExample() {
    boolean condition = someBooleanMethod();

    if (condition) {
        System.out.println("Condition is true.");
        return;
    }
    System.out.println("This line of code is unreachable.");
}

private static boolean someBooleanMethod() {
    return true;
}
```

In this example, we have `someBooleanMethod`, which always returns `true` (imagine some logic implemented by some unreadable code, not just this simple statement). This code snippet will compile, but the second `System.out` will never be executed. So, you have to refactor your code: you could fix the `boolean` method if that's the case or just drop it and delete the `if` condition.

- **Class cast exceptions**, on the other hand, are runtime exceptions in Java that occur when you try to cast an object to a type that is not compatible with the object's actual type. In other words, you're trying to convert an object into a type that it is not, resulting in an exception:

```
public void classMismatchExample(){
    Object i = 6;
    String s = (String) i; //this will throw an exception
    System.out.println(s);
}
```

This is a very simple problem that is usually detected by your IDE while you're writing code, but still, that is an example of static analysis.

Some static analysis tools can also detect some bad practices; one of the most common is a class implementing a compareTo method but then you're using equals. When you implement the compareTo() method, it's important to ensure that you also override the equals() method. This ensures consistency in how objects of the class are compared for ordering and equality:

```
Person person = new Person();
Person anotherPerson = new Person();
if(person.equals(anotherPerson)) {
    System.out.println("They're equal");
} else {
    System.out.println("They're not equal");
}
if(person.compareTo(anotherPerson) == 0) {
    System.out.println("They're equal");
} else {
    System.out.println("They're not equal");
}
```

The result of this method is probably not what we wanted:

```
They're not equal
They're equal
```

That's because the equals method is not correctly implemented in our Person class, and we're using the one coming from Object. If our class implements **Comparable**, then it's not a good thing to use equals on it. To avoid any misbehavior, you could just override equals using compareTo:

```
@Override
public boolean equals(Object o) {
    if (this == o) return true;
    if (o == null || getClass() != o.getClass()) return false;
    return this.compareTo(o) == 0;
}
```

- Finally, a good static analysis of your code can detect **duplicated code**, which in my opinion is the most common smell I've come across; static analysis tools can recognize code fragments that are repeated and flag them for developers' attention (often, this step can be done directly by your favorite IDE).

Security

Static analysis of code is essential for security as it plays a pivotal role in identifying and mitigating security vulnerabilities. By thoroughly examining the source code of an application or system before it is executed, static analysis helps to enhance the overall security posture of software. One of the significant benefits of static code analysis is its ability to reduce security vulnerabilities, such as **cross-site scripting** (**XSS**) and injection attacks, which are common and potentially devastating threats to the integrity and confidentiality of data and the smooth operation of applications. Here are some more benefits:

- **Detection of XSS vulnerabilities**: Static code analysis scans the source code for any instances where user inputs, such as form fields or URL parameters, are not properly validated or sanitized. This meticulous examination helps identify potential entry points for malicious code injection. For example, in the context of a web application, static analysis can pinpoint locations where user-supplied data might be directly included in HTML or JavaScript code. This information is invaluable in fixing these issues as it adds proper input validation and output encoding, thereby thwarting XSS attacks.

- **Mitigation of injection attacks**: Static analysis is highly effective in detecting vulnerabilities that can lead to injection attacks, including SQL injection, which can compromise the database and sensitive data. By analyzing the code, it can flag any instances where user inputs are used directly in SQL queries, without proper parameterization or escaping. Developers can then modify the code so that it uses prepared statements or stored procedures, effectively preventing injection attacks.

- **Library and component vulnerability scanning**: We can extend the analysis to dynamically linked libraries and third-party components. We should regularly scan for known vulnerabilities in libraries and dependencies used by the application. Automated tools can help identify outdated or susceptible components, ensuring that the software relies on secure and up-to-date code.

- **Early detection and prevention**: One of the key advantages of static code analysis is its ability to detect vulnerabilities at an early stage of the development process. This early detection is crucial because addressing security issues at later stages, such as during testing or in production, can be considerably more expensive and disruptive. Static analysis empowers development teams to address vulnerabilities as they write the code, reducing the likelihood of security issues making their way into the final product.

By addressing these vulnerabilities at their root, organizations can minimize the potential for security breaches and the associated risks and costs.

Cyclomatic complexity

Static analysis of code can also be used to calculate and keep the cyclomatic complexity of the code itself under control. Let's try to understand what it is. Simply put, **cyclomatic complexity** is like counting the different ways you can walk through a piece of code. If there are fewer routes and they're not too complicated, the cyclomatic complexity is lower, and the code becomes easier to read and get.

To reduce cyclomatic complexity, you "just" have to write clean code, but apply all the advice we gave in the previous chapters and remove all the code smells that you get. Static analysis can help you, for example, in detecting methods or functions that are too long, duplicated code, or dead code (that is, code that is never used at runtime); it can also help you reduce the number of decision structures (that's a big deal: try to avoid as many `if` statements as possible in your code to reduce the complexity) and help you avoid flag arguments in methods.

We're not going to look at this in too much detail here, but we think it's generally interesting to understand how to calculate cyclomatic complexity for a simple method. Let's suppose you have the following code:

```
public int calculateSum(int a, int b) {
    if (a > 0) {
        return a + b;
    } else {
        return a - b;
    }
}
```

You can calculate cyclomatic complexity for functions, modules, methods, or classes in a software program using control flow graphs. It should be easier to draw the control flow graph for the `calculateSum` method than to explain what a control flow graph is. It represents all the possible paths of execution of your program and it looks something like this:

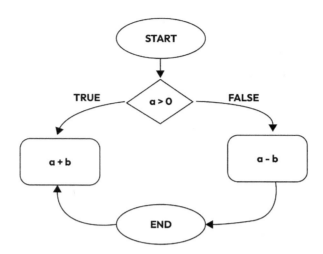

Figure 7.1 – The control flow graph for the calculateSum method

The previous diagram represents the control flow graph for the calculateSum method. We can see a **START** node, from which starts an edge that goes into a conditional node; depending on the condition (**TRUE** or **FALSE**), the flow goes through one edge or another (**a+b** or **a-b**). They both end at the **END** node.

To calculate the cyclomatic complexity, there's a simple formula: $M = E - N + 2$. Here, we have the following:

- **M** represents the cyclomatic complexity
- **E** is the number of edges in the control flow graph
- **N** is the number of nodes in the control flow graph

In our case, it would be $M = 5 - 5 + 2 = 2$.

In general, a piece of code with a cyclomatic complexity value exceeding 11 is considered overly complex and brings challenges for testing and maintenance.

The following are some common cyclomatic complexity values that are used by static analysis tools:

- **1-4**: Low complexity – relatively easy to test
- **5-7**: Moderate complexity – manageable
- **8-10**: High complexity – suggests the need for refactoring to improve testability
- **11 and above**: Very high complexity – extremely challenging to test

The code's complexity level also impacts its testability. The higher the cyclomatic complexity, the more difficult it is to create comprehensive tests. The cyclomatic complexity value indicates the number of test cases required to achieve 100% branch coverage.

Exception (mis)handling

Exceptions in Java programs are not always treated as they deserve; defects coming from their mishandling are common and often underestimated. Handling exceptions correctly in Java is vital to preventing program crashes, maintaining data integrity, providing a better user experience, enhancing debugging, improving security, and maintaining code quality. Properly handled exceptions help your software recover gracefully from errors and meet regulatory requirements when necessary.

Static analysis tools can help us detect some common exception mishandling; we're going to see some of them here.

Consider the following snippet:

```
Person person = null;
try {
    String name = person.getName(); //throws NPE
} finally {
    throw new IOException();
}
```

As you can see, an IOException is thrown in the finally block; in general, throwing exceptions in the finally block is considered a smell since it could hide some other exception being thrown in the try block. In this case, the expected output would be a NullPointerException.

Also, employing the return statement within a finally block can introduce confusion. This rule's significance lies in the fact that when the code throws an exception, the return statement can discard it. Let's see how by changing a bit of the previous code snippet:

```
Person person = null;
try {
    String name = person.getName(); //throws NPE
} finally {
    return;
}
```

The NullPointerException is thrown, but the finally block containing the return statement is just swept under the carpet. Nothing happens.

The last smell in exception handling we're going to see is when we close a stream into the `finally` block and something fails. What happens if `close()`, when invoked on a stream, fails and there are other instructions to be executed after it? Those instructions are simply not executed:

```
public static void copyFiles(String sourceFileName, String
destFileName) {
    InputStream inputStream = null;
    OutputStream outputStream = null;
    try {
        inputStream = Files.newInputStream(Paths.get(sourceFileName));
        outputStream = Files.newOutputStream(Paths.get(destFileName));
        copy(inputStream, outputStream);
    } catch (IOException e) {
        // handling exception
    } finally {
        try {
            inputStream.close();
            outputStream.close();
        } catch (IOException e) {
            throw new RuntimeException(e);
        }
    }
}
```

The `copyFiles` method copies one file to another (we're omitting the internal copy method for conciseness), opening two streams (`inputStream` and `outputStream`). As you can see, in the `finally` block, the two streams are closed in the same `try` block: if the first one fails, the other one will stay open.

Now that we've seen what we're looking for when we perform static code analysis, let's get to know some tools that can help us. As usual, consider the next few sections as suggestions to deepen your knowledge so that you can improve the quality of your code day by day.

Automated static analysis tools

Automated static analysis tools, such as SonarQube, Checkstyle, FindBugs, and PMD, play a crucial role in the software development process by helping developers maintain code quality, identify potential issues, and adhere to coding standards. These tools are instrumental in ensuring that software projects are not only functionally correct but also maintainable and robust.

SonarQube and SonarLint

SonarQube is a comprehensive tool that's designed for continuous code inspection. Its primary function is to analyze code bases automatically, pinpointing potential issues such as bugs, security vulnerabilities, and code smells. By integrating seamlessly into the **continuous integration and continuous deployment (CI/CD)** pipelines, SonarQube ensures that each build undergoes a deep examination for code quality. This process includes identifying and reporting on areas that may require improvement or attention.

One of the notable features of SonarQube is its ability to perform security vulnerability detection, which is crucial in today's software development landscape where security is a top priority. This tool offers a holistic view of the code base, helping development teams maintain a high standard of code quality throughout the entire development life cycle. Additionally, SonarQube provides historical analysis, allowing developers to track changes in code quality over time. This historical perspective proves invaluable in assessing the effectiveness of code improvements or identifying potential regressions.

SonarQube and **SonarLint** often go together, like *Batman* and *Robin*. SonarLint is a lightweight IDE extension and serves as a valuable companion to SonarQube, offering developers a means to address code quality issues directly within their IDEs. SonarLint operates in real-time, providing instant feedback as developers write code. By integrating with popular IDEs such as Eclipse, IntelliJ IDEA, and Visual Studio, SonarLint seamlessly becomes a part of the local development environment.

One of SonarLint's strengths lies in its language support, which covers a variety of programming languages. This versatility allows developers to apply consistent code quality standards across different projects and code bases. Importantly, SonarLint can be configured to synchronize with SonarQube, ensuring that developers adhere to the same rule sets locally as those enforced by the centralized analysis performed by SonarQube.

In essence, SonarQube and SonarLint work hand-in-hand to create a robust system for maintaining and enhancing code quality. SonarQube provides centralized, comprehensive analysis, while SonarLint brings that analysis directly into the developers' local environments, enabling them to proactively address issues during the coding process. Together, these tools contribute significantly to the overall goal of producing high-quality, secure, and maintainable code.

Checkstyle

Checkstyle is an open source tool that enforces coding standards and conventions for Java code. It checks the source code against a set of predefined rules and reports violations. Checkstyle is highly configurable, allowing development teams to customize and enforce their own coding standards. Some of the key features of Checkstyle are as follows:

- **Customizable rules**: Checkstyle allows you to define your own coding rules or use predefined rule sets based on established coding standards such as Sun Code Conventions, Google Java Style, and more. You can define rules about indentation, line length, variable naming, import order, and so on.

- **Integration**: Checkstyle can be integrated into popular IDEs and build systems, making it seamless for developers to incorporate code checks into their development workflows

- **Continuous Integration**: It is often integrated into **Continuous Integration** (**CI**) pipelines, ensuring that code quality checks are performed automatically whenever code changes are committed
- **Report generation**: Checkstyle generates detailed reports, making it easy for developers to identify and fix code violations

FindBugs

FindBugs is a static analysis tool for identifying bugs and potential security vulnerabilities in Java code. It uses static analysis to detect issues in bytecode, making it particularly valuable for finding problems that might not be apparent from the source code alone. Here are some of the key features of FindBugs:

- **Bug detection**: It is designed to find a wide range of bugs, including null pointer dereferences, thread synchronization problems, and performance bottlenecks
- **Integration**: Like Checkstyle, FindBugs can be integrated into various development environments and CI/CD pipelines
- **User-defined checks**: Developers can create custom bug detectors for project-specific issues
- **Community support**: FindBugs has an active community that maintains and updates the tool, ensuring it remains relevant and effective

FindBugs reviews your code by looking at its bytecode – that is, without needing to access the original source code. But because its analysis isn't always perfect, FindBugs can sometimes raise warnings that aren't real issues. The rate of these false warnings reported by FindBugs is less than 50%.

PMD

PMD is a static source code analyzer for various programming languages, including Java. It focuses on code quality and identifies potential issues, redundancies, and complex code patterns. PMD offers the following key features:

- **Multiple languages**: It supports multiple languages, not just Java, making it versatile for projects with diverse code bases
- **Rule-based analysis**: It analyzes source code against a set of predefined rules that can be customized based on project requirements
- **Code duplication detection**: PMD can detect duplicate code fragments, helping developers maintain cleaner and more maintainable code
- **Integration**: PMD can be integrated into different IDEs and build systems (PMD offers an extension for Visual Studio Code, making it convenient for developers working in this popular IDE)

Using tools that check code for mistakes is important in both the place where we write code (IDEs) and in the system that keeps an eye on our code as we work (CI pipelines). These tools help us find mistakes early, which is very helpful.

In our code writing environment (IDE), these tools help us spot problems as we write the code, making it less likely for errors to show up later.

In our code monitoring system (CI pipeline), these tools make sure the code we write follows the rules and standards we set. This keeps the quality of our code high and makes sure we don't accidentally break things that used to work.

One of the great things about these tools is that they make sure everyone on the team follows the same rules. This helps our code be more organized, easier to understand, and generally better. These tools also save us time and money. They help us find and fix problems early, which is cheaper and faster than waiting until later when problems can be much harder to solve.

At the end of the day, using these tools makes our code better, helps us work together more easily, and keeps our code secure and safe from mistakes.

With that, we've taken a quick look at static analysis, focusing on what to look for and how to look for it. Unfortunately, static analysis alone is not enough. Clean code is one thing – efficient code is another. It is strictly necessary to analyze the code while it is running.

What is dynamic analysis?

While static analysis is done on the code, its complementary version, **dynamic analysis**, is done on the program while it is running. This approach involves analyzing the code during execution, rather than just inspecting the source code, or performing static analysis, which examines code without executing it. Dynamic analysis provides insights into how a program behaves in real-world scenarios and helps identify issues that might not be apparent through static analysis alone.

If you have ever done some unit testing or some debugging, well, you did some kind of dynamic analysis. But there is much more to this. Dynamic program analysis involves collecting diverse insights about a program's behavior, which includes understanding variables' value assignments, the sequence and timing of function calls, data structure manipulations and modifications, memory allocation and usage, utilization of system resources, and the detection of encountered errors. This information is essential for purposes such as bug and security vulnerability identification, program performance enhancement, verification of program adherence to its requirements, and gaining a deeper understanding of the program's operational principles.

There are many examples of dynamic program analysis; let the journey begin.

Debugging

As trivial as it may seem, **debugging** is the most widely used technique for dynamic program analysis; maybe it's the single activity we do the most in our industry – yes, certainly much more than writing the code or designing the architectures. And yes, we know that by implementing some good habits in respect of testing (such as **test-driven development** (**TDD**)) the need for debugging should be minimal, ideally zero, but in the real world, it isn't always possible to do so.

Since it's such a popular activity, we won't dwell too much on debugging. However, I would like to draw attention to some aspects that some people might underestimate, especially at the beginning of their professional careers.

For effective debugging, try to reproduce the bug first; from experience, this can be a difficult phase, sometimes much more difficult than the resolution itself. It involves having it explained to you what was done to produce that bug (in case you haven't noticed it yourself) and reproducing the same input that generated the problem or at least an input of the same type. It is not even granted that you can use a debugger, actually: for example, if you can't reproduce the problem in an environment where you can use the debugger (for example, your local host), you'll need to use some other technique, such as logging. By logging the program's state at key points, you can track down the source of the error more easily. As we already know – and it's the key target of this whole book – refactoring can help you debug. Sometimes, it could just look like a game, but refactoring your code and making it cleaner will likely help you understand what's happening.

Although it is widely used as a technique, I must point out that crying and banging your head on the keyboard does not work to fix bugs; on the other hand, do not hesitate to ask for help. This can also be an exceedingly difficult thing.

Profiling

Even the most skilled development teams may find that a few lines of code don't achieve peak performance right from the start. To uncover the most efficient methods for improving code speed, it must undergo evaluation, debugging, and review.

Software engineers (and quality assurance professionals) must take some steps to guarantee that their code is as swift, smooth, and flawless as possible.

Profiling is the process of measuring and analyzing the runtime behavior and performance characteristics of a program. The primary goal of profiling is to identify bottlenecks, performance issues, and areas for optimization in the code. This is crucial for improving the efficiency and speed of a program. Profiling can be applied to various types of software, including desktop applications, web applications, and server-side software.

There are many different profiling tools available, and they can be used to collect several types of data, as shown here:

- **CPU usage**: This data shows how much CPU time the program is using

- **Memory usage**: This data shows how much memory the program is using

- **Function call frequency**: This data shows how often each function in the program is being called

- **Function execution time**: This data shows how long each function in the program is taking to execute

- **Resource usage**: This data shows how many various system resources, such as disk I/O and network bandwidth, the program is using

Once the profiling data has been collected, it can be analyzed to identify bottlenecks. A bottleneck is a part of the program that is slowing it down. For example, a function that is called very often and takes a long time to execute may be a bottleneck. Once the bottlenecks have been identified, they can be fixed by optimizing the code. For example, the bottleneck function may be rewritten to make it more efficient. Profiling is a valuable tool for improving the performance of software. It can be used to identify and fix bottlenecks, and to make sure that the program is using system resources efficiently.

Profiling has practical applications in various fields. For instance, web application developers can employ profilers to identify performance bottlenecks in their applications, allowing them to optimize the code for quicker loading. Similarly, game developers use profilers to improve frame rates by identifying and optimizing problematic sections of their games. Server administrators also make use of profilers to pinpoint resource-intensive processes, enabling them to reduce the server's resource burden.

Lots of tools are used to profile running Java applications. Sometimes, they are included in your IDEs in their plugin/extensions, such as NetBeans or Eclipse. One of the most used and common tools is VisualVM, a visual tool integrated into the **Java Development Kit** (**JDK**) that provides a wide range of profiling, monitoring, and diagnostic capabilities, including CPU profiling, memory profiling, and thread analysis.

VisualVM provides a user-friendly graphical interface for monitoring and analyzing Java applications. It offers a wealth of visual data and performance metrics, making it easier to identify and address performance issues. One of VisualVM's key features is its Java profiling capabilities. It allows developers to profile their applications to identify bottlenecks, memory leaks, and other performance-related problems. You can perform CPU profiling, thread analysis, and memory profiling, which are essential for improving the efficiency and reliability of Java applications.

When your application starts freaking out and you don't know exactly what is happening (for example, everything starts slowing down), one of the best chances (and one of the most desperate, at the same time) is to make a so-called "heap dump" or "memory dump." A **memory dump** is essentially a snapshot of the contents of a computer's memory (RAM) or a specific process's memory at a given point in time.

This snapshot captures the state of the system or application at the moment it was created. Memory dumps serve various important purposes, including debugging software errors and crashes, analyzing security incidents and malware infections, investigating system crashes, and optimizing memory usage in applications. They come in different types, such as complete memory dumps (for hardware-related issues), kernel memory dumps (for operating system issues), process memory dumps (for application-specific debugging), and mini dumps (for smaller and more manageable data). Memory dump analysis is crucial for gaining insights into system and software behavior and is an essential tool in resolving a wide range of computing issues.

VisualVM (like other profiling tools) allows you to capture heap dumps and thread dumps, which are essential for diagnosing memory-related issues and analyzing thread behavior in your Java application.

Fuzzing

Fuzzing, also known as **fuzz testing**, is an automated software testing approach where unconventional, often random, and invalid data is provided as input to a computer program. The program's responses are closely monitored for anomalies such as crashes, violations of built-in code rules, or potential memory issues. Fuzzers are typically employed to assess software programs that rely on structured inputs, such as file formats or protocols that distinguish between valid and invalid data.

A good fuzzer generates partially valid inputs that are "valid enough" to avoid immediate rejection by the input parser but are "invalid enough" to uncover unanticipated program behaviors, especially in corner cases that may not have been adequately addressed.

In a security context, the most valuable input to fuzz is often data that traverses a trust boundary. A **trust boundary** is a point where data or program execution transitions between different trust levels or where data and commands are exchanged between entities with varying privileges. Trust boundaries can be found at distinct locations in a system where all subsystems and their data have equal trust. For instance, an execution trust boundary occurs when an application gains elevated privileges, such as root access. A data trust boundary occurs when data originates from an untrusted source, such as user input or a network socket. For instance, it's more critical to fuzz code that's responsible for handling file uploads from any user, as it crosses a trust boundary, than code dealing with a configuration file accessible only to privileged users.

Every fuzzer can be put into one of two categories:

- **Mutation-based fuzzers**: These fuzzers start with existing data samples and make changes to them to create new test cases. They take an original input or test case and then modify it in various ways, such as changing random bits or values, to see if these modifications trigger unexpected behavior or vulnerabilities in the software being tested. Mutation-based fuzzers are good at finding certain types of bugs or vulnerabilities, especially when you have an initial set of valid inputs to work with.

- **Generation-based fuzzers**: These fuzzers build test cases by understanding the structure and rules of the target protocol or file format. Instead of modifying existing data samples, they generate new data that follows the specific format and logic required for testing. These fuzzers are good at exploring different aspects of a program or system because they can create a wide range of test cases based on their knowledge of the protocol or file format.

Now, we'll delve into subcategories within these two groups. There's no universally agreed-upon list of fuzzing categories, but I liked the approaches described in the book *Fuzzing: Brute Force Vulnerability Discovery* (see *Further reading*), so I'll try to resume them.

Pre-generated test cases

As mentioned earlier, the **pre-generated test cases** method, exemplified by the PROTOS framework, starts by studying a specific specification. It involves understanding supported data structures and acceptable value ranges. Test cases are then crafted as hard-coded packets or files, designed to test boundary conditions or challenge the specification itself. These test cases prove valuable for assessing how accurately the specification has been implemented on various systems. While this method requires substantial upfront effort in test case creation, its advantage lies in its reusability across multiple implementations of the same protocol or file format. A limitation, however, is that fuzz testing is finite as there's no random element; once the list of test cases is exhausted, fuzzing concludes.

Random

The **random approach** is the simplest yet least effective method. It involves hurling pseudo-random data at the target while hoping for the best (or worst, depending on your perspective). Surprisingly, vulnerabilities in critical software have been uncovered using this technique. The challenging part is identifying the cause of an exception or a server crash resulting from tons of random bytes. Capturing the traffic with a sniffer is essential to facilitate debugging, often requiring extensive time in a debugger and disassembler. Debugging stack smashing can be especially troublesome as the call stack becomes corrupted.

Manual protocol mutation testing

Manual protocol mutation testing is even less sophisticated than random fuzzing. It doesn't involve an automated fuzzer; instead, the tester becomes the fuzzer. By entering inappropriate data into the target application, the goal is to crash the server or provoke undesired behavior. It's a straightforward, cost-effective approach that's often applied to web applications, allowing the analyst to rely on experience and intuition during the audit.

We think that this approach is sometimes referred to as **hallway usability testing**, even though a usability test is something different than testing the program's correctness. If you're interested in what hallway usability testing is, take a look at the *Further reading* section.

Mutation or brute-force testing

Brute-force testing involves taking a valid sample of a protocol or data format and continuously modifying every byte, word, or string within that data packet or file. While this approach requires minimal upfront research and is relatively easy to implement, it's somewhat inefficient because it may waste CPU cycles on data that cannot be interpreted. Nevertheless, it can be fully automated, and it relies on a collection of known good packets or files for testing. Examples of brute-force file format fuzzers include FileFuzz for Windows and notSPIKEfile for Linux.

Automatic protocol generation testing

In **automatic protocol generation testing**, the tester initially studies and understands the protocol specification or file definition. Instead of creating hard-coded test cases, a grammar is developed to describe the protocol's operation. Static and fuzzable variables are identified within the packet or file. The fuzzer works by looking at templates, creating fuzzy data, and then sending the changed data to the target. How well this works depends on the tester's skills in finding the parts of the specification that are likely to cause problems during the parsing process. Notable examples are SPIKE and SPIKEfile. However, this method demands time to create the grammar or definition upfront.

We just wanted to give you a general smattering of concepts that we have often seen put in place without a real "structurization" of what was being done. As usual, we do not pretend to be exhaustive but simply wish to spark some curiosity in you regarding this subject.

Symbolic execution

Symbolic execution stands as a program analysis method in which programs are run with symbolic inputs rather than concrete ones. Simultaneously, it preserves a path condition (see the *Cyclomatic complexity* section to learn what a *path* is) that evolves each time a branch instruction is encountered, encapsulating the constraints on the inputs that lead to that specific point within the program. In other words, it works by replacing real data with symbolic values as input and describing program variable values as symbolic expressions. This way, the program's results are expressed as functions of these symbolic inputs.

To create tests, this method relies on solving the gathered constraints using a constraint solver. Symbolic execution is also handy for finding bugs since it inspects the program as it runs for errors or assertion violations and creates test inputs that can trigger these issues.

It is also seen as a sort of **white-box fuzzing** because you are fuzzing (see the previous section) but you have the knowledge of how the program works (yes, also of the code – it's also something in between static and dynamic analysis).

Consider this very trivial Java method:

```
void doSomething() {
    int x = getInput();
    int z = x + 2;
    if (z > 20) {
        throw new RuntimeException();
    } else {
        System.out.println("OK");
    }
}
```

This method does indeed do something, so its name does not lie, but it doesn't do anything meaningful. It's just a means to explain how symbolic execution would work on it.

In a regular execution (often called "concrete" execution), the program operates as follows: it reads a specific input value (for example, 10) and assigns this value to the variable, x. Subsequently, the program executes the addition (z = x + 2) and the conditional branch, which, in this case, results in a false evaluation and OK as the output.

During symbolic execution, the program operates differently. It reads a symbolic value, represented by a symbol such as λ, and assigns this symbol to the variable, x. The program then continues with the addition, setting z to $\lambda + 2$. When it encounters the if statement, it evaluates the condition as $\lambda + 2 > 20$. At this stage, the symbol λ can take on any value, and symbolic execution splits into two distinct paths by «forking.» Each path retains a copy of the program state at the branching point along with a path condition.

In this example, one path is associated with the $\lambda + 2 > 20$ path condition, leading to the execution of the if branch, while the other path is tied to the $\lambda + 2 <= 20$ path condition, resulting in the execution of the else branch. Both paths can be independently symbolically executed.

As the paths reach their conclusion, which might happen due to an exception (for example, throwing a RuntimeException) or program termination, symbolic execution figures out a specific value for λ by solving the path constraints for each path it explores. These specific values can be thought of as real-world test cases, which can be instrumental for tasks such as bug reproduction. In this particular case, the constraint solver would establish that to throw the RuntimeException, λ needs to be greater than or equal to 18.

We must admit that this technique is not used much and presents several downsides. For example, as you can easily guess, the greater the cyclomatic complexity of the program, the greater the complexity of the symbolic execution; this technique does not scale at all as the complexity of the program increases. In addition, the efficiency of this analysis technique depends largely on the efficiency of the program itself. There are other contradictions that I invite you to observe in the *Further reading* section.

Taint tracking

Taint tracking, often referred to as **information flow tracking** or **data flow tracking**, is a technique that's used in computer security and software analysis to monitor the flow of data within a program or system to identify potential security vulnerabilities. Taint tracking works by marking data as *tainted* if it comes from an untrusted source, such as user input or a file from the internet. The taint tracker then tracks the flow of this tainted data through the program to identify any operations that could potentially lead to a security vulnerability. Tainted data can include things such as passwords, personal information, or any data that should not be exposed or manipulated by unauthorized users.

Here's how taint tracking typically works:

1. **Data labeling**: Taint tracking systems label certain data as "tainted" or "untrusted" when it originates from external sources, such as user inputs. For example, if a user provides a password as input, that password data is labeled as tainted.

2. **Data flow monitoring**: The system then monitors how this tainted data flows through the program. It keeps track of which variables, functions, and components the tainted data interacts with.

3. **Violations detection**: Taint tracking mechanisms continuously check if tainted data is used in a way that could compromise security. For example, if tainted data is used in a database query, sent over a network, or included in a response, the taint tracking system can flag this as a potential security risk.

4. **Alerts generation**: When a potential security violation is detected, the system can generate alerts, log the event, or take some other predefined action to mitigate the risk. This helps in identifying and fixing security vulnerabilities:

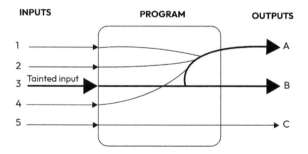

Figure 7.2 – One of the possible inputs is marked as tainted (because it comes from an untrusted source) and its flow through the program is tracked until its possible outputs

For example, a taint tracker could be used to identify SQL injection vulnerabilities in web applications. SQL injection vulnerabilities occur when an attacker can inject malicious SQL code into a web application's database queries. This can allow the attacker to read or modify data in the database, or even execute arbitrary code on the web server. A taint tracker could be used to identify SQL injection vulnerabilities by marking all user input as tainted. The taint tracker would then track the flow of this tainted data through the web application's code to identify any operations that could potentially lead to a SQL injection vulnerability. For example, if the tainted data is used in a database query without being properly sanitized, the taint tracker would flag this as a potential vulnerability.

A small digression – what is SQL injection?

Even if it is not strictly related to taint tracking, we think it is worth knowing what **SQL injection** is.

SQL injection is a common and dangerous type of cyber-attack where an attacker can manipulate a web application's SQL query by injecting malicious SQL code. This can potentially lead to unauthorized access, data theft, or even data manipulation. But how can this happen? Suppose you have a web application that takes user input to search for a specific user in a database using the following SQL query:

`SELECT * FROM user WHERE username = 'input';`

Here, the input is taken directly from `user` input, and the application does not properly validate or sanitize this `input`.

An attacker can exploit this vulnerability by inputting the following as their username:

`' OR '1'='1`

The SQL query would then look like this:

`SELECT * FROM users WHERE username = '' OR '1'='1';`

The `'1'='1'` condition is always true, so the query effectively selects all rows in the `users` table, allowing the attacker to bypass any authentication and access all user data.

To prevent SQL injection, you should use parameterized queries or prepared statements provided by Java's **Java Database Connectivity (JDBC)** API or some other popular frameworks, such as Hibernate. Here's how you can rewrite the vulnerable code so that it becomes secure:

```
String userInput = getUserInput();
String sqlQuery = "SELECT * FROM users WHERE username = ?";
PreparedStatement preparedStatement = connection.prepareStatement(sqlQuery);
preparedStatement.setString(1, userInput);
ResultSet resultSet = preparedStatement.executeQuery();
```

In this example, a parameterized SQL query is created using `PreparedStatement`, where `?` is a placeholder for the user input. The user input is then safely set as a parameter using the `setString` method (note that no quotes and no string concatenation are involved). The query is executed, and the results are processed securely.

By using parameterized queries like this, you can prevent SQL injection attacks because the JDBC driver handles the input as data rather than executable SQL code. This ensures the user input is treated safely and doesn't interfere with the query's structure.

Taint tracking can be used to identify a variety of other security vulnerabilities, such as XSS, command injection, and insecure path traversal. It can also be used to track the flow of sensitive data, such as credit card numbers and social security numbers.

Using taint tracking offers various advantages, including the ability to uncover security vulnerabilities in software that would be difficult or even impossible to identify through alternative testing methods. This approach also allows you to monitor sensitive data flow, helping to mitigate the risk of data breaches. Moreover, it provides a means to establish security sandboxes, effectively isolating untrusted code from trusted components.

Nonetheless, taint tracking presents several challenges. Its implementation can be intricate, requiring expertise in software security and taint tracking. It may introduce a performance impact on the monitored program, and it can result in a significant number of false positives, which can be time-consuming to investigate.

It is worth noticing that some programming languages, such as Perl, Ruby, or Ballerina, natively support *taint checking*, a feature that proceeds variable by variable, forming a list of variables that are potentially influenced by outside input. More information can be found in the *Further reading* section.

Summary

In this chapter, we added another tool to our toolbox for writing and maintaining clean code and efficient software: code analysis. We learned that we can do it in two ways: by checking the code before it's even run (statically) and by watching the code as it runs (dynamically). We tried to figure out what kind of problems we should look out for in each of these analyses, and we also found some tools and techniques that can help.

Just like the other stuff we've covered, this chapter is meant to give you ideas for going deeper. Code analysis is often seen as something extra, like an optional step, but it's a crucial part of making a project efficient and easy to maintain. So, don't underestimate its importance!

Besides the times when you do analysis and improve your work, it's crucial to keep a certain level of quality in your everyday tasks. You can make a significant difference with minimal, targeted effort by using some simple but effective methods. In the next chapter, we'll explore some of these methods.

Further reading

- Cyclomatic complexity: `https://www.geeksforgeeks.org/cyclomatic-complexity/`

- SonarQube documentation: `https://docs.sonarsource.com/sonarqube/latest/`

- PMD documentation: `https://pmd.github.io/pmd/index.html`

- FindBugs manual: `https://findbugs.sourceforge.net/manual/index.html`

- An introduction to CheckStyle: `https://www.baeldung.com/checkstyle-java`

- Getting started with VisualVM: `https://visualvm.github.io/gettingstarted.html`

- M. Sutton, A. Greene, and P. Amini, *Fuzzing: Brute Force Vulnerability Discovery*, by Addison-Wesley Professional

- Hallway usability testing: `https://www.techopedia.com/definition/30678/hallway-usability-testing`

- Limitations of symbolic execution: `https://en.wikipedia.org/wiki/Symbolic_execution#Limitations`

- Taint checking in programming languages: `https://en.wikipedia.org/wiki/Taint_checking`

Part 3: Further Learning

Apart from the actual act of refactoring, it's crucial to keep up a certain level of quality in your everyday work. There are small but powerful ways to achieve this goal, making a big impact with minimal, focused effort. We'll discuss things like how you format your code, manage versions of your code, and work together with others through techniques like pair programming.

After we've covered everything about fixing up classes and packages, let's zoom out and look at the big picture: architecture. Even if your code is good, things can go wrong if the way different parts interact is not well-managed. We'll talk about signs to watch out for and what to do instead to keep everything running smoothly.

This part has the following chapters:

8
Crafting Quality Every Day

While trying to give you advice on keeping your code clean and your design clear, it's also important to talk about some practices that will help you little by little, day by day. Apart from dedicating specific moments to refactoring, maintaining a consistent level of quality in your day-to-day work is essential for the overall health and efficiency of your software development process. Achieving this doesn't always require extensive time or effort; small, targeted actions can make a significant difference. By incorporating the practices we're about to describe into your daily routine, you can not only prevent the accumulation of technical debt but also improve the overall quality and maintainability of your code base. These efforts may seem small in isolation but, collectively, they can have a substantial impact on the long-term success of your software projects.

In this chapter, we're going to cover the following main topics:

- Code versioning
- Code formatting and style
- Code reviews
- Pair programming
- Documentation
- Why you're doing what you're doing
- A hard dose of reality

Code versioning

I have a soft spot for code versioning, and that's weird, I get it. It was one of the first things I had to learn the hard way when I started working right after graduation. Incredibly, no one had ever mentioned code versioning throughout my entire computer science studies. This makes me think that maybe my degree program was lacking in this regard, and it shows how important code versioning is in the life of a developer from day one.

Anyway, let's get to the point. To tell you what code versioning is, I could start by saying that it is something that can save your day when things go wrong; I'll admit that it sounds a bit too generic as a description, so I'll go into detail.

Version control is like a time machine for your files. It keeps track of all the changes you make so you can easily jump back to any previous version when needed. This system is usually referred to as a **versioning control system** (**VCS**) and there are many implementations of them. With a VCS, you can turn back the clock on individual files or the entire project, check how things have changed over time, figure out who messed with something that's causing trouble, identify when an issue was introduced, and much more. Plus, using a VCS means that if you mess things up or lose files, you've got a safety net for easy recovery, and it doesn't add much complexity to your workflow. Changes are typically marked with a code, often called the "revision number," "revision level," or just "revision." For instance, the original set of files is labeled "revision 1." When the first change happens, it becomes "revision 2," and this pattern continues. Every revision comes with a timestamp and the name of the person who made the change. Revisions can be compared, restored, and, in some cases, merged, making it a powerful way to manage the evolution of files. The advantages of a VCS increase as the complexity of the project increases and the number of team members increases.

As we already said, VCSs are useful for reverting errors; in case of trouble, you can restore your class, your package, and your module to a previous version that was still okay and start again. But this is not the only reason why everyone in this industry must use a VCS.

Developers can collaborate and team up on a project using VCSs. They can all access the database at the same time to check out past versions, making it simpler for them to collaborate effectively, regardless of their geographical locations. Version control also allows developers to maintain a historical record of changes, attributing them to specific contributors. This capability empowers them to roll back to earlier document versions and gain insights into how various team members' contributions have shaped the project's evolution. In the realm of collaborative development, it's essential to have a clear understanding of the commits being added to the repository and the reasons behind these commits to prevent conflicts and ensure the stability of the source code. Collaborative platforms (for example, GitHub and GitLab) that are built around VCSs offer centralized repositories (we'll jump into that later), tools for issue tracking and management, as well as threaded discussions and forums. These features streamline a team-oriented approach to the software development life cycle.

Graph structure

In graph theory, think of revisions like a tree growing from a main line. Picture *branches* coming out of this main line, forming a tree shape. Even though it's more complex and looks like a graph, you can simplify it in your mind as a "tree with merges" for practical use.

Revisions happen one after another over time and can be put in a specific order, either by their revision number or the time they were made. Each revision is based on the ones before it, but sometimes, you can completely replace an earlier revision by getting rid of everything and putting in new stuff. In the simplest case, with no extra branches or undoing, each revision is only connected to the one just before it, making a straight line. The latest version is called the **HEAD** revision. In graph theory terms, if you think of each revision as a point and each connection between revisions like an arrow (usually going from older to newer, following the timeline), this setup makes a straight-line graph:

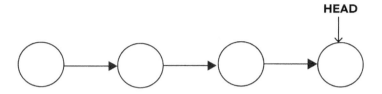

Figure 8.1 – A very basic sequence of revisions

When there is branching (that is, there are different paths) or we have to get back to an older revision, creating a situation where a revision depends on one older than the one just before it, the graph changes into a directed tree. In this tree, each point may have more than one next point. This creates multiple endpoints, representing revisions without any more changes (the "latest revision on each branch"). In theory, the tree may not have a favorite endpoint (the "main" latest revision), but usually, one endpoint is chosen as the **HEAD**. If a new revision is based on the **HEAD**, it either becomes the new **HEAD** or starts a new **BRANCH**:

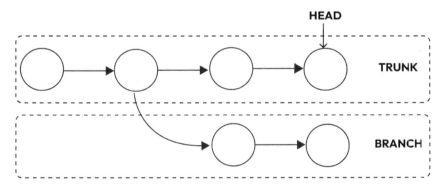

Figure 8.2 – Branching from the trunk

The list of revisions from the starting point to the **HEAD**, called the trunk or mainline in graph theory, makes a simple straight-line graph. However, if a revision can be based on more than one previous revision (when a point can have more than one parent), it's called a **MERGE**. This is one of the trickier parts of revision control. It often happens when changes occur in different branches (usually two), and these changes are combined into one branch that includes both sets of changes. If these changes overlap, it can be hard or even impossible to merge them without manual help or rewriting (these situations are known as **conflicts**):

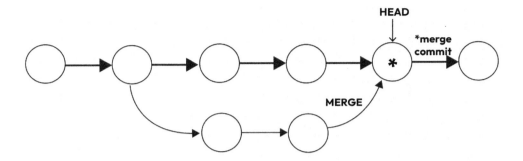

Figure 8.3 – Merging a branch into a trunk (a merge commit is created)

When merges happen, the graph stops being a tree, as points can have more than one parent. Instead, it becomes a rooted **directed acyclic graph** (**DAG**). This graph doesn't have cycles "by definition" because parents always existed in the past, it's rooted because it has a starting node given by the very first commit and it's directed because you can navigate through it only in a given direction (we could say the direction of time) and never in the opposite direction. If there's a trunk, merges from branches are like "external" additions to the tree. The changes in the branch are bundled as a patch, and applied to the **HEAD** of the trunk, creating a new version without directly mentioning the branch and keeping the tree structure. So, even though the actual relationships make a DAG, you can think of it as a tree with merges, and the trunk itself is a straight path.

In addition to performing the **MERGE** operation, code versioning systems also offer the option to perform the so-called **rebase**. This action shifts the whole branch of new changes to start from the latest point in the main branch. It includes all the recent changes in the main branch. However, instead of making a **MERGE** commit, rebasing rewrites the project history by making entirely new commits for each original commit in the branch. Putting it more simply, it's like you take the whole branch and "attach" it at the end of the main one:

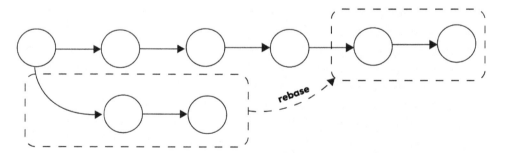

Figure 8.4 – Rebase operation

Rebasing has a big advantage because it makes your project history cleaner. It does this by removing the extra merge commits that git merge often creates. Additionally, rebasing creates a completely straight-line project history, allowing you to trace the development from the latest feature to the very start of the project without any diverging paths.

Now that we've seen how a VCS works at a general level, it's time to take a look at how the three main types worked before and how they work now.

Local VCSs

Though quite ancient, this approach has fallen out of use, especially in professional settings – I haven't even witnessed its use. Yet, as the initial example of a VCS, it's worth mentioning it so that we can contrast it with modern practices.

In the past, a common version control method involved duplicating files into a separate directory, sometimes with timestamps for meticulous record-keeping. Despite its simplicity, this method was error-prone, with users easily losing track of their current directory and making unintended modifications or overwrites. To tackle these issues, programmers developed local VCSs with straightforward databases to log changes made to files under revision control.

Here is an example of a local VCS:

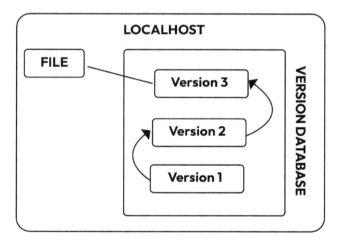

Figure 8.5 – A local VCS

One of the most popular tools of this kind was RCS, which has been a thing for a while; it was also distributed among macOS's Developer Kit.

Centralized VCSs

To address collaboration challenges among developers using different systems, **centralized version control systems** (**CVCSs**) such as CVS or Subversion were created. These systems store all versioned files on a central server, allowing multiple users to access and retrieve files:

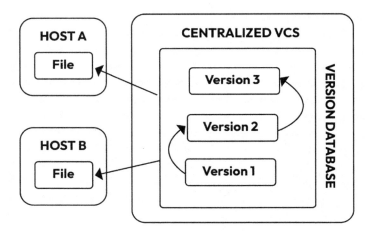

Figure 8.6 – A CVCS schema

While this method facilitated project coordination and administration, it had a major drawback – the centralized server was a single point of failure. If it went down, collaboration and file-saving became impossible, and data loss risked the entire project history. This limitation led to the evolution of today's VCSs.

Distributed VCSs

A **distributed version control system** (**DVCS**) is a type of VCS that allows multiple users to work on a project while having their own local copies of the entire project's repository. In a distributed CVS, each user has a complete copy of the project's history and can make changes independently on their local copy. These changes can be tracked, merged, and shared with others seamlessly.

One of the most well-known distributed CVS systems is **Git**. Git enables developers to work on a project offline, make commits to their local repository, and then synchronize their changes with a central repository or other team members' repositories when they are ready. Here is a DVCS schema:

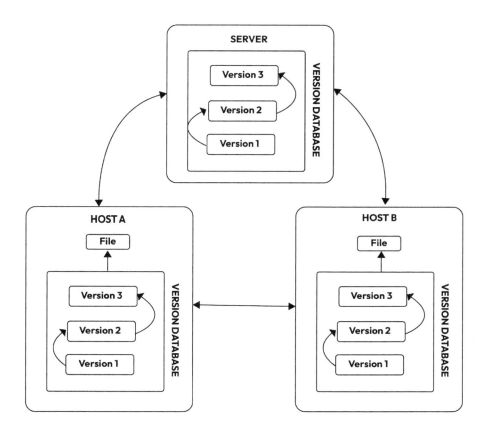

Figure 8.7 – A distributed VCS schema

Distributed CVS systems offer several advantages, such as increased flexibility, improved collaboration, and better handling of projects with geographically distributed teams. Each contributor has a full copy of the project's history, which provides redundancy and makes it harder to lose data. Additionally, DVCS systems allow for more branching and merging capabilities, making it easier to manage concurrent work on the same project.

Branching strategies

To keep your code base organized and have a smooth workflow, it's a good idea to follow what's called a **branching strategy**.

Branches are like separate workspaces for developers to build new features or fix issues in a software project. We saw that branches can be combined with the main code when the work is finished. This separation helps you avoid mixing up changes and makes it easier to fix mistakes. If everyone works on their branch, no one should mess up what others are doing.

A branching strategy is a plan that software teams use for writing, combining, and deploying code when they use VCSs. It's like a set of rules that tells developers how to work with the shared code.

This strategy is crucial because it keeps things organized and prevents problems when many developers are working at the same time. Without it, there could be conflicts when everyone tries to add their changes simultaneously. This would slow down the process of getting code ready to use – and cause a certain amount of frustration!

By following a branching strategy, developers can work together without causing issues. It lets teams work on different things at the same time and release code faster with fewer conflicts. It's all about having a clear process for making changes to the code; you can set up your own branching models, of course, but there are a bunch of them that have become quite successful over the years. The one we're about to show will use only Distributed VCSs since are the only ones that are still in use.

Trunk-based development

Trunk-based development is a way of working where all developers make their changes directly in the main part of the code, which we call the **trunk**. This is the part of the code that's ready to be used in the project. Developers are encouraged to save their work often and use special techniques to manage changes that aren't ready yet.

We also focus on automated testing, meaning the computer checks if the code is working well all the time. We do this to make sure any changes we make are tested thoroughly before they are used in the project.

Sometimes, if a task takes a long time, a developer might create a separate branch from the main code, make changes there, and then bring those changes back to the main part when they're done. But the main idea in trunk-based development is to use separate branches as little as possible and have everyone work together on the main part of the code most of the time. The following diagram represents a very simple sequence of commits (a graph made by only one, linear path) that have been done on a single branch:

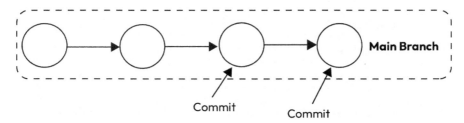

Figure 8.8 – In trunk-based development, each commit is done on the main branch

Here's how the trunk-based branching model works in detail:

1. **Work in the main code**: Instead of making separate branches, work directly in the **MAIN** (trunk) branch.

2. **Make small, frequent updates**: Make small and regular changes to the code. This makes it easier to check and reduces the chances of problems.

3. **Use continuous integration (CI)**: Frequently combine and test the code to catch issues early, prevent conflicts, and keep the code ready for release.

4. **Merge changes often**: Regularly bring your changes back into the main code, keeping it current and lowering the chance of conflicts.

At first glance, it doesn't seem so bad. There are some pros – for instance, it encourages teamwork and quick feedback (there could be a merge conflict or a failing test), helps find problems early and fix them fast, speeds up adding new features, keeps the code organized by having everyone work on one branch, and lowers the complexity of dealing with many branches. When applied together with **test-driven development (TDD)** and a **continuous integration/continuous deployment (CI/CD)** pipeline, you can guarantee that your code is still working correctly. Under a certain number of circumstances, it can be a valid approach.

But there's a great drawback: this model is not scalable since it might not work well for big teams or complex projects. If the main code goes bad, everything is affected. Moreover, we need strong automated testing and CI. As I mentioned previously, it can be a valid alternative if some conditions (conditions that, to tell the truth, should always be put in place) are respected.

Let's see something a bit different.

Feature branching

Feature branching is a widely used approach where a fresh branch is made for a particular feature or code change. This lets developers work on the feature separately without messing with the **MAIN** branch. Once the feature is finished, it can be merged back into the **MAIN** branch using a pull request.

> **What is a pull request?**
>
> A **pull request** is a mechanism used in version control systems, such as Git, to propose changes to a codebase. It is a request to merge a set of changes made in a feature branch into the main or target branch. The process typically involves a developer creating a branch, making changes, pushing those changes to a remote repository, and then submitting a pull request for review by others. The pull request allows team members to discuss, review, and test the proposed changes before they are merged into the main codebase, helping maintain code quality and collaboration in software development projects. More on this in the *Further reading* section.

This request permits other team members to inspect the changes and propose adjustments or enhancements before adding the feature to the **MAIN** branch:

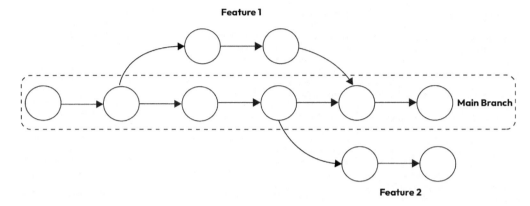

Figure 8.9 – In feature branching, each new feature is developed on a dedicated branch

Again, let's see the workflow in detail:

1. **Set up feature branches**: For each of the tasks you're working on, create a dedicated branch. Each of these branches should originate from the **MAIN** branch.

2. **Develop the feature**: Implement your feature into the **Feature** branch and commit as many times as you need. This branch must contain only commits related to that particular feature and nothing else (when I say nothing, I mean nothing: remember that this change set will go straight to production one day – you don't want to mix things up).

3. **Initiate a pull request**: When your development is complete and you've tested everything and you're happy with that, you can create a pull request to merge your changes into the **MAIN** branch.

4. **Examine and approve**: The changes are checked by other developers, who will give their approval or suggest some modifications (basically, they can start a conversation). In this way, potential issues and errors can be caught before the code becomes part of the **MAIN** branch.

5. **Merge the feature branch**: Now that your feature has been implemented, and the pull request has been examined and approved, the **Feature** branch can be merged back into the **MAIN** branch.

6. **Tidy up**: Delete the **Feature** branch.

As you can see, we have raised a bit the complexity of getting the **MAIN** branch to stay as clean as possible. The primary goal is to maintain the stable version on the **MAIN** branch while supporting concurrent feature development. In general, the code can be well-organized and tested (no merges into the **MAIN** branch until all tests are passed). Change tracking is improved. Using this strategy, we can insert code reviews in our workflow (see the next section).

On the other hand, new challenges arise when we're managing and updating multiple branches, with potential delays in merging changes into the **MAIN** branch due to lengthy reviews. Of course, having multiple branches can create conflicts.

Now, let's look at a very, very popular branching strategy.

GitFlow

GitFlow is a way of managing branches in Git. It mainly uses two long-lasting branches, **MAIN** and **DEVELOP**, which stay throughout the project's life. It also uses short-lived branches such as **FEATURE**, **RELEASE**, and **HOTFIX**. These are created when needed and removed once they've done their job.

The **MAIN** branch holds the stable, ready-to-use code, while the **DEVELOP** branch is where all the active development happens. **FEATURE** branches are for working on new features or changes, **RELEASE** branches help with getting ready for a new release, and **HOTFIX** branches are for quickly fixing critical problems in the production code.

GitFlow is a bit hard to understand at first. On the **MAIN** branch, we have the stable version, and on the **DEVELOP** branch, we have the "next" version. Each **FEATURE** branch hosts a specific feature that is being developed:

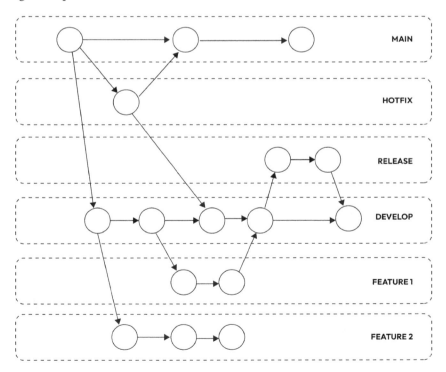

Figure 8.10 – GitFlow schema

Here's the detailed workflow:

1. Start working on a branch called `develop`. Use this branch for your current development; this branch must be created from the `main` branch.

2. Then, when you begin working on something new (or on a bug fix), create `feature` branches; these must be created starting from the `develop` branch.

3. When you've finished working on your feature, just merge your feature branch into `develop`.

4. When it's time to prepare for a new release, create a `release` branch from the `develop` branch. Assign a clear and descriptive name, incorporating the version number, such as "release/1.0." Test it deeply to identify and address any bugs, ensuring its readiness for production.

5. When the release is ready, combine it with the main part and mark it with a version number. Use a pull request to have the code checked and approved by other team members.

6. Start over again. Once the release is done, go back to the `develop` branch and start over with a new `feature` branch.

   Some critical problems may arise due to something that is in the main branch; in this case, we want to follow a faster procedure, and not risk deploying the feature we're still developing.

7. Make a hotfix branch from the main. This branch is crucial for quickly fixing important problems or bugs in the production code that can't wait for the next release. It's like a priority lane for bug fixing.

8. Once the hotfix is done and has been tested, merge it into both the `develop` and main parts to ensure the fix works for both ongoing development and the production code.

This approach offers a structured approach to code change management, separating ongoing development from stable releases and promoting the use of short-lived **FEATURE**, **RELEASE**, and **HOTFIX** branches. Code reviews and testing are even more facilitated. At the end of the day, GitFlow provides a predictable development flow.

On the other hand, it is undeniably more intricate than other branching strategies. Also, it may lead to a larger number of branches (you have to create a branch even for really small features or issues); consequently, there's potential for merge conflicts. It is also clear that GitFlow requires a certain level of discipline and adherence to the process, and some may perceive it as overly prescriptive or inflexible.

In summary, no branching model is perfect. Analyze your need and choose one; no one says that it cannot be a mix of the models we just presented. I often saw, for instance, **HOTFIX** made directly into the **MAIN** branch and other times a **HOTFIX** branch opened, depending on the complexity involved in the fix. Also, consider that merging is often time-consuming: not only is the merge itself in case of conflicts but also the fact that usually, a merge requires a new build. If your build is slow, merging your branch to the **MAIN** branch could take time.

Best practices

Although it might sound like a simple task, almost like saving a file in the cloud so that you don't lose it if your computer gets stolen, managing files and project versions is another crucial aspect of improving your project management. Speaking from experience, it's good not to underestimate this matter; it's one of the things that sets someone who cares apart. Here are some tips we feel like sharing; as usual, it's all quite flexible and based on our experience.

Make it a habit to commit to your work frequently and at the earliest opportunity. By doing this, you ensure that each commit captures a specific set of related changes. Keep your commits small and focused on a single task or feature. However, remember not to commit unfinished work as this can potentially disrupt the stability of the code base and create issues (golden rule: do not break the build on the main branch!). Instead, break your work into smaller, logical chunks, and commit them as you complete each part (or use a feature flag if you feel like that's the case). This practice helps maintain a clean and reliable version history, making it easier to track the evolution of your project and collaborate effectively with your team.

Always run tests on your code before you commit changes. Testing helps ensure that a commit is not just functioning as expected but also that it doesn't introduce any unintended problems or errors into the code base (golden rule: do not break the build on the main branch! Yes, I know I already said that). This step is crucial because sharing untested commits with your fellow developers can lead to confusion, disruptions in the project, and a lot of extra work down the line. By rigorously testing your changes before committing, you not only safeguard the stability of the project but also demonstrate your commitment to quality and collaboration within the development team. It's a smart practice to help maintain a smooth and efficient workflow, building trust among your colleagues, and reducing the need for extensive debugging or troubleshooting later on. Remember, a well-tested commit is a valuable contribution to the project.

When writing a commit message, aim for clarity and conciseness. The summary should be a brief yet informative glimpse into the nature of your changes, emphasizing their intent and how they distinguish themselves from the previous state of the code. In addition to a well-written summary, consider providing a more detailed description of your changes in the body of the commit message. This helps fellow developers, and even your future self, understand the context and significance of your modifications. Another valuable practice is linking your code changes to relevant work items or issues, enhancing traceability and project management. By associating your commits with specific tasks or tickets, you create a more organized and transparent system for tracking the progress of your work. For example, a common practice for Jira users (Jira is a very popular issue tracker) is to include the issue ID in the commit message. At the end of the day, your commit message serves as a crucial communication tool within your development team. A well-structured message ensures that your contributions are easily understood and integrated into the project's development history, facilitating collaboration and maintaining a clear record of your work.

One last piece of advice: when managing sensitive information such as passwords, it is crucial to exercise vigilant caution. Avoid the inadvertent exposure of production passwords and adopt alternative methods for secure storage. One recommended approach is to leverage a specialized system such as Vault, which provides a secure and centralized repository for managing sensitive credentials. By steering clear of committing production passwords directly and opting for such dedicated systems, you enhance the overall security posture of your data handling practices. This proactive approach not only mitigates the risk of inadvertent leaks but also ensures a more robust and scalable solution for safeguarding critical authentication information.

Code formatting and style

Here's another part of our job that may seem basic, but no one talks about it... except when something goes wrong! From my experience, I believe that this is one of the things where developers have different ideas, maybe not entirely, but after all, we are precise people, and we all have our little quirks in how we arrange the code. As unimportant as it may seem, formatting the code correctly is important.

Code formatting means arranging your computer program in a neat and organized way. It's like making sure your writing follows specific rules so that it's easy to read and understand. When you format your code, you decide on things such as how much space to leave between lines, where to put curly braces, and how to name things. This makes your code more readable, consistent, and easier to work with.

There are various rules and habits to follow when arranging code in Java, but, in our opinion, it's also something very intuitive, almost like a natural skill for us software engineers. We'd bet that even without discussing it, we all know which one we prefer between the following two code snippets. Here's the first one:

```
public class Main {

    public static void main(String[] args) {
        System.out.println("Hello there!");
    }

}
```

Here's the second one:

```
public class Main {
public static void main(String[] args) {
System.out.println("Hello there!");
}
}
```

We think we all prefer the first snippet, and that's because the second one lacks proper indentation, which is the first and crucial aspect of how we format our code. However, no matter the style, the entire team needs to stick to the same standard, which means a set of internal rules that we all expect everyone to follow. Rules need to be established for each of the aspects that govern code formatting; let's take a look at the main ones.

Indentation

We use indentation to help us move through a file's structure. If you think about it, a Java source file is a hierarchy of elements: we have the entire file, and then we have the classes inside it Within classes, there are methods, and within methods, we have blocks, and so on, in a repeating pattern, including `if` statements, loops, and more. To help us navigate through all of this, we use indentation. Without indentation, even the simplest methods would be hard to understand. As we've mentioned before, code is designed to be run by machines but also to be understood by humans:

```
public void isEven
        (Integer number) {if (number
    % 2 == 0) {System.out
        .println("Even number");
    } else {System.out.println("Odd number");}}
```

Understanding this very simple code takes much longer if the method is not properly indented. This code prints one string if the given number is even and another if it's odd. Understanding this method would have been much quicker if it had been indented correctly:

```
public void isEven(Integer number) {
    if (number % 2 == 0) {
        System.out.println("Even number");
    } else {
        System.out.println("Odd number");
    }
}
```

There are mainly two aspects related to indentation: when to break to a new line and how much to move the indented code to the right. For example, you can choose to indent the code with a tab or four spaces, or whatever you prefer, so long as everyone follows the same style.

There are some widely used standards and conventions, such as **Oracle's Java Code Conventions** and the **Google Java Style Guide** (both of which are mentioned in the *Further reading* section). The first one recommends using four spaces for indentation, while the second suggests two. As you can see, it's a pretty diverse world of choices! But, as I've mentioned before, what's important is that everyone on the team uses the same set of rules.

Braces and whitespaces

Braces play a crucial role in delineating code blocks in Java. The two most prevalent brace styles are the **One True Brace Style (1TBS)** and **Allman Style**.

In 1TBS, the opening brace is placed at the end of the line, and the closing brace is put on a new line, indented to align with the opening line, like this:

```
if (number % 2 == 0) {
    System.out.println("Even number");
} else {
    System.out.println("Odd number");
}
```

In Allman Style, both the opening and closing braces are positioned on their individual lines, maintaining the same indentation level as the starting line:

```
public void isEven(Integer number) {
    if (number % 2 == 0)
    {
        System.out.println("Even number");
    } else
    {
        System.out.println("Odd number");
    }
}
```

No matter which style you choose, it's crucial to consistently apply it throughout your code base. Furthermore, always include spaces around operators to enhance readability:

```
int x = y + z;
```

Both Google and Oracle use 1TBS. Also, Robert Martin's *Clean Code* suggests this. For what it is worth, we also suggest it!

Line length and wrapping

A simple guideline for the length of lines in your code is to keep them between 80 and 100 characters (Oracle says 80, Google says 100). Fun fact: the 80-character limit for code lines can be traced back to Herman Hollerith, who won the contract for processing the 1890 US Census. He used 80-column punched cards to handle the data. His company later evolved into IBM.

By keeping your lines between 80 and 100 characters, your code will be easy to read on different screen sizes and resolutions. If a line gets too long, you can split it into multiple lines while following these examples:

- When you have lots of things separated by commas in a method call, you can break the line after a comma:

```
String carFeaturesFormatted = String.format("Make: %s, Model:
%s, Version: %s, Price: %s",
        make, model, version, price);
```

- If you have a long math expression, you can break the line before an operator:

```
int totalPrice = priceFare1 * factor1
        + priceFare2 * factor2
        + priceFare3 * factor3;
```

- When you have a long condition, you can wrap it like this:

```
if (cond1 && someMethod(argument1, argument2, argument3)
        || cond2 && anotherMethod(argument4, argument5)) {
    // code
}
```

Since the && operator has higher precedence than the || operator, line wrapping aligns with this logic, making it easier to read.

- For long string concatenations, you can wrap them like this:

```
String message = "Dear " + name + ",\n"
        + "Thank you for your subscription to " + newsLetterName
+ ".\n"
        + "The price of your subscription was " + price + ".\n"
        + "Regards,\n"
        + "The Newsletter Team";
```

However, note that the combination of string formatting and text blocks in Java 17 should allow us to bypass this problem. A **text block** refers to a language feature that allows you to define multiline strings in a more readable and maintainable way. It's a way to embed blocks of text without the need for cumbersome concatenation or escape characters. For example:

```
String textBlock = """
    This is a
    multiline
    text block.
    """;
```

- When using Lambda expressions, you can align wrapped lines with the opening delimiter like this:

```
catalogue.stream()
        .filter(film -> film.getGenre().equals("Sci-Fi")
                && film.getLength() > 180)
        .forEach(item -> System.out.println(item.getTitle()));
```

As Google's style guide says, you should never split a line right next to the arrow in a Lambda, except when the Lambda's body is just a single, unbraced expression; then, you can put a line break right after the arrow.

Comments and documentation

You can comment on Java code in three ways:

- Use Javadoc comments (/** . . . */) for describing classes, interfaces, methods, and fields (these are sometimes called documentation comments)

- Use single-line comments (//) for brief explanations, clarifications, or marking TODOs (there are sometimes called implementation comments)

- Use block comments (/* . . . */) for more extended explanations, especially when explaining intricate algorithms

The Google Java Style Guide has a specific section for Javadoc's comments only since they are the most important ones. Documentation (Javadoc) is crucial to explain to others how to use your code, and that's why is important to be strict when you write it... because you write it, right?

Since we've already discussed everything about the form that comments should take in code, let me say a few words about the substance of comments. Comments for generating Javadoc are crucial, no doubt about it. They don't explain how the code works but rather the behavior of the method. They clarify any specifics about the parameters and the situations in which exceptions are raised.

However, I've often seen comments being misused. First and foremost, commenting out code that is considered unnecessary is not a good practice. If the code is unnecessary, please delete it. If you're concerned about making mistakes, remember that VCSs act as a safety net, allowing you to retrieve deleted code with minimal effort.

At times, I've come across comments related to the implementation. In the case of particularly complex code that's hard to follow, a comment can be helpful. However, it should never be seen as a substitute for cleaning up the code to make it more understandable. If the code isn't written well, don't think you can fix it by adding comments. Rewrite the code. Additionally, it's common for such comments not to get updated when the logic of the method changes. The method does one thing, but the comment says something else, leading to confusion.

Other types of comments that I don't find particularly useful, except for rare exceptions, are the infamous TODO and FIXME. If you know you need to fix something, just fix it. If you can't do it right away, record the task in your task management system (for example, Jira) and move on. Putting FIXME in the code only adds confusion. When someone sees that FIXME in 2 years, they'll wonder, "Why hasn't it been fixed yet? Maybe it's not important." The same goes for TODO.

In summary, we advise you to write as few comments as possible in your code. Instead, focus on explaining why you're making a particular choice and the reasons that led you down one path instead of another. As Robert Martin says in *Clean Code*, you have to explain your intent.

Naming conventions

Naming conventions play a vital role in enhancing program comprehension and improving code readability. They serve as a set of guidelines that, when followed, make code more accessible and easier to grasp. These conventions not only contribute to readability but also convey essential information about the purpose of an identifier. This additional context helps developers understand the role of the identifier, whether it represents a constant, package, class, or another entity within the code. These conventions are essential tools for effective code communication and can significantly aid in the comprehension and maintenance of software systems.

Both Google's and Oracle's conventions define in-depth rules for naming the various components and they have many touchpoints:

- Google's style guide specifies that identifiers are made up of ASCII letters and digits, and occasionally, underscores, as specified by the \w+ regular expression. Special prefixes or suffixes such as `model_`, `cModel`, and `c_name` are not used in identifier names.

- **Class and interface** names are usually in `UpperCamelCase`, which means the first letter of each word is capitalized. Class names are typically related to things and are usually nouns, such as `Student` or `ImmutableList`. Interface names can also be nouns or noun phrases, such as `Set`, or they might sometimes be adjectives or adjective phrases, such as `Serializable`. When it comes to naming annotation types, there aren't specific rules or widely accepted conventions. Google's style guide also specifies that for test classes, their names end with `Test`. If a test class covers a single class, it takes the name of that class and adds `Test` to the end.

- **Method** names are usually written in `lowerCamelCase`, where the first letter is in lowercase and subsequent words are capitalized, such as `sendMessage` or `stop`. Method names are typically related to actions or what the method does, and they are like verbs or phrases, such as `sendNotification` or `initialize`. Google's style guide also specifies that method names in the `JUnit` test could have underscores to separate different parts of the name. Each part is also written in `lowerCamelCase` – for example, `publishPost_translateToUserLanguage`. There isn't a single correct way to name test methods, so you have some flexibility here.

- **Constant** names follow `UPPER_SNAKE_CASE`, meaning they are written in all uppercase letters with words separated by a single underscore. Constants are like unchanging values in your code. They are represented as `static final` fields, which means they never change once they are set. These constants are deeply immutable, meaning they can't be modified in any way, and they don't have methods that cause any noticeable side effects. Examples of constants include simple data types such as numbers, text (strings), unchangeable value types, and even things set to `null`. But here's the key: if anything about this value can change or be observed differently over time, it's not a constant (you could have guessed that).

- **Parameter names** are typically written in `lowerCamelCase`, where the first letter is lowercase, and subsequent words are capitalized. When it comes to naming parameters in public methods, it's a good practice to avoid using single-character names whenever possible. As Robert Martin's *Clean Code* states, using more descriptive names makes it easier for others to understand the purpose of the parameter (just think about naming a parameter `x`).

- **Local variable names** are typically written in `lowerCamelCase`. Even if a local variable is declared as `final` and remains unchanged, it's not regarded as a constant, and therefore, it should not be named like a constant.

Automated tools

We cannot think of implementing all these rules by hand every time we write a line of code. Well, it used to be done that way once, but even I am not old enough to have seen it! Fortunately, we have automatic tools at our disposal that help us on various levels.

For example, **integrated development environments (IDEs)** play a significant role in supporting code formatting by providing tools and features to help developers adhere to coding standards and automatically format their code. IDEs facilitate code formatting by performing auto-indentation – that is, automatically indenting code blocks – making it easier to read and understand the code's structure. Indentation can be customized according to the coding standards of your project. Furthermore, most IDEs allow developers to define and customize code style preferences. These preferences include settings for indentation, brace placement, line wrapping, and naming conventions. Developers can tailor these settings to match the coding standards of their project or organization. IDEs come with built-in or customizable code formatters that automatically format your code based on the defined coding style preferences. These formatters ensure that your code follows the established standards consistently.

But don't worry, you don't have to set up all the nitty-gritty of your IDE's formatting settings details; most of them – especially the most used ones – have the chance to export the so-called **code style formatter**. You just have to discover how your IDE does it (or just google it), export your file, and make sure everyone in the team is using that file, importing it in their IDE. When you format your code in your IDE – via the relative command or shortcut – the code style will be the same for everyone... everyone who's using the same IDE, of course. Yes, because these code styles are specific for each IDE; NetBeans' one is different from Eclipse's one.

There are many solutions to this problem. For example, you could try to manually edit your exported code style file (which is always a text file) so that it adapts to the destination IDE; however, I don't feel like advising you to do that. A possible solution could be to use a cross-IDE tool, a tool that is essentially the same for everyone. For example, there is a tool called **CodeConfig** (`https://editorconfig.org`) that allows you to configure a code style and can be installed on numerous different IDEs (many, such as IntelliJ, support it natively). Alternatively, you could move the problem somewhere else.

If you're working on a Java project, you're probably using a build automation tool such as Gradle or Maven. These tools allow you to compile code, among other things, and, in general, simplify the entire development life cycle. As you know, there are various plugins available for these tools. Some of them directly modify the code itself – in this book, we've seen examples such as Lombok and MapStruct.

Some plugins intend to check your code for any problems with code style. One of the most famous is Checkstyle. The Apache Maven Checkstyle Plugin (see the *Further reading* section) integrates the Checkstyle tool into your Maven build process to enforce coding style and standards on your Java source code. Checkstyle is an open source static code analysis tool that checks your Java code against a set of predefined coding conventions and style rules. You define your coding style rules and preferences in a Checkstyle configuration file, typically named `checkstyle.xml`. This file specifies which coding standards you want to enforce, such as naming conventions, indentation, and formatting rules. Then, the Apache Maven Checkstyle Plugin is configured in your project's `pom.xml` file. You specify the Checkstyle rules file and other settings to be used during the build. When you run a Maven build (for example, via `mvn clean install`), the Apache Maven Checkstyle Plugin is executed as part of the build process. It scans your Java source code files for violations of the defined coding standards. If Checkstyle detects any violations, it generates a report that lists the issues found in your code. This report can be viewed in various formats, such as HTML or XML. You can configure the plugin to either fail the build if violations are found or generate a warning report without failing the build. The choice depends on your project's requirements. The Apache Maven Checkstyle Plugin is useful to get an overview of any problems you might have, but it does not fix them for you.

Some plugins handle code formatting. By integrating these plugins into your development process, you can ensure that your code is automatically formatted with every build, without the need for manual intervention. A Maven plugin that you could use is **maven-formatter-plugin** (`https://code.revelc.net/formatter-maven-plugin`), which, by default, supports the "Eclipse style" but can be configured with any code style. We haven't eliminated the complexity of the "file transfer" step, but we've integrated code formatting into our development cycle. But we can be even smarter than that.

In software companies, CI/CD tools such as GitLab or Jenkins are now widespread. If you're new to the concept, a CI/CD pipeline is an automated workflow that streamlines the software development and delivery process. It starts with CI, where developers frequently merge their code changes into a shared repository. Automated builds, testing, and code analysis are performed to ensure code quality and identify issues early. **Continuous delivery (CD)** follows CI and involves deploying code changes to staging or pre-production environments. Additional testing and quality checks are conducted to simulate production conditions. After successful testing, the code can be automatically deployed to the production environment.

When it comes to formatting and styling code, you can set up an automatic system that checks how code is written. Every time new pieces of code are pushed into the repository, this automatic system checks if the code follows formatting rules. Depending on how we set up this system, it can be a simple check that tells us if the code isn't written correctly, or it can be stricter and stop the process if there are serious issues (though this rarely happens). Furthermore, this system can do something really helpful: it can fix poorly written code so that it follows the shared rules of our group or company. In practice, this system "re-commits" the same pieces of code, but this time, they are formatted correctly. This means we might not have to worry about fixing the code manually anymore.

One last side note: formatting code in the same way is also important to reduce merge conflicts and unintentional code commits. Let's imagine that Developer A uses `CodeStyleA`, while Developer B uses `CodeStyleB` (as expected). Developer A makes a small change, let's say a five-line method, inside a class. Being diligent, they initiate code formatting for the entire class using their IDE. Since Developer A is using their personalized `CodeStyleA`, they will likely unintentionally commit other parts of the class that weren't the intended focus of the change. This results in lines that were altered by Developer A but, in a way, weren't supposed to be. On the other hand, Developer B is making changes to the same class but in a different place. When they need to push their code, they find the same lines changed by Developer A, but only because Developer A *incorrectly formatted* the code. This may seem like an edge case, but it's not uncommon – I've seen it happen many times. It's not a disaster by any means, but it's time wasted that can be saved with a bit of care.

Now that we've discussed code versioning and style, let's talk about a practice that can't be emphasized enough.

Code reviews

Code reviews, often also called **peer reviews**, are a very powerful tool for developers' daily work. We could almost say that they are fundamental, but the truth is that under certain conditions, it is possible to choose whether to perform them or not, provided, however, that if not, other methodologies are implemented. But let's go in order and try to understand what a code review is.

A code review can be implemented in slightly different forms, but it typically consists of submitting a piece of code to one or more developers who did not write that code; these people are usually referred to as "reviewers." So, for example, if you own a certain task and you developed the relative code, before deploying it in production (or usually even before merging your feature branch on your main branch, depending on your "framework"), your code is reviewed by some other teammate who did not write a single line of that code. The aim is not to judge and the benefits are vast.

First of all, there is a sort of quality assurance. It allows developers to catch and rectify defects, bugs, and vulnerabilities in the code before it reaches the end users. By detecting issues early in the development process, code review significantly reduces the cost and effort required to fix them in later stages of development or after deployment.

Beyond catching bugs, code review can also reveal design flaws and inefficiencies in the code. By discussing and suggesting improvements during code review, developers can refine the software's architecture, making it more robust and scalable.

Maybe even more important – but this is arguable – is knowledge sharing. Code review is a learning opportunity for all team members. It promotes knowledge sharing and mentorship, where experienced developers can guide less experienced ones. This collaborative aspect fosters a culture of continuous learning and improvement within the development team.

Code review ensures that the code adheres to a consistent coding style and follows the project's coding guidelines. This consistency makes the code base more maintainable and understandable, especially when multiple developers are working on the same project. Remember, your code is only clean if everyone on the team thinks it is!

Then comes one of my favorite aspects: that code review encourages effective communication within the development team. Developers engage in discussions about the code, which can lead to a better understanding of the project's goals and requirements, resulting in a more aligned and cohesive team. This, in my opinion, also encourages a culture of feedback, which is crucial within companies and teams; it is one of the moments in which we learn to communicate our feedback effectively and, above all, in which we learn to receive it, appreciating it for what it is – that is, a gift to our professional growth. Trust the touchy-feely – the code review is one of the most learned moments.

A code review becomes more effective if you set some sort of rules, I dare almost say limits to what you are going to observe: are we looking for inefficiencies, are we trying to make the code cleaner, are we looking for bugs, are we doing all these things? No problem, just agree and set expectations. Keep code review sessions short and sweet. Decide on what works for your team, such as maybe sticking to a rule of not going over 1 hour or reviewing more than 200 lines of code at a time. This keeps things productive.

As much as possible, use tools and automation. For example, tools such as GitHub help us with code reviews, with the ability to compare different versions of code, write comments, and more. Automatic tools for static code analysis, which were already addressed in the previous chapters, allow us – if integrated into pipelines, for example – to avoid the most common inaccuracies such as the organization of imports, code formatting, and so on.

Again, the human factor is fundamental. Try to be constructive in giving feedback and try to be "open-minded" in receiving it; it's not a race, it's a cooperation between equals. The goal must only be to achieve a common result and to do it together. Code review should be a constructive process, not a blame game. Use polite language and provide suggestions for improvement rather than criticizing the author. The goal is to enhance the code, not demotivate the developer. Make sure everyone on your team, whether they're new or experienced, takes part in code reviews. It helps newer team members learn about the code and allows them to have their work checked by more experienced developers. This way, the workload can be balanced, and it's easier to manage when someone is absent or leaves the team.

Sometimes, appointing a moderator or lead developer to facilitate the code review process can be a key element in maintaining its effectiveness. They serve as a guiding force, ensuring that the review discussions stay productive and on track. The moderator's responsibilities encompass structuring the review process, clarifying expectations for both authors and reviewers, mediating discussions, and balancing feedback. They also play a vital role in prioritizing issues, documenting outcomes, and mentoring less-experienced developers.

To be honest, there are also some disadvantages in code reviews – that is why they're sometimes not well-seen by tech-illiterate managers.

The review process has the potential to extend the time it takes to release a software update. This delay occurs because reviewers and authors must collaborate to address issues, which can be time-consuming. Furthermore, reviewers may not be able to expedite the review process due to their existing workload. However, this hurdle can be mitigated through the utilization of code review tools equipped with automated testing capabilities. These tools effectively identify common errors, thereby freeing up valuable developer time that can be redirected toward tackling more complex software engineering challenges.

Developers often find themselves juggling a substantial workload, and the need for a code review can divert their attention from other critical tasks that demand their immediate attention. This diversion poses a dilemma for team members who must choose between completing their ongoing responsibilities or pausing their work to conduct a code review. In either scenario, work somewhere within the organization is delayed. To alleviate this issue, team members can implement strategies such as a reviewer rotation system or maintain a list of domain experts who can share the reviewing burden. These measures prevent any single developer from becoming overwhelmed by a multitude of review requests.

When developers are tasked with reviewing a substantial code alteration, the review process tends to consume a considerable amount of time. Assessing large code changes can be particularly challenging, and reviewers may feel compelled to expedite the process to meet deadlines, potentially compromising the quality of feedback. An effective solution to this challenge is the practice of incremental code development. This approach allows reviewers to examine smaller code segments multiple times, as opposed to grappling with a massive code change all at once. This not only enhances the quality of the review but also streamlines the overall process.

There are different types of code reviews, which we will list in order of effectiveness, starting with the one that we think is the least effective.

Email pass-arounds

Email pass-arounds are a common way of dealing with small issues and tiny bits of code. You can do this by sending emails or using code tools. In an email pass-around, the person who made the code changes sends an email to those who need to check it. It's like looking at someone's screen over their shoulder, and it's quite easy to use. You don't need a lot of training, and you can start right away. Of course, think of "email" as "a direct message to someone…" I mean, who uses email to communicate with their teammates nowadays?! It can, of course, be a Slack message, or a "merge request" on GitLab… anything.

The advantages of using email pass-arounds include ease of setup, remote and asynchronous review possibilities, and automatic reviews in some code management systems.

However, there are drawbacks to email pass-arounds, such as the time it takes to collect necessary files, difficulty in tracking and following conversations within email threads, the absence of a definite end date for the review, uncertainty about whether the changes were implemented, and challenges in measuring its effectiveness. In all honesty, I found references to this practice only "in literature;" I've never seen it happen.

Code review automation tools

Teams sometimes use automated tools to save time and ensure they deliver high-quality code. These tools can automatically collect and display code changes, streamline feedback through comments, and even help find and fix vulnerabilities using **static application security testing (SAST)**.

Think of these tool-assisted reviews as a valuable addition to other review methods. They help maintain coding standards, identify vulnerabilities, collect data efficiently, and streamline the review process. However, some teams might be tempted to rely solely on these tools and skip involving team members in code reviews. It's crucial to view these tools as enhancements to the process rather than replacements.

Tool-assisted reviews can simplify data collection and metrics, and free up developers to focus on their work. There are some disadvantages, too, that rely on the developer's need to manage and maintain the tools – some tools are often really expensive and do not completely remove the necessity of a human review.

In-person (or remote) teamwork reviews

In these reviews, two developers work together, either in person or through a shared screen online. One developer is the author who made the code changes, and the other is the reviewer. The author explains the changes they made and why they chose those solutions. The reviewer asks questions and gives suggestions, kind of like how team members work together when pairing. The author can make small changes during the review and note bigger fixes for later.

Advantages are pretty straightforward: in-person meetings (sometimes, they're also called over-the-shoulder reviews) are easy to set up and complete, and of course, can be done remotely. They're quicker than pair programming (which we'll delve into in a minute).

However, it can happen that the reviewer may not be as connected to the code; in this case, a lot of time would be needed to explain the background and all of the nitty-gritty of the code – or, even worse, the review would be done hastily, quicker than necessary. In this context, there could be some lack of objectivity; without knowing the context (basically, all the code under review just "rained" over the reviewer's head), you can't be sure that all the needed implementations were made. In general, it's tricky to understand how well the code is doing.

Now, we're getting to what we think is the most effective review technique, even though it's not entirely a review technique. Pair programming is a lot more than that.

Pair programming

Perhaps it is simplistic to talk about pair programming as a mere code review technique, but this is just the starting point.

Pair programming is a software development technique that requires each feature to be created by a pair of programmers, working on the same workstation (also, consider being able to do it remotely by sharing the screen). A person writes the code and is called the driver; the other, the navigator, makes a sort of instant revision of every line that is written at the time it is written. The driver focuses on the details of the implementation, while the navigator takes a broader view, reviews the code, and helps with problem-solving.

It is a very powerful technique that has many advantages and – inevitably – some disadvantages. Let's get to know them.

Advantages

The quality of the software improves: programmers are led to bring their different experiences together, bringing different points of view and different approaches. Pair programmers work closely together throughout the development process, discussing design decisions, code structure, and potential improvements in real-time. Having two sets of eyes on the code can lead to cleaner code, fewer bugs, and more robust solutions. What's best, the navigator can catch errors and suggest improvements as they arise. Two minds working together often lead to more creative and effective problem-solving. Programmers can bounce ideas off each other and explore different solutions. Since code is reviewed in real-time, it's more likely that issues are spotted and corrected before they become major problems, reducing the debugging and maintenance effort.

Another immediate advantage is knowledge sharing. Pair programming helps distribute knowledge and expertise among team members (or even among members of different teams, who are working together to bring in their respective knowledge). It's an effective way to transfer skills and best practices from more experienced developers to less experienced ones. Pair programming can be more powerful than any knowledge-sharing session.

Also, to be considered is a certain element of team building and improvement of communication in general within the team. By collaborating closely, you can hone all those soft skills needed in your daily work with other people and maybe even your feedback culture.

Moreover, pair programming increases focus – it significantly boosts focus by minimizing distractions. The shared responsibility between the "driver" and "navigator" fosters a concentrated mindset, reducing the likelihood of drifting. This collaborative approach ensures constant code review and real-time communication, creating an environment where both individuals are actively engaged in problem-solving. In essence, pair programming not only deters distractions but actively cultivates a focused and productive development atmosphere. Something may change when pair programming is done from a remote location, but not that much.

One factor to consider is the level of seniority of the two programmers, both in general and on the individual task. For example, pairing two experienced developers could be the right choice to boost productivity. A pair made by two novice developers is unlikely to happen, even if it could bring some problems, given my lack of what we could call a "role model." Anyway, it's still better than two novice programmers working independently. The expert-novice pair is one of the most common; this kind of pairing can foster the introduction of fresh ideas as less experienced individuals are often more inclined to question established practices. Simultaneously, the experts, while being asked to clarify established methods, are encouraged to reevaluate them. Nonetheless, within this pairing dynamic, a novice who feels intimidated might become a passive observer, hesitating to actively engage. Similarly, certain experts may lack the patience necessary to facilitate productive participation from novices. Some refer to this phenomenon as "watch the master."

Disadvantages

The first disadvantage – perhaps the most obvious one, and the one that your tech-illiterate manager might argue with – is that with pair programming, you have two people doing the work of one. If this is not true (we have previously seen all the advantages and peculiarities of pair programming, in which the roles are distinct and several jobs are carried out at the same time) it is true that pair programming is resource-intensive as you have two programmers who take care of the same task. In a world where there are never enough developers to do all the work, this could be a problem to address.

It is also undeniable that the code will be ready in a longer time; if two people take care of the same task, it is obvious that the "busy" tasks will be fewer in absolute number. In the case of very tight deadlines, this could be a problem.

It would be better, then, to balance the level of seniority of the two programmers involved so as not to create "watch the master" situations or excessive tutoring of a junior resource.

In our opinion, pair programming needs to be properly modulated. Not all tasks are suitable for pair programming. Let's imagine a repetitive task without too much-added value, something that is not complicated from any point of view – it is just very long. The added value that a possible driver can give would be very small; in that case, it would be much better, in our opinion, to opt for a classic "delayed" code review process.

Moreover, pair programming might not be for everybody: some people just don't get along, or others prefer to work individually. In this case, it's better not to force the hand on this practice, or start with short sessions (let's say, an hour or so).

I have used pair programming a lot in my career, and I must point out that it has also happened that some colleagues did not feel suitable for pair programming, especially in contexts where the percentage of time for which this practice is carried out is greater than individual programming. Some people prefer to work alone, perhaps exploring freely, following only the logical thread of their thoughts and perhaps converging with teammates only later. The humble advice we would like to give in these cases is not to force the hand with pair programming or in any case to agree at a team level – as trivial as it may be, I think it is the only thing that can work in this case.

A very interesting paper about the costs and benefits of pair programming can be found in the *Further reading* section.

Styles of pair programming

Pair programming is hard. You have to be extremely focused, especially – I would say – in the role of the navigator. Pair programming can be both exhausting and fulfilling. Typically, most programmers can only effectively pair for about 5 to 6 hours a day. Therefore, it's important to schedule breaks and regularly switch pairs. There are many ways in which you can manage your pair; in the following sections, we'll see some of them.

Driver and navigator

This is the classic pair programming style. The **driver** is the individual in control of the keyboard, concentrating on accomplishing the current small task while temporarily setting aside broader concerns. They are encouraged to vocalize their actions as they perform them. The **navigator**, who's positioned as an observer while the driver operates the keyboard, actively assesses the code in real-time, provides guidance, and communicates their thoughts. The navigator maintains awareness of larger issues and potential bugs, taking note of prospective next actions or obstacles as they arise.

A typical workflow typically follows these steps:

1. Start with a well-defined, preferably small task.

2. Reach a consensus on a singular, manageable objective at a time. This can be defined by a unit test, for example.

3. Regularly interchange roles and the keyboard. This shared, active participation maintains energy levels and enhances comprehension. What does "regularly" mean? We'll see shortly.

4. In the role of the navigator, refrain from getting lost in the immediate tactical details of coding since the driver focuses on those. Your responsibility is to step back and complement your partner's tactical approach with medium-term thinking. Jot down upcoming tasks, potential roadblocks, and ideas on sticky notes. Discuss them after the completion of the current tiny goal to avoid disrupting the driver's workflow.

Ping-pong pairing

The **ping-pong pairing** technique is closely aligned with TDD and is particularly effective when you have a well-defined task that can be approached in a test-driven manner:

1. "Ping": Developer A initiates by creating a failing test.

2. "Pong": Developer B responds by writing the code necessary to make the test pass.

3. Developer B then takes the lead by initiating the next "ping," which involves creating the next failing test.

4. After each "pong," it's common practice to collaboratively refactor the code. This step aligns with the "Red – Green – Refactor" approach, which we encountered in the previous chapters.

Strong-style pairing

Strong-style pairing is a method that helps people learn by working closely together. It's like a mentor teaching a newbie.

The main rule is, "Before you do something on the computer, talk to someone else about it." In this method, the experienced person usually guides the less experienced one. The important thing is that the learner must trust the teacher and not worry if they don't understand everything at first. Questions and discussions can happen after they try things out.

This method is a bit like having someone watch over your shoulder, but it's really good for teaching. It's best for getting started with new things, but you shouldn't use it too much. The goal is for the learner to become more independent over time. That's when you know the teaching has worked.

Time management

It's important to manage your time in pair programming; deciding how long a person should remain a driver and how long they should be a navigator greatly changes the developer experience in pair programming. A very well-known technique – but I must say very little used – is the **Pomodoro technique**.

This method can be integrated with most of the pairing approaches mentioned, helping maintain focus. Pair programming can be tiring, so having prompts for breaks and switching roles is beneficial.

The Pomodoro technique is a time management method that was developed by Francesco Cirillo in the late 1980s. It's designed to help people enhance productivity and maintain focus. For all the non-Italian speakers out there: "*Pomodoro*" means "*tomato*" and it refers to a simple Pomodoro-shaped kitchen timer.

Here's how this technique works:

1. **Set a timer**: Choose a task you want to work on. Set a timer for 25 minutes, which is called one "Pomodoro." During this time, you commit to working on the task with full concentration.

2. **Work intensely**: While the timer is running, work on your task with focused, undivided attention. Avoid distractions, such as checking your phone or email. I'm not saying that you should also ignore calls from your wife, but it's strongly recommended; to use this book as an excuse.

3. **Take a short break**: When the timer rings after 25 minutes, take a short 5-minute break. Use this time to relax, stretch, or do something unrelated to work. It's a brief reward for your focused effort.

4. **Repeat**: After the short break, go back to another 25-minute Pomodoro session. Keep repeating these cycles of work and short breaks.

5. **Longer break**: After completing four Pomodoro sessions (totaling 2 hours of work), take a longer break of 15-30 minutes. Use this time to recharge and plan your next tasks.

The Pomodoro technique aims to leverage the benefits of focused, concentrated work while preventing burnout. It encourages you to break your work into smaller, manageable chunks with built-in breaks. This method can help improve time management, reduce procrastination, and boost overall productivity. It's particularly useful for tasks that require deep concentration, not only programming; we think it should be taught at school.

The Pomodoro technique can be used to manage pair programming sessions; whenever a Pomodoro ends, the driver and navigator switch roles. You decide if this technique is good or if it is too "rigid." These and all the others are just suggestions – it's up to you to find the right size and the right pace of work.

Documentation

When we talk about documentation, we can talk about a lot of things. In general, the term *documentation* refers to the process of creating and maintaining written records and materials that describe various aspects of a software project. This documentation serves multiple purposes and is essential for the successful development, maintenance, and understanding of software systems.

In simple terms, this means we can have different kinds of documentation in software development – some very technical, and others not so much.

Requirements

Requirements documentation is where you define what the software should be like. It's like the building plan for the software.

Requirements documentation in software development is like making a detailed wish list or set of instructions for what a new piece of software should do. It's a way to precisely define and describe what the software needs to achieve and how it should behave. This documentation outlines the features, functions, and qualities the software should have to meet the needs of its users or the business.

This documentation is crucial because it acts as a guide for the software developers. It helps them understand the expectations and goals set by the clients or stakeholders. Think of it as a blueprint that details the foundation and boundaries within which the software will be designed, built, and tested. Requirements documentation is like drawing a map that shows the path for building the right software that fulfills specific needs and functions as intended.

Requirements documentation is a phase that comes after the collection and analysis phases. I refer you to the *Further reading* section for more in-depth information. Once gathered, it's uncommon for requirements to be simply written in a lengthy and formal textual document. According to our experience, what happens more often is that spreadsheets or specialized tools are used. If spreadsheets are used, each requirement is typically represented by a row, and each attribute of the requirements, such as an ID, a description, a priority, a reporter, and so on, is represented by a column. The same information, and often much more, is managed through specific software for "issue tracking," such as Jira or Redmine. Requirements documentation then becomes the collection of information – the issues – stored in these tools. It's widely used, especially in Agile development frameworks.

Architecture documentation

Architecture documentation, also known as **software architecture description**, is a unique form of design document. If design documents derive directly from the code, architecture documents are a step forward (someone says they're the third derivative, starting from the first one, which is the code). These documents contain very little information that is specific to the code itself; the nitty-gritty of the implementation must be kept away. They don't explain how to code a particular function or why a specific function is designed the way it is. Instead, they outline the general requirements and reasons that lead to the creation of such functions. A well-crafted architecture document is concise in details but rich in explanations – also rich in images and graphs, I would say. It might offer suggestions for lower-level design but delegates the actual exploration and trade studies to other documents.

Architectural documentation is probably the first thing that a new member of your team would read. That's one of the reasons why we're saying it's crucial: software architecture documentation helps different people involved in a project to have a common understanding of how the system works.

One way to document your architecture is the typical one: just draw a bunch of boxes on a whiteboard and connect them with arrows and lines! Or... there's a more structured approach called **C4**.

The C4 approach, also known as the **C4 model**, is a framework for visualizing and documenting software architecture. It was created by Simon Brown and is designed to provide a clear and concise way to represent and communicate the architecture of a software system. C4 stands for **Context**, **Containers**, **Components**, and **Code**, which are the four levels of abstraction in this model:

1. **Context diagram (C1)**: This is the highest level and provides an overview of the entire system, showing its interactions with external entities and systems. It helps establish the system's boundaries and its place in the broader ecosystem.

2. **Container diagram (C2):** The next level, the container diagram, focuses on the high-level building blocks within the system. It represents containers, such as web servers, databases, mobile apps, and more, and shows how they interact with each other.

3. **Component diagram (C3):** Below containers, the component diagram delves into the internal structure of each container, breaking them down into individual components or services. This level provides more detail about how each container works internally.

4. **Code (C4):** At the lowest level, you have the actual source code, where the details of the individual components are documented. This level includes class diagrams, code snippets, and other fine-grained details.

The C4 approach is a way to create a hierarchy of visual representations to describe and understand a software system's architecture. It helps in simplifying complex systems, making it easier to communicate and collaborate on software design and development.

Diving deeper into this approach would be a bit outside the scope of this book, so I suggest that you visit the official C4 website. A link has been provided in the *Further reading* section.

Technical documentation

Technical documentation covers a lot of stuff, and it even includes architectural documentation. But in this case, I wanted to point out a specific kind of documentation. It's the one that gets into the nitty-gritty details, such as code, modules, APIs, microservices, and other low-level stuff. It's way more detailed than what you'd usually find in architectural documentation.

Documentation can come in various shapes and sizes, ranging from elaborate design documents to straightforward README files. The choice of format depends on the specific product, system, or service being described. Regardless of the form it takes, the primary goal of technical documentation is to assist developers in resolving issues without requiring them to undertake additional research.

Even if is often disregarded, technical documentation is crucial; unfortunately, it's also very hard to do and very time-consuming. It's the very first thing that is ignored when your time runs out. "We'll do it" and you never will. So, our suggestion here is to include the writing of the documentation in your daily work; in other words, in your software development life cycle. For example, you could agree on a "definition of done" (a checklist or set of criteria that determines when a task or project is considered completed and meets the required quality standards) that includes documentation.

There are various types of documentation you should take care of.

- **SDK documentation:** SDK documentation provides instructions for integrating new software into an existing application. It covers software usage, capabilities, and interactions with other applications, making it essential for developers to enhance app features.

- **Source code documentation:** Source code documentation includes code examples to guide developers in software usage. Focus on explaining necessary parts rather than everything in the code.

- **Release notes**: Release notes are technical documents detailing changes in a new product release, such as new features, bug fixes, and known issues. Developers and testers use them to grasp what's new.

- **Knowledge base documentation**: This document houses knowledge that developers can use for software development and maintenance. It covers tools, languages, methods, design principles, how-to guides, troubleshooting, and FAQs, fostering knowledge sharing and efficiency in software development.

- **API documentation**: API documentation explains how a program's interface functions, offering details about methods, parameters, and what the API returns. It may come as tutorials or guides, aiding developers in understanding and using the API.

There are a couple of tools we want to suggest that can improve your API documentation and automate it – partially, at least.

Swagger

The first one is really widespread, and it's called **Swagger**. Swagger is an open source framework and a suite of tools that enables you to design, build, and document RESTful web services. It provides a way to describe and document the functionality of an API in a standardized and machine-readable format, often in JSON or YAML.

Swagger offers several key benefits, apart from the documentation itself: it can also generate client and server code in various programming languages, reducing the effort needed to integrate with the API. A very useful feature is that it includes tools for testing and debugging APIs, making it easier to identify and resolve issues. Last but not least, Swagger uses the **OpenAPI Specification** (formerly known as the **Swagger Specification**), a widely adopted standard for describing RESTful APIs. This promotes consistency and interoperability among different systems and developers.

How can you integrate Swagger into your application? It's a piece of cake, especially if you're using Spring Boot. Supposing you're using Maven, it's enough to add a couple of dependencies in your POM file. If you're using also **Spring Boot 3**, it's only one:

```
<dependency>
    <groupId>org.springdoc</groupId>
    <artifactId>springdoc-openapi-starter-webmvc-ui</artifactId>
    <version>2.2.0</version>
</dependency>
```

In other cases, you will have to add some other dependencies and a couple of configurations. Nothing difficult and nothing long. You'll find an excellent tutorial in the *Further reading* section

And then? Nothing – that's it! Now, let's suppose we have a "classic" REST controller written in Java, something like this:

```
@RestController
public class EmployeeController {

    //fields and constructors...

    @GetMapping("/employees")
    Collection<Employee> findAll() {
        return repository.findAll();
    }

    @PostMapping("/")
    public ResponseEntity<Employee> create(@RequestBody CreateEmployee
employee) {
        Employee createdEmployee = repository.create(employee);

        URI uri = buildResourceUri(createdEmployee);

        return ResponseEntity.created(uri)
        .body(createdEmployee);
    }

    // buildResourceUri method implementation...
}
```

As you can assume from the @RestController annotation, this class exposes its public methods as public APIs. The first one returns a list of employees and takes no input parameters (it doesn't handle HTTP statutes, nor pagination... it's just an example!); the second one is needed to insert a new employee and it has a body defined by the Employee class. Swagger can understand all of this and automatically generate an OpenAPI-compliant documentation. The following screenshot is just a part of the huge JSON that is generated by Swagger to adhere to the OpenAPI standard:

```json
{
  openapi: "3.0.1",
  info: {
    title: "OpenAPI definition",
    version: "v0"
  },
  servers: [
    {
      url: http://localhost:8080,
      description: "Generated server url"
    }
  ],
  paths: {
    "/": {
      post: {
        tags: [
          "employee-controller"
        ],
        operationId: "create",
        requestBody: {
          content: {
            "application/json": {
              schema: {
                $ref: "#/components/schemas/Employee"
              }
            }
          }
        },
        responses: {
          "200": {
            description: "OK",
            content: {
              "*/*": {
                schema: {
                  $ref: "#/components/schemas/Employee"
                }
              }
            }
          }
        }
      }
    },
    "/employees": {
      get: {
        tags: [
          "employee-controller"
        ],
        operationId: "findAll",
        responses: {
          "200": {
            description: "OK",
            content: {
              "*/*": {
                schema: {
                  type: "array",
                  items: {
                    $ref: "#/components/schemas/Employee"
                  }
                }
              }
            }
          }
        }
      }
    }
  },
  components: {
    schemas: {
      Employee: {
        type: "object",
        properties: {
          id: {
            type: "integer",
            format: "int64"
          },
          name: {
            type: "string"
          },
          role: {
            type: "string"
          }
        }
      }
    }
  }
}
```

Figure 8.11 – Huge JSON generated by Swagger

This JSON has been left intentionally incomplete since it is... well, incomprehensible for the human brain. Luckily enough, Swagger kicks in with a UI that interprets all this madness and gives us a beautiful web page. Something like this:

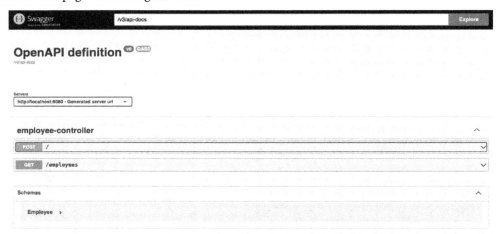

Figure 8.12 – Two very basic endpoints exposed by swagger-ui

This is the very basic version of it. By clicking on the single endpoint (that is, one of those writings in colorful boxes, such as /**employees**), you'll get its details, and you can also try it out:

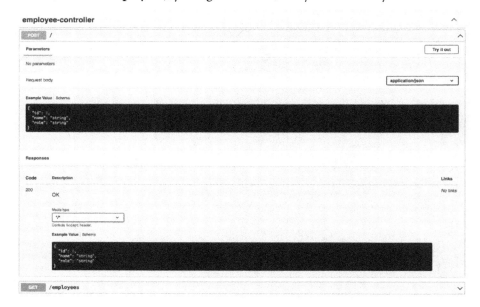

Figure 8.13 – By clicking on a single method, some more details will be displayed

With Swagger annotations, you can detail your API documentation as much as you like. In the `POST` method that creates a new employee, you can see a parameter of the `CreateEmployee` type that represents the body for the `POST` call. The fields of that class could be annotated like this:

```
@Schema(name = "Employee name", example = "John Doe", required = true)
private final String name;

@Schema(name = "Employee role", example = "Software engineer",
required = true)

private final String role;
```

Swagger would generate the following output:

Figure 8.14 – Details of the request body rendered by swagger-ui

A tool like Swagger, with its UI, guarantees massive value with minimum effort. Keeping your documentation up-to-date should be also simpler because everything – the code and its documentation – is in one place.

Spring REST Docs

The second tool I would suggest to document your (REST) APIs is called **Spring REST Docs**. Spring REST Docs is a part of the Spring Framework, a popular framework for building Java-based enterprise applications. Specifically, Spring REST Docs is an extension for documenting RESTful APIs developed using Spring. It helps developers create accurate and consistent documentation for their RESTful web services by leveraging tests written in Spring Framework.

Here's how Spring REST Docs typically works:

1. Developers write tests for their REST API endpoints using the Spring Framework's testing tools. These tests can include HTTP requests and responses.

2. Spring REST Docs processes these tests and generates documentation based on the test results. It can generate documentation in various formats, such as AsciiDoc, Markdown, or HTML. This is a very cool thing: documentation is kept up-to-date in case of changes in the code.

3. The generated documentation can be included in the API documentation, making it easier for other developers or consumers to understand how to use the API effectively.

Spring REST Docs is especially useful in projects where maintaining accurate and up-to-date API documentation is crucial. By using actual tests to generate the documentation, it ensures that the documentation accurately reflects the behavior of the API. This approach promotes consistency between the code and its documentation and helps developers and consumers better understand how to interact with the API.

Good practices for documentation

Writing and maintaining documentation is fundamental yet hard. Doing it the right way is not very common – not at all! – and will take your team to the next level. Here's some advice based on our experience and also on our mistakes.

Incorporate documentation into the development flow

One common reason software teams skip documentation is that they're always waiting for that perfect moment when they have loads of free time. But let's face it – in the fast-paced world of software, that moment rarely arrives with all the new projects and initiatives on the horizon.

So, here's the hack: make documentation a natural part of your design process. Think of it as a crucial step that's part of the whole deal, not some extra task you squeeze in later. Sure, it might add a bit more time, but that extra effort will pay off when you need to handle or expand your system down the road. Plus, your team will be all set to tackle those unexpected curveballs like pros.

Write comprehensive documentation

Comprehensive documentation for your software architecture is an absolute must for ensuring the seamless maintenance and expansion of your systems. This documentation functions as a valuable resource, particularly when crucial members of your engineering team move on, safeguarding essential knowledge from being lost. Moreover, it streamlines the process of conveying vital information about the system to a diverse range of stakeholders.

While there may be those who argue that code alone suffices as documentation (I would agree with that, actually, but only if you add the adjective "good" to the word "code"), it is vital to acknowledge that comprehensive documentation offers invaluable context for decision-making and is accessible to both technical and non-technical stakeholders.

Up-to-date documentation

Maintaining up-to-date documentation is essential as outdated documentation can lead to the same issues as having no documentation at all. Documentation that accurately reflects the current state of the system is crucial to ensure informed decision-making and to prevent critical errors caused by referencing outdated information during updates or changes.

Tailored documentation for specific audiences

Customizing software architecture documentation to cater to specific audiences is essential. Not all stakeholders have the same information requirements, and attempting to fit all the details into a single document can hinder the ease of finding information. It might even discourage individuals from using the documentation altogether.

To ensure the effectiveness of documentation, it's crucial to provide the appropriate level of context for the intended audience. For instance, business executives may not require in-depth technical and code details, whereas engineers may find it challenging to fulfill their responsibilities without access to such technical specifics.

We can give you all the advice in the world, and guide you toward all the best practices possible, but unfortunately, we must acknowledge that these good habits are sometimes unwelcome to non-technical individuals. In the next section, we'll have a chat about it.

A hard dose of reality

The aspects we've talked about, as well as many others, will help you add activities to your daily work that will make your code, your project, and your work better. By including all of this in your development cycle, maybe right from the beginning of a project, it will undoubtedly be easier to be diligent in this regard.

However, we must tell you something undeniable – sometimes, some of these practices can cause disagreements between tech-savvy and non-tech-savvy people. What we've noticed is that there's often a very different view of how work is organized, especially in terms of tasks. Of course, even the concept of code quality may not matter at all to certain managers or partners who are not used to writing code. But let's go step by step.

For example, pair programming can be seen by management as resource-intensive because it requires two developers to work on the same task, potentially increasing labor costs. It could also be because the target is arguably more long-term. However, management often prioritizes short-term project goals, such as meeting deadlines and immediate deliverables, which may not align with the collaborative nature of pair programming. The benefits of pair programming, such as improved code quality and reduced defects, often manifest in the long term. However, these benefits may not be immediately visible to management, which can lead to skepticism. In general, there could also be a simple lack of familiarity: some managers may not be familiar with the practice and may be hesitant to introduce a process they don't fully understand. Also, introducing pair programming may disrupt established workflows within the organization, leading to resistance from management.

Documentation also suffers some of these perceived fears. Why stop documenting something that is already working? Why not go ahead and do another task instead? Some managers may not fully understand the importance of documentation in terms of reducing errors, enhancing collaboration, and easing onboarding of new team members. This lack of understanding can lead to underestimating its value. Also, some managers may perceive the time spent on documentation as time that could be used for more coding or direct project work, potentially leading to underutilization of developer resources.

Between the two, I have to say that pair programming is the practice that meets more resistance, at least from my point of view. All the practices that we've covered in this chapter are important, but getting along is also crucial! Try to introduce all of these practices or at least some pieces of them; try to adapt, try to prioritize. To address concerns, developers, and management can engage in open communication to explain the long-term advantages of pair programming, documentation, and so on, how they can improve code quality and project quality, reduce defects, and enhance knowledge sharing. They can also discuss how it can lead to faster problem-solving and overall efficiency in the development process. Management can work to strike a balance between immediate project needs and the long-term benefits of such practices.

The importance of knowing what you're doing

In this more informal part of this chapter, we want to offer one last piece of advice about the things you do every day. It's not just a technical tip; it's more like advice from a friend, something I wish someone had told me when I started my career.

When you work on a project, a task, or anything else, always keep in mind why you chose to do it. Ask yourself, "Why am I doing this?" It's not just about staying motivated; there's more to it than that.

First of all, this will help you avoid feeling like a random monkey hitting keys on a keyboard. It will also help you understand how your work contributes to the development of a project or a company. Having clear goals for your work, whether they're short-term, medium-term, or long-term, will keep you focused on your task without getting distracted by other things. If your work has a specific purpose, and even better, if that purpose is something you believe in, your productivity will increase, and your work will be better.

Knowing why you're doing something, and understanding the purpose behind it, will lead to better decision-making. When faced with doubts or uncertainties, having a clear goal in mind will guide your choices and prevent future disappointments. When we have detailed plans for specific actions at both upcoming milestones and our ultimate goals, every decision appears to align seamlessly.

One of the decisions you'll have to make includes prioritizing your tasks within a project. Should you do one thing before the other? Which task will take more time compared to the value it will generate? Well, if you know what you're doing – in other words, if you have a clear goal – this will likely assist your decision-making and set a smoother path toward project completion.

If you know your goal, you can probably also understand how far you are from reaching it. In other words, knowing your "why" helps you measure your progress. Imagine a team or a developer who is simply told to do something, completely disconnected from the context, something like "Write a method that returns this output given this input" – I don't think this happens much after school, but let's say it does. This person wouldn't have the slightest idea of how their work is contributing and where they stand on the journey toward the final goal. This person would do a worse job.

In a book on refactoring, it's important to mention that understanding the "why" behind things helps in writing better code and, when necessary, refactoring it more effectively. Writing down the reasons for doing something, perhaps in a comment alongside complex code, can assist developers in rewriting it more efficiently. This, along with good test coverage and everything we've already discussed in the previous chapters, greatly aids both the comprehension of the current code and any potential rewriting efforts.

Ask questions, and keep asking yourself and others. If you're in a position where a manager or a partner is guiding you on task prioritization – for instance, if you work within a framework that involves a product owner – always ask why one thing is chosen over another. What benefits will it bring? How much will it cost, and how much will it earn for the company? Is there data to support this decision? I'm not saying to start a war, absolutely not, but always try to "challenge" your colleagues in this sense.

Summary

In this chapter, we tried to provide you with some advice on introducing small but significant changes that will greatly benefit your work. We explored how you can version your code and offered some branching models that the community has found effective over the years. Versioning your code is important, but let's version beautiful code! We discussed how code reviews can be helpful and how to incorporate them into your everyday work. We dedicated an entire section to a particular form of code review, which is pair programming. We also delved into documentation, distinguishing between various types and providing guidance, especially for technical documentation of REST APIs. Lastly, we addressed the real-world implementation of these practices, which can sometimes face resistance, particularly in medium to small-sized companies.

In the next chapter, we'll take a step back and discuss how these various elements communicate with each other. We'll talk about best practices, identify issues (bad smells), and provide some advice on refactoring your architectures.

Further reading

- *Extreme Programming Explained: Embrace Change*, by Kent Beck, Addison-Weasley

- On pair programming: `https://martinfowler.com/articles/on-pair-programming.html`

- Llewellyn's strong-style pairing: `https://llewellynfalco.blogspot.com/2014/06/llewellyns-strong-style-pairing.html`

- *Costs and benefits of pair programming*, by A. Cockburn and L. Williams: `https://collaboration.csc.ncsu.edu/laurie/Papers/XPSardinia.PDF`

- A great tool for remote teams who want to use Pomodoro: `https://cuckoo.team/`

- *Pull Request*, an article by Martin Fowler: `https://martinfowler.com/bliki/PullRequest.html`

- GitFlow original post: `https://nvie.com/posts/a-successful-git-branching-model/`

- How to write a good commit message: `https://www.freecodecamp.org/news/how-to-write-better-git-commit-messages/`

- The Google Java style guide: `https://google.github.io/styleguide/javaguide.html`

- Oracle Java conventions: `https://www.oracle.com/technetwork/java/codeconventions-150003.pdf`

- About comments and formatting, *Chapters 4* and *5* of Robert C. Martin, *Clean Code*, Pearson

- Introduction to the Apache Maven Checkstyle Plugin: `https://www.baeldung.com/checkstyle-java`

- About collecting, documenting, and managing software requirements: *Chapter 2* of Giuseppe Bonocore's *Hands-on software architecture in Java*, Packt

- The C4 model for visualizing software architecture (`https://c4model.com/`) and Giuseppe Bonocore's *Hands-on software architecture in Java*, *Chapter 1*, Packt

- Tutorial for setting up Swagger by Baeldung: `https://www.baeldung.com/swagger-2-documentation-for-spring-rest-api`

- Spring REST docs: `https://docs.spring.io/spring-restdocs/docs/current/reference/htmlsingle/`

Beyond Code – Mastering Software Architecture

At this point, everything should be crystal clear about why and how to constantly refactor your code; in general, why it's important to have a clean, readable, and easily maintainable code base. But in today's development world, it's highly unlikely that we'll have just one application, one component; it's much more realistic to have various components interacting with each other. If it's true, as it is, that according to Conway's Law, a company is structured and organized in a way that mirrors its software systems, it's crucial to have a cohesive yet scalable ecosystem – not just robust but resilient and, frequently mentioned, clean. Because even clean code can lead to epic disasters if interactions between various services are poorly managed.

In this chapter, we'll tackle the following topics:

- What is an architecture?
- Architectural patterns
- Monolith to microservices
- Bad smells in the microservices architecture

What is an architecture?

Having come this far, we've realized that writing code is just a small part of our job. We need to focus on writing code that not only works but is also easy to read and maintain. We've learned that there are many small adjustments we can make to make our work simpler and smoother. Now, let's take a step back and think further: Is our job really only about code? Is writing good code (whatever that means) the only thing, even though it's broad and complex, that we need to do well? If we're asking this question, you can guess that the answer is: not at all! Just like in the movie *Ratatouille* where Chef Gusteau says, "*Anyone can cook*," here, we can paraphrase his words and say that *anyone can code*. It takes a little, in fact, to learn to write some lines of Java code or maybe even in some other simpler language. In recent months, technologies related to **artificial intelligence** (**AI**) have exploded, which can literally write code for us. But what is really challenging is not just writing code or even pieces of software that work together but doing it well. As Robert C. Martin says, *"Getting software right is hard."*

Software architecture is like the blueprint for a software system. It's the plan that outlines how different parts of the software work together. This involves making decisions about how to design things to meet specific goals. It includes elements such as the different pieces of software, how they connect to each other, and the rules for organizing them. So, software architecture is basically the high-level design that guides the creation of a software system.

The architecture of a software system is like the design or structure created by the people building it. It's determined by how the system is divided into parts (components), how these parts are organized, and how they talk to each other. In simpler terms, it's how the different pieces of the software are put together and work together. This is only one definition of architecture, shaped by the *Clean Architecture* book by Robert C. Martin. Reading Martin Fowler's works, instead, gives us another (funnier) definition of what architecture is: the collective knowledge that experienced developers have about the design of a system and the set of decisions you hope to make correctly at the beginning of a project.

We hope it's a bit clearer what we mean by software architecture, but maybe it will be even clearer when we've explained its goals. On goals, the ideas seem quite clear in literature: good architecture makes things work better. The reason for creating a good architecture is to make it easier to develop, deploy, operate, and maintain the software system it holds.

Development

As long as there's a small, single team handling the entire project, people may think that architecture isn't that important; in fact, it's seen as almost an obstacle. This is why many projects, especially in the startup phase, often don't have a proper architecture. However, as the project expands, rush to the rescue as soon as possible! In fact, it's challenging to work with different teams on the same project, on the same module; it becomes necessary to divide the module itself into well-defined parts ("how" is a whole different story). Simply dividing the initial component into multiple components is not enough, though. It needs to be done carefully, understanding how these components will interact with each other. Otherwise, there's a risk that from a single component, different ones may simply develop independently, each doing its own thing. And if everyone goes their own way, it's difficult to work on new features or fix existing problems. If a software system is difficult to develop, it's unlikely to have a long and healthy lifespan. Therefore, the system's architecture should be designed to make development easy for the team or teams working on it.

Deployment

Deployability means how easily and reliably software can be set up and run in a reasonable amount of time (ideally, with a single click). If there's a problem with the new setup, it should be possible to go back to the previous one without too much trouble. With the rise of virtualization and cloud systems, and as software systems get bigger, it's the architect's job to make sure setting up the software is done efficiently and predictably, reducing the overall risk for the system.

Unfortunately, many times, people don't think about how to set up a system when they're first building it. This can result in designs that make the system easy to create but really hard to get up and running.

For example, when starting to build a system, developers might opt for an architecture that includes a certain number of services and components. It might seem like a good idea for various reasons, such as smoother development and each piece working independently. However, during deployment, the team realizes that some of these services are interconnected and rely on each other to function properly. Deployment then becomes challenging, as you may need to deploy not only one service but also interconnected ones. If architects had considered the system setup from the beginning, they might have chosen fewer services, a combination of services and in-house components, and a more integrated approach to managing connections.

System operation

System operation involves the day-to-day management and execution of a computer system or software application. It includes tasks such as running the software, keeping an eye on its performance, applying updates and fixes, ensuring security, handling backups, assisting users, and addressing issues as they arise. Essentially, it's the ongoing effort to keep the system running smoothly and meeting user needs.

The influence of architecture on system operation is generally considered not as significant as its impact on development, deployment, and maintenance. Most operational challenges can be addressed by increasing the system's hardware resources without causing major changes to the software architecture; this scenario is quite common. Inefficient software architectures can often be made to function effectively by merely adding more storage and servers. The affordability of hardware compared to the cost of human resources means that architectures causing obstacles in operation are not as expensive as those hindering development, deployment, and maintenance.

Just because the impact of bad architecture on operations is easily fixable doesn't mean it's not an important aspect. Even though the so-called "hardware" (which often translates to buying cloud computing services from companies such as **Amazon Web Services** (**AWS**), Google, or Microsoft) costs less than people and time, it doesn't mean it's inexpensive or an insignificant cost. An inefficient architecture that requires a disproportionate number of resources compared to the value it brings (whether economic or otherwise) should be a concern.

Maintenance

Software maintenance refers to the ongoing process of managing and updating software to ensure it continues to meet the needs of users and remains effective over time. It involves making modifications, fixing bugs, improving performance, and adapting the software to changes in the environment or user requirements.

In this case, we could make a direct comparison with the architecture of buildings to understand how it impacts the manageability of a project. Imagine two buildings, two residences: one very complicated and sophisticated, unique in its kind; it has special aesthetic and technological features created specifically for the occasion, refined materials, and unique solutions. The other building is a classic European apartment complex, with straight facades and identical windows, common and sturdy materials, very similar to others encountered before. In the case that I have to make a change or solve a problem, in which building do you think it would be easier to operate?

Out of all the parts of a computer program, keeping it up and running is the most expensive. The constant need for new features and fixing mistakes takes a lot of time and effort from people. The main cost of keeping a program going comes from searching through the existing code and dealing with risks. Searching through the code, called **spelunking** by Robert C. Martin in his book *Clean Architecture*, takes time and money to figure out the best way to add something new or fix a mistake. When making these changes, there's always a chance of accidentally causing new problems, which adds to the risk and cost.

Having a well-thought-out plan for how the program is set up can really help cut down on these costs. If the program is split into different parts and each part is kept separate through stable connections, it makes it much easier to add new things without accidentally causing problems. This kind of planning reduces the risk of unintended issues and makes maintenance less costly.

Now that we have seen what architecture is and why it's important, let's discover the main types of architecture we can have.

Architectural patterns

In software, we can organize things in different ways, and these organized structures are called **software architecture patterns**. Many of them have been tried and proven to work well for solving different problems. Each pattern arranges things in a specific way to fix particular issues in software.

But let's keep it interesting and not dive into a super long list of these patterns. Instead, we'll look at a few of the most important and commonly used ones. This way, we can understand the main ideas without getting overwhelmed by all the possibilities.

Layered architecture

The **layered architecture pattern** (also called the **n-tier architecture pattern**) is probably the most widely used design approach. It's the go-to standard for many Java **Enterprise Edition** (EE) applications, and it's well-known among architects, designers, and developers. This pattern closely aligns with typical communication and organizational setups in most companies, making it a logical and common choice for developing business applications.

In the layered architecture pattern, components are organized into horizontal layers, each with a specific role in the application (such as presentation or business logic). While the pattern doesn't prescribe a fixed number of layers, common setups have four: **presentation**, **business**, **persistence**, and **database**. Sometimes, the business and persistence layers are combined for simplicity. Smaller apps might have three layers, while larger ones could have five or more.

Each layer has a distinct responsibility. For instance, the presentation layer handles user interfaces and communication, while the business layer executes business rules. Layers create abstractions, simplifying tasks. The presentation layer focuses on displaying information, not retrieving it. Similarly, the business layer concentrates on business logic, leaving data retrieval to the persistence layer, which then passes data to the business layer for processing and onward to the presentation layer for display:

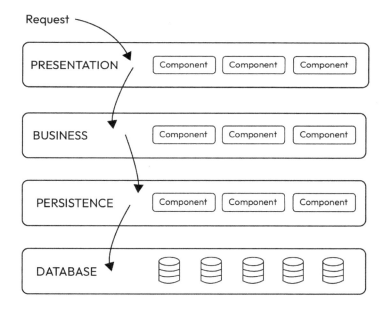

Figure 9.1 – Layered architecture

The layered architecture pattern excels in separating concerns among components. Each layer focuses solely on its relevant logic—presentation in the presentation layer, business in the business layer, and so forth. This classification simplifies role and responsibility models, making development, testing, governance, and maintenance straightforward. Defined component interfaces and limited scope contribute to this ease.

Notably, every layer in the architecture is marked as closed, a crucial concept in this pattern. A **closed layer** means a request must pass through the immediate layer below it before reaching the next one beneath. For instance, a request from the presentation layer travels through the business layer, then to the persistence layer, and finally reaches the database layer.

Monolithic application architectures

In a layered architecture, as we said, the concept involves organizing different components or functionalities of a system into distinct layers. But these layers can be interpreted in two ways:

Different applications/deployments: In this interpretation, each layer is considered a separate application or deployment. Each layer represents a self-contained unit with specific responsibilities. For example, you might have a presentation layer, business logic layer, and data access layer deployed as separate applications. This approach promotes modularity and facilitates scalability and maintenance.

Components inside the same application (monolith or N-tier): Alternatively, the layers can be viewed as components within the same application. In a monolithic architecture or an N-tier architecture, different layers exist within a single application's codebase. For instance, you could have a presentation layer handling user interfaces, a business logic layer managing application rules, and a data access layer interacting with the database—all within the confines of a single application.

Both interpretations are valid, and the choice between them depends on the specific architectural design goals and requirements of the system.

Microservices

There are many lengthy books about **microservices**, and it would be impossible to tell you everything here and now. However, we should at least give you a general overview of the topic because for years – and perhaps still today – they have been one of the main trends in our industry.

Microservices architecture, commonly abbreviated as microservices, is a specific way of structuring applications. In this architectural style, a large application is broken down into smaller, independent parts, each with its distinct set of responsibilities. This approach enables the creation of more modular and manageable components within the overall system. To represent this, we could put an example of a very common application, having a microservice dedicated to searching for items, another one handling the order, another one dealing with accounting issues, and a last one dealing with notifying users via email, push, and so on. Here is an example of microservices architecture:

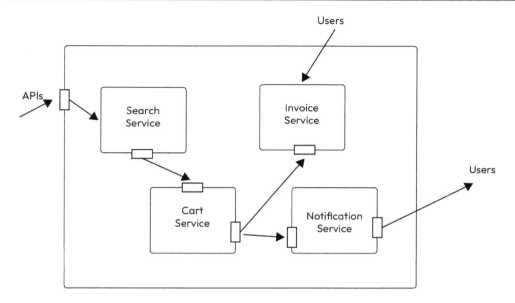

Figure 9.2 – An example of microservices architecture

In the context of microservices, an application can consist of numerous internal microservices, each handling a specific function. When a user makes a request, the microservices work together to compose and fulfill that request. This decentralized and modular nature of microservices offers flexibility, scalability, and easier maintenance compared to monolithic architectures where all functionalities are tightly integrated into a single, large application.

Understanding the concept of a service component is crucial within this pattern. Instead of viewing services in a microservices architecture, it's more beneficial to consider service components. These components can vary in size, ranging from a single module to a substantial part of the application. Service components house one or more modules (that is, Java classes) representing either a specialized function (such as providing traffic information for a specific location) or an autonomous section of a comprehensive business application. Determining the appropriate level of granularity for service components stands as a significant challenge in the context of microservices architecture. Nobody I know is completely satisfied with that!

Another essential idea in the microservices architecture pattern is its distributed nature. In this framework, all components within the architecture are completely independent of each other and are accessed through various remote access protocols (such as **Java Message Service (JMS)**, **Advanced Message Queuing Protocol (AMQP)**, **Representational State Transfer (REST)**, **Simple Object Access Protocol (SOAP)**, **Remote Method Invocation (RMI)**, and so on). The distributed aspect of this architecture pattern is instrumental in achieving remarkable scalability and deployment characteristics.

In a microservices architecture, finding the right granularity for service components is a significant challenge. If they are too coarse-grained, you might miss out on the benefits of this pattern (deployment, scalability, testability, and loose coupling). On the other hand, overly fine-grained components can lead to service orchestration demands, turning your lean microservices architecture into a complex **service-oriented architecture** (**SOA**) with added complexity, confusion, and cost.

Detecting the granularity challenge is possible by looking for signs such as orchestrating service components from the user interface or **application programming interface** (**API**) layer, indicating components may be too fine-grained. Inter-service communication for a single request may also suggest incorrect granularity or improper partitioning based on business functionality.

If service-component orchestration persists regardless of granularity, it might signal that a microservices architecture may not be the ideal choice. The distributed nature of this pattern makes maintaining a single transactional unit across components challenging, requiring complex transaction compensation frameworks for rollback, adding unnecessary complexity to this otherwise simple and elegant architecture.

The microservices architecture offers a myriad of advantages that significantly impact the development and operation of large, complex applications:

- **Continuous delivery and deployment**: One of the key strengths of the microservices architecture is its facilitation of continuous delivery and deployment. This means that updates, enhancements, or new features can be seamlessly integrated into the application without disrupting its overall functionality.

- **Modular and easily maintained**: Microservices are designed to be small and modular, allowing for easy maintenance. Each service is focused on a specific business capability, making it more straightforward to understand, update, and troubleshoot.

- **Independent deployability**: A notable feature is the ability to independently deploy services. This ensures that changes or updates to a particular service do not require a comprehensive redeployment of the entire application, leading to more efficient development processes.

- **Scalability on a service level**: Microservices empower teams to independently scale services based on their specific demands. This granular scalability optimizes resource utilization and responsiveness, enhancing the overall performance of the application.

- **Autonomous teams**: The microservices architecture fosters team autonomy, enabling different teams to work independently on specific services. This autonomy streamlines development cycles, allowing teams to innovate and iterate at their own pace.

- **Experimentation with new technologies**: Embracing microservices allows for easy experimentation and adoption of new technologies. Since services can be built and deployed independently, teams can explore and implement cutting-edge tools or frameworks without overhauling the entire system.

- **Enhanced fault isolation**: In the microservices model, faults are isolated to individual services, preventing a failure in one service from cascading and affecting the entire application. This improves the overall resilience and robustness of the system.

Of course, no technology is perfect, and the microservices system has some problems and challenges. Let's delve into significant challenges and issues associated with the microservices architecture:

- **Service identification**: Determining the optimal set of services can be a demanding task. Selecting the right services that effectively represent distinct business capabilities requires careful consideration and planning.

- **Complexity of distributed systems**: Microservices involve the creation of distributed systems, adding a layer of complexity. This complexity extends to the development, testing, and deployment phases, posing challenges in ensuring seamless integration and operation.

- **Coordination for feature deployment**: Deploying features that span multiple services necessitates meticulous coordination. Ensuring that various services work harmoniously to deliver a unified functionality demands careful planning and execution to avoid disruptions.

- **Decision-timing dilemma**: Determining the opportune moment to adopt the microservices architecture is a challenging decision. Knowing when the benefits outweigh the drawbacks and aligning the transition with organizational needs requires thoughtful evaluation.

Addressing these challenges is crucial for successfully implementing the microservices architecture.

Event-driven architecture

This is another common type of architectural pattern that can also be seen as a nuance of microservices. To put it simply, it involves designing a structure that recognizes events happening in the system—something that occurs—and making it react by producing some kind of result. The examples of "things that can happen" are potentially endless: a user signs up for the platform, a third-party system calls one of our webhooks, and an error occurs during some kind of process. For each of these events, one or more components will be listening and responding to the event itself. But let's try to be a bit more formal in our definition.

An **event** refers to a change in state or, more expansively, any observable occurrence that can be detected and documented by an application or device. These events can then be communicated and exchanged with other applications and devices. Within your enterprise, every incident—be it customer requests, updates in inventory, sensor readings, and the like—constitutes an event.

An **event-driven architecture** is a way for decoupled services to talk to each other using events, which are like little messages about changes or updates. This is a pretty common approach in modern apps with microservices.

In this setup, there are three main parts:

1. **Event producers**: These are the creators of events and publish them to the router; for example, "a purchase is completed."

2. **Event routers or event brokers**: These are the organizers who decide where each event should go. For example, you can imagine something like "a completed purchase should result in sending an email to the customer."

3. **Event consumers**: These are the parts of the system that want to know about certain events; for example, a component that receives some data about a completed purchase and reacts by sending an email to the customer.

The cool thing is these different parts don't have to know too much about each other. They just send out these little event messages, and the other parts can choose to listen and react or not. In our examples, the component that completes the purchase doesn't know a thing about what will happen next; it just publishes an event. The consumer, who is in charge of sending an email, doesn't have to know anything about the purchase completion process. This makes things flexible because, for instance, you can update how the payment system works without messing up how the mailing system works. They are like separate teams that can do their own thing without always checking with each other. This can often translate into two actually different teams working more or less separately.

Sometimes, an event can also be referred to as a message; the terms are often interchangeable. A bit more specific is the concept of a command: unlike an event that defines a change of state in some data or entity within the domain, a command explicitly requires something to be done. The implicit aspect is that in this case, the one carrying out the action and publishing the event is aware of something that is supposed to happen afterward. Technologically, however, almost nothing changes. Here is a diagram of event-driven architecture:

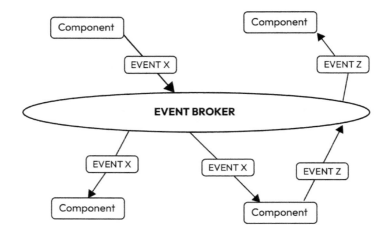

Figure 9.3 – Event-driven architecture

There are several advantages to embracing an event-driven architecture:

- The first is probably **independent scaling and fault isolation**: by adopting an event-driven architecture, the ability to scale and manage failures independently becomes a key benefit. As already mentioned, these are also benefits of microservices. Through the decoupling of services, each service interacts solely with the event router, rendering them agnostic to the existence of other services. Consequently, in the event of a failure in one service, the rest can continue to function seamlessly. The event router serves as an elastic buffer, adept at handling surges in workloads and ensuring overall system stability.

- The **development is more agile** because the event-driven model eliminates the need for custom code to poll, filter, and route events. Instead, the event router autonomously manages these tasks, automatically filtering and pushing events to consumers. This streamlined process significantly accelerates development cycles by minimizing the heavy coordination traditionally required between producer and consumer services. Developers can focus more on implementing business logic rather than dealing with intricate event-handling intricacies.

- When you have an event router acting as a centralized hub for auditing applications and establishing policies, you get **effortless auditing**. These policies can dictate access controls, limiting who can publish and subscribe to the router and specifying permissions for users and resources to access data. Additionally, the event router facilitates the encryption of events both during transit and while at rest, enhancing data security measures.

- You usually also have some **cost reductions**: event-driven architectures operate on a push-based model, triggering actions only when an event is present in the router. This contrasts with continuous polling, leading to reduced network bandwidth consumption, lower CPU utilization, decreased idle fleet capacity, and fewer SSL/TLS handshakes. The result is a more cost-effective system that maximizes resource efficiency by minimizing unnecessary operations, providing both economic and operational benefits.

In the world of event-driven setups, there are two main ways things work: the pub/sub model and the event streaming model.

Pub/sub model

Pub/sub stands for **publish/subscribe** or **publisher/subscriber**. This system functions using a messaging framework built on event stream subscriptions. Once an event takes place or is published, it is sent to subscribers who have expressed interest in that particular information. This method guarantees timely notification of relevant parties regarding unfolding events.

Event streaming

Unlike the pub/sub model, the event streaming model involves the recording of events in a log. Here, event consumers do not subscribe to an event stream; instead, they have the flexibility to read from any segment of the stream and can join the stream at their convenience.

There are some different types of event streaming, the main ones being:

- **Event stream processing**: Leverages a data streaming platform such as Apache Kafka to intake events and handle the processing or transformation of the event stream

- **Simple event processing**: An action is promptly triggered in the event consumer as soon as an event occurs

---

Apache Kafka

The most widely tool used for event streaming is Apache Kafka. Apache Kafka stands out as a powerful distributed data streaming platform, widely recognized as a top-tier solution for event processing. Renowned for its versatility, this platform excels in managing the seamless flow of event streams in real-time, encompassing tasks such as publishing, subscribing, storing, and processing data. Designed to meet the demands of diverse use cases, Apache Kafka particularly shines in scenarios where high throughput and scalability are paramount.

One of the distinctive features of Apache Kafka is its ability to efficiently handle a spectrum of data-sharing tasks without the need for intricate point-to-point integrations. This characteristic not only streamlines the overall architecture but also plays a pivotal role in reducing latency to an impressive millisecond scale. By offering a robust foundation for real-time data processing, Apache Kafka empowers organizations to harness the potential of timely insights and responsive analytics.

In essence, Apache Kafka emerges as an indispensable tool for industries and applications where the rapid exchange of information is critical. Its architecture not only supports the simultaneous handling of numerous events but also ensures that the system can effortlessly scale to accommodate growing demands. This combination of flexibility, scalability, and low-latency processing positions Apache Kafka as a preferred choice for businesses seeking a reliable and efficient solution for their data streaming and event processing needs.

The natural evolution of an event-driven architecture, especially one that adopts the event streaming pattern, is reactive architecture.

Reactive architecture

In recent years, a new way of doing things in the Java world has become popular, and it is called the **reactive paradigm**. Let us try to understand the basic ideas. As usual, we don't expect you to fully grasp the reactive paradigm in just one part of a book. The *Further reading* section is there for you, so you can explore more about it!

The term *reactive* is employed in the realm of reactive systems (not only in Java), and it was coined in the 2014 Reactive Manifesto, a collaborative effort by the community to develop responsive and distributed systems. The manifesto emphasizes the creation of systems that must be:

- **Responsive**: The system promptly responds with minimal and predictable delays to inputs to enhance user experience. For example, in a web application following reactive principles, user interface components are designed to update quickly in response to user interactions. For instance, when a user clicks a button, the system responds immediately, providing feedback without noticeable delays.

- **Resilient**: In the face of a component failure, the system gracefully handles it, minimizing the impact on overall system availability and responsiveness. For example, consider a microservices architecture where one service fails due to a temporary issue. A resilient system would handle this failure gracefully, perhaps by rerouting requests to an alternative instance of the service, ensuring that the overall system remains operational (**Circuit Breaker pattern**).

Circuit Breaker pattern

Connecting to the concept of resilience, it's worth talking about the **Circuit Breaker** pattern; it is a design pattern to improve the resilience of a system. It is used to handle faults and failures in a distributed or remote service by detecting and preventing repeated failures. The pattern is inspired by the electrical circuit breaker, which automatically interrupts the flow of electricity when a fault is detected to prevent damage to the electrical system.

A circuit breaker operates by wrapping a function call (such as a remote service call) and monitoring for failures. When a certain threshold of failures is reached, the circuit breaker "trips" and stops allowing calls to that function for a specified period. During this time, the system can take alternative actions, such as returning a fallback response or retrying the operation after a delay. This prevents the system from repeatedly trying to call a failing service, which could lead to degraded performance or complete system failure.

If you'd like to implement a circuit breaker in your Java application, the most used libraries are probably **Hystrix** and **Resilience4j**. Developed by Netflix, Hystrix is a widely used library for implementing the Circuit Breaker pattern in Java. It provides **fault tolerance** (**FT**) and **latency tolerance** (**LT**) features for distributed systems. Resilience4j is a lightweight, modular library for handling failures in Java 8+ and functional programming styles. It provides several resilience patterns, including Circuit Breaker, Rate Limiter, Retry, and Bulkhead. If you're using Spring Boot, **Spring Cloud Circuit Breaker** offers a unified abstraction layer for various circuit breaker implementations. This framework presents a uniform API that developers can use within their applications, granting the flexibility to select the circuit breaker implementation that aligns most effectively with their specific application requirements. The supported implementations at the moment of writing are Resilience4j and Spring Retry.

- **Elastic**: The system can adapt to varying workloads, maintaining consistent response times. For example, an elastic system could automatically scale its resources up or down based on demand. During peak usage, additional server instances might be provisioned to handle the increased load, and they can be scaled down during periods of lower demand.

- **Message-driven**: Systems aligned with the manifesto employ a message-driven communication model. For example, in a distributed application, components communicate through messages rather than direct method calls: instead of invoking a remote service synchronously, a system following the message-driven approach might send a message asynchronously and continue processing other tasks while awaiting a response.

A reactive architecture follows all these indications, emphasizing the propagation of changes and the declarative specification of the system's behavior in response to those changes. In reactive systems, an often-used paradigm is the Actor Model.

The Actor Model

I think it's worth mentioning the **Actor Model** because it's truly interesting, serving as the foundation for reactive systems. The Actor Model is nothing new: it was introduced by Carl Eddie Hewitt in 1973 as a theoretical model for managing concurrent computation. Its practical relevance became evident as the software industry recognized the challenges associated with implementing concurrent and distributed applications. In other words: managing threads is not suitable anymore and we do not have faster CPUs; we only have CPUs with more cores!

An actor is a *self-contained computational unit*, embodying several crucial characteristics that distinguish it within the Actor Model:

1. **Encapsulation of state and logic**: An actor encapsulates both its state and a portion of the application logic. This encapsulation ensures that an actor's internal workings are shielded from direct external access, promoting modular and maintainable code.

2. **Asynchronous message interaction**: Actors communicate exclusively through asynchronous messages, avoiding direct method calls. This design choice enhances the responsiveness of the system, as actors can continue processing messages independently without waiting for immediate responses.

3. **Unique address and mailbox**: Each actor possesses a unique address and maintains a mailbox for incoming messages. The address serves as a distinct identifier in the system, while the mailbox provides a mechanism for other actors to deliver messages asynchronously.

4. **Sequential message processing**: Messages in an actor's mailbox are processed sequentially in the order of their arrival. The default implementation of the mailbox often adopts a **First-In-First-Out** (**FIFO**) queue, ensuring predictable and ordered execution of messages.

5. **Tree-like hierarchy**: The actor system is organized in a hierarchical, tree-like structure. This hierarchy facilitates the organization of actors, with each actor having a specific place and role within the larger system.

6. **Dynamic actor operations**: Actors can dynamically create other actors, send messages to any actor within the system, and initiate their own termination or that of actors they have spawned. This dynamic behavior allows for flexible and adaptive system architectures.

Making programs that do many things at the same time is tricky because we have to make sure different parts of the program don't interfere with each other. The Actor Model makes it easier by letting us write code that can run independently without getting tangled up in these issues.

Instead of directly asking another part of the program to do something and waiting for it to finish, we can send a message and keep going. This means the part sending the message doesn't have to wait around for a reply. A system using this feature is usually referred to as a **non-blocking system**.

Using messages also helps prevent problems that can happen when many parts of the program are working at the same time. Messages are like notes passed between different parts, and they get dealt with one after the other, so there's no confusion.

Another good thing about the Actor Model is that if something goes wrong, such as a part of the program not doing what it's supposed to, the actors can tell their "boss" about it. The boss can then decide whether to fix the problem or just start over with a fresh attempt. This way, the whole program can keep running smoothly even if there are hiccups along the way.

In Java, you can leverage the Actor Model by using **Akka**, a toolkit and runtime for building highly concurrent, distributed, and fault-tolerant systems. It provides abstractions for managing concurrency, making it easier to develop scalable and resilient applications. In the *Further reading* section, there's a simple tutorial about it.

We have quickly covered several broad and somewhat complex concepts; much of it relies on modern, non-monolithic architecture. Let's now say a few words about one of the main trends of recent years: breaking the monolith!

Monolith to microservices

A **monolithic architecture** refers to a traditional approach in software design where an entire application is built as a single, unified code base. In a monolithic architecture, all components and modules of the application are interconnected and interdependent. This means that the code for the user interface, business logic, and data access layers, among others, is tightly integrated into a single executable or deployment unit.

In a monolithic architecture, the entire application is developed and maintained within a single code base, making it a cohesive unit. All modules and components within the application are closely connected and share the same resources, such as databases and servers; therefore, the entire application is deployed as a single unit, making updates and releases a coordinated process. One advantage of the monolithic architecture is that it often uses a uniform technology stack throughout the entire system; the main disadvantage is that scaling a monolithic application typically involves replicating the entire application, which can be less efficient than scaling individual components independently.

While monolithic architectures have been the standard for many years and have certain advantages, such as simplicity in development and deployment, they also pose challenges, especially as applications grow in size and complexity. The move away from monolithic architecture has led to the adoption of alternative architectural patterns, the most common being microservices. This has been quite a mantra for the last few years, and there are lots of books and articles about that. We'll just say a few words so that you don't feel completely unprepared!

Our first piece of advice is: don't treat a monolith like it was necessarily evil because, well, it depends. In some cases, the monolith is OK. For example, if you have a small-scale application with limited complexity and traffic, the overhead of managing a microservices architecture might outweigh the potential benefits, especially if requirements don't change that much. A monolith can be simpler to develop and maintain in such cases. Also, you could have limited resources: microservices often require specialized knowledge and additional infrastructure, which might not be feasible for smaller teams. Transitioning from a monolith to microservices requires time, effort, and potentially additional resources. If your organization is constrained in terms of time, budget, or expertise, maintaining the monolith might be a pragmatic decision. But the main reason could be that your monolith *just works*: if your monolithic application is stable, performs well, and meets the current and foreseeable future needs of the business, there might not be a compelling reason to undergo the complexity of transitioning to microservices.

While the benefits of microservices are evident, the transition from monolith to microservices comes with its own set of challenges. Entire books have been written on the argument, so we'll just give you a couple of hints:

- **Data management**: The transition to microservices introduces a paradigm shift in data management. In a monolith, data is often stored and accessed within a unified database. However, in a microservices architecture, data is distributed across multiple services. This decentralization of data can lead to challenges in ensuring consistency and maintaining transactional integrity. Organizations must grapple with issues such as data synchronization, versioning, and cross-service transactions to avoid data inconsistencies and ensure the reliability of their applications.

- **Service communication**: Efficient communication between microservices is paramount for the success of the architecture. Unlike monolithic applications, where function calls can be internal, microservices communicate over a network. Choosing appropriate communication protocols and mechanisms becomes crucial to facilitate seamless interactions between services. Decisions regarding synchronous or asynchronous communication, API design, and message formats require careful consideration to optimize the performance and reliability of the entire system.

- **Operational complexity**: The move to microservices introduces a new level of operational complexity. Managing a distributed system involves orchestrating the deployment and scaling of multiple services. Monitoring the health and performance of each service, logging relevant information for debugging purposes, and ensuring the overall reliability of the system become intricate tasks. Organizations need robust tools and practices for distributed tracing, logging aggregation, and monitoring to effectively navigate the operational challenges posed by microservices.

- **Cultural shift**: Beyond technical considerations, transitioning to microservices often necessitates a cultural shift within development teams. Embracing a DevOps mindset, where development and operations teams collaborate closely throughout the **software development life cycle (SDLC)**, becomes essential. **Continuous integration** and **continuous deployment (CI/CD)** practices need to be adopted to enable rapid and reliable releases. This cultural transformation requires a commitment to automation, collaboration, and a shared sense of responsibility among team members.

Each of the previous points hides a world of challenges behind them. These challenges, while surmountable, underscore the need for a thoughtful and well-executed transition.

It would be really difficult, naive, and maybe even arrogant to try to guide you in just a few words through the transition to adopting a microservices architecture. I have been involved several times in projects where this transition took years and sometimes wasn't even fully completed. It's a lengthy process that requires great attention, especially in deciding how big a microservice should be. However, we can offer you some insights to understand what to pay attention to if you find yourself involved in such a transition (and it's quite likely!):

- **Incremental adoption**: One of the best practices for a successful transition to microservices involves adopting a strategy of incremental changes rather than a sudden, big-bang overhaul. Organizations often find it prudent to start the migration process by identifying and transitioning non-critical services first. This phased approach allows teams to gain experience with microservices while minimizing the impact on the overall system. It also facilitates the identification and resolution of challenges on a smaller scale before tackling more critical components.

- **Effective communication**: In a microservices architecture, where services communicate over a network, establishing clear and effective communication channels is paramount. Organizations should define and adhere to well-defined APIs to ensure seamless interaction between services. This not only enhances the reliability of the system but also facilitates the independence of services, enabling teams to evolve and update services without disrupting the entire application. Effective communication is foundational to achieving the modularity and flexibility that microservices promise.

- **Automated testing**: Comprehensive automated testing is a linchpin of successful microservices adoption. Given the distributed nature of microservices, thorough testing is essential to catch issues early in the development and deployment process. Test suites should cover unit testing, integration testing, and **end-to-end** testing for each microservice. Automation not only accelerates the testing process but also provides a safety net for frequent deployments, ensuring that changes to one service do not inadvertently break the functionality of others. Consider adopting contract testing.

- **Monitoring and logging**: Operational complexities introduced by microservices necessitate robust monitoring and logging solutions. Organizations should invest in tools that enable real-time monitoring of service health, performance metrics, and potential issues. Centralized logging allows for efficient debugging and troubleshooting across distributed services. Proactive monitoring and logging not only aid in maintaining system reliability but also contribute to a proactive approach to system optimization and performance enhancement.

- **Cultural alignment**: Transitioning to a microservices architecture is not only a technological shift but also a cultural one. Fostering a culture of collaboration, shared responsibility, and continuous learning is crucial for the success of the transition. Teams should embrace a DevOps mindset, where development and operations collaborate closely, and there is a shared sense of ownership for the entire system. Continuous learning and knowledge sharing ensure that teams are equipped to adapt to the evolving landscape of microservices and embrace the agility it brings to software development.

These best practices try to provide a roadmap for teams and organizations navigating the complex terrain of transitioning from monolithic architectures to microservices.

When you have some kind of microservice architecture in place or, better, while designing it, you'll want to be aware of some bad smells you could spot quite easily.

Bad smells in the microservices architecture

Just as there are **bad smells** in code – issues that hide between methods and classes – there are also problems related to how software components work together in a software architecture. These are recurring patterns or, rather, anti-patterns, and when we see them, we should be suspicious and take action if needed. Let's take a look at some of the most common ones.

Shared persistence

"Don't cross the streams," as the *Ghostbusters* used to say. It's a bit like what happens with shared persistence. We talk about shared persistence when two or more microservices share the same persistent data, such as a database, a **Redis** instance, or a cache. This can cause a few problems. First, if services *A* and *B* try to read and write to the same data layer at the same time, synchronization problems can occur. What one service reads might have been written by another, and vice versa.

However, the most significant issue, in my opinion, is the interdependence that arises when you need to make changes to the data structure itself. For example, simply changing, adding, or removing a column from a database table could become a big problem and might require modifying both microservices, even if one of them isn't affected by the change. If we wanted to represent this situation in a very simple yet effective way, we would have a diagram like this:

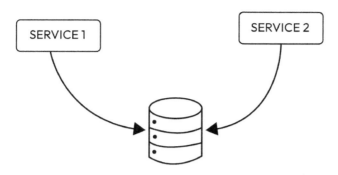

Figure 9.4 – Two (micro) services rely on the same data storage

The most obvious solution is to maintain a separate data storage layer for each microservice. This means that each microservice owns its data, and it's responsible for providing functions to access that data. When someone needs to use that data, they'll use the microservice as a kind of **data abstraction**. They won't need to know where or how the data is stored. Data owned by a specific microservice should not be duplicated elsewhere.

However, it's essential to note that having a non-shared data storage layer doesn't necessarily mean having a separate database for each microservice. It depends on the granularity of the service. For example, if you have a microservice that handles customers and their shipping addresses (such as in an e-commerce platform), you might have a database specific to this service. Customers and addresses are likely interconnected, so you might have relational tables linked; for example, by a foreign key. If you want to make your microservices more granular, say, a customer service and an address service, you can't have completely separate and unrelated databases. However, you can ensure that the customer service writes to the CUSTOMER table and the address service writes to the ADDRESS table. These tables will be related by a foreign key but will remain distinct. Data integrity will be guaranteed (also) by the properties of the relational database (**ACID properties**):

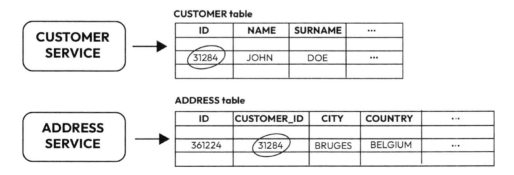

Figure 9.5 – Two services use different tables of the same database, which
are related by the id-customer_id foreign key relationship

Now, we've told you how it should be, but we also need to tell you that this doesn't always happen, especially during the transition from a monolithic system to microservices. You may have to share the data storage layer for a while. However, our advice is to avoid this situation as much as possible and resolve this issue as soon as you can.

Shared libraries

Sharing persistence (data storage) leads to coupling problems, and the same goes for sharing libraries. One of the first things we discussed in this book, and generally emphasized in studies and work, is the principle of **Don't Repeat Yourself** (**DRY**). Do things once, do them well, and reuse your code as much as possible. This is certainly a mantra to follow, but in the case of architecture (especially a microservices architecture), one must be very cautious.

Let's imagine having two services – two components that use the same shared library, always written and managed by us. If we need to make a change to this library, we will not only have to handle the change in the library itself but also update the dependency in the microservices, and perhaps even change the code if needed (this depends on whether we change the method signatures or not).

The example we are discussing involves only two microservices and one library. However, within an architecture, there can be many interrelated components: component A is connected to component B, which is connected to component C, and so on. Modifying a library can potentially lead to a difficult-to-control ripple effect, triggering a chain of retesting, rebuilding, and redeploying that can be quite costly.

I'm not saying here not to use shared libraries. Shared libraries are crucial for avoiding code duplication among software components. Take logging, for instance. Custom logic, such as formatting or concealing sensitive data such as customer details, is often required. Now, picture each component with its unique implementation. Consider the wasted developer hours if it's not identical across components. Aggregating logs becomes challenging, and slight implementation differences can lead to inconsistent labeling.

Something such as the recent log4j vulnerability poses a significant challenge if this implementation is spread all around the code base. Fixing it per microservice or component demands substantial effort. Conversely, with a custom logging library using log4j internally, addressing the vulnerability only would require action at a single point. **Logging** is a universal feature in microservices, making it an excellent candidate for a shared library. Other examples include security, monitoring, async communication, and handling exceptions.

Also, adding a middle layer between the code and external tools is really helpful. It protects the main part of the program from changes in those tools. This makes it easier to put new features in or fix problems. It also makes the code easier to read and work on with a team. After a year of doing this, it's clear that it makes our software stronger and more flexible.

I'm trying to say here that while good architecture implies decoupling the different parts of the application, shared libraries do exactly the opposite. On the other hand, they reduce repetition, and that's good! We have to find a balance. There's no one-size-fits-all rule for every situation. You need to consider each case individually. In general, it could be said that it's worth creating a shared library whenever you need to write code that doesn't depend on the specific subject of the module you're working on. The examples mentioned earlier (logging, security, monitoring, and so on) are things that can be used in different situations, no matter what specific area you're working in.

There are different ways to handle your shared libraries. You could either set up a distinct repository for each needed library or use a single repository (referred to as a **monorepo**; more on this in the *Further reading* section) that houses multiple libraries. The crucial point is to have some form of separation. For instance, you could have a single repository covering monitoring, security, and logging projects. Each project would be self-contained, except for any necessary dependencies.

It's really important to keep the user's decisions and logic inside a kind of protective bubble; this is crucial in programming and when making shared libraries. **Encapsulation** is like a shield that stops unwanted access and keeps data safe from being leaked. That's why it's a must when you're building shared libraries. Let's imagine you're making a library with code specific to a certain company, such as a tool to put files into storage. The parts that the user works with need to be designed in a general way, avoiding names such as *S3FileUploader* (because S3 is Amazon's storage service). But why avoid these names? Well, think about this: what if in the future you want to switch to Azure Blob (which is like Microsoft's version of Amazon S3)? If you had named things specifically to Amazon, all your users would have to change their ways of doing things. So, it's better to use more general names, such as *FileUploader*. Believe me, it'll save you a bunch of time and work in the long haul.

Keep your library code clean. Even though many people may contribute to the shared library, avoid turning it into a big, complicated thing! Before adding a new library, think about it a lot. When you do add one, think about how it might change and who will use it. Don't just make it for your own needs; that makes it hard for others to use or add to.

Don't put domain-specific code in there! Even shared business code probably doesn't belong there. Even if it means each component that uses it has to copy it, a user model that starts the same for all components is still business-related logic that shouldn't be in the library. That's because different services might need to change later to fit their specific business needs. It's not good if they all use the same model because it might have things that don't relate to other microservices or even break them if they want to rename or change some of the logic. So, when working with a single repository, it's a great idea to use conventional commits to talk about changes in the code. Follow some commit conventions you'll find among the team, such as starting each commit with *fix* when you're fixing something. This is helpful when someone else is trying to understand the history of the repository, what was done, and where things are in the code.

Last but not least, when you're dealing with a shared library that is a client library to another service, you could think about generating it. Rather than writing a shared library to interact with APIs in a system, it's more effective to create an API specification. This specification can then be used to automatically generate API clients for various languages and services. Something really cool we did once was to include and use a library called **Feign**, a Java-based declarative web service client developed by Netflix. It simplifies the creation of HTTP clients for RESTful services by allowing developers to define requests using annotations and interface methods. Feign integrates with Netflix Ribbon for load balancing, supports various data formats, and provides fallback mechanisms for enhanced application robustness. It's commonly used in microservices architectures for efficient communication between services.

Direct communication

One of the primary motivations behind designing good architecture is the desire for improved flexibility and easier maintenance of the overall system. This flexibility is crucial for accommodating changes within the application, including modifications to the API of individual services or adjustments to the communication protocols between services.

However, a challenge arises when clients communicate directly with different services. This direct communication model diminishes some of the benefits of a good architectural design, particularly regarding flexibility. When clients are tightly coupled to the specific addresses of other services, the ability to relocate or split these services becomes problematic. In essence, the address of a service becomes a fixed point, making it difficult to make structural changes to the system without impacting its clients. Additionally, when a service is publicly exposed, there is a constant need to maintain backward compatibility in its API to avoid disrupting existing clients. This is usually considered an anti-pattern, and we're going to represent it with the following diagram, where you can see different types of devices connecting directly to the exposed services:

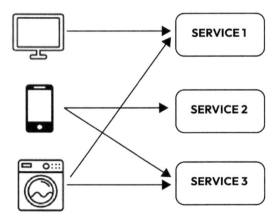

Figure 9.6 – Different clients for different devices directly call the services

There are many possible solutions to avoid this anti-pattern. Let's see a couple of them.

API gateway

An **API gateway** is a server or service that acts as an entry point for a collection of services. Its primary role is to provide a centralized and unified point of entry for clients (such as mobile apps, web applications, or other services) to interact with various components. It basically sits between the client and server, providing other essential functions. Here is a diagram of an API gateway:

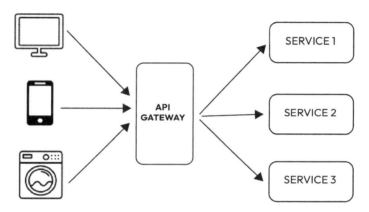

Figure 9.7 – All of the clients of the different devices pass through the same API gateway

For example, API gateways usually provide **request routing**: an API gateway routes incoming requests from clients to the appropriate service(s). It acts as a traffic cop, directing requests to the relevant service based on factors such as the endpoint, version, or other criteria.

The API gateway can **aggregate multiple requests** from clients into a single request to reduce the number of round trips between the client and the services. This is beneficial for optimizing performance and reducing latency. Similarly, the API gateway can **aggregate responses** from multiple services before sending them back to the client. This can reduce the number of requests needed from the client and enhance overall system efficiency.

Load balancing distributes incoming requests across multiple instances of a service to ensure optimal resource utilization and prevent overload on any single instance. The API gateway can handle this load balancing to enhance the system's scalability and reliability.

The API gateway usually centralizes **authentication and authorization** processes. It can enforce security measures such as validating API keys, handling user authentication, and ensuring that only authorized clients can access specific services.

To improve performance, the API gateway can implement **caching** strategies. It can store and retrieve responses from services in a cache, reducing the need to recompute or fetch the same data repeatedly.

The API gateway often includes **monitoring and analytics** tools to track the performance and usage of microservices. This information can be valuable for identifying bottlenecks, optimizing resource allocation, and ensuring the overall health of the system.

An API gateway can enforce **rate limits** on incoming API requests to prevent abuse or overuse of resources. This involves setting a maximum number of requests a user or client can make within a specified time frame.

Throttling can also be implemented through **quotas**, where clients are allocated a certain number of resources or requests over a defined period. Somehow related to quotas is the concept of **monetization**: API gateways can track the usage of APIs by clients and implement usage-based billing. This involves charging clients based on the number of requests, data transferred, or other relevant metrics.

An alternative to the API gateway pattern is the **Backend for Frontend** (**BFF**) pattern.

Backend For Frontend (BFF)

The term *BFF* refers to a design pattern in software development where a separate backend is created for each frontend application or user interface. This approach is particularly common in the context of microservices architectures and is aimed at optimizing the interaction between frontend and backend components.

In a traditional web application, there is usually a single backend that serves data and functionality to various frontend clients. However, as applications become more complex and diverse, with different platforms (web, mobile, and so on) and user experiences, managing all these requirements within a single backend can become challenging.

The BFF pattern addresses this challenge by creating specialized backend services for each frontend or client type. Each BFF is tailored to the specific needs of the corresponding frontend, providing a more efficient and targeted interface between the two layers. This allows frontend developers to have more control over the data and services they need, without being constrained by a monolithic backend that serves multiple purposes. Please be mindful that the BFF functions as a "proxy," filtering and adjusting requests from a shared set of backend (BE) services to a particular frontend (FE) client. It is essential that the BFF does not duplicate backend business functionalities in theory, as doing so would compromise the integrity of the application. Here is a diagram of the BFF pattern:

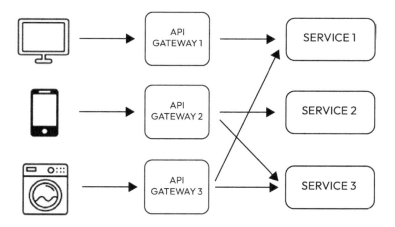

Figure 9.8 – In BFF, we have a gateway for each type of client

In contrast to the earlier diagram, in this setup, each device type links to its dedicated API gateway tailored to its requirements. These gateways act as a kind of cover, hiding the services in the background and decoupling the devices from direct connections to these services.

There are several advantages to using the BFF pattern:

- **Specialization**: Each BFF can be optimized for the specific requirements of its associated frontend, leading to better performance and user experience

- **Autonomy**: Frontend and backend teams can work more independently, as changes to one do not necessarily affect the other, provided the API contracts are maintained

- **Scalability**: Different frontends may have varying scalability needs, and BFFs allow for more fine-grained scalability planning based on individual requirements

- **Flexibility**: BFFs can adapt to the technology stack and architectural choices that are most suitable for the specific frontend they serve

It's important to note that while the BFF pattern offers advantages, it also introduces some complexities, such as the need to manage multiple backend services. Proper communication and coordination between frontend and backend teams, as well as adherence to well-defined API contracts, are crucial for the success of this pattern.

Summary

In this chapter, we've dived into the meaning of the term *architecture* and checked out its main variations. We've seen why having a clean, maintainable, and scalable architecture is important, and we've got some hints on how to achieve it (make sure to dig deeper in the *Further reading* section). We've looked at the main architectural patterns, from the (relatively) simpler ones to the slightly more complex ones designed for larger systems. We've also discussed what to watch out for when trying to break the monolith – moving from a monolithic architecture to a microservices one. Speaking of the latter, we've taken a quick look at some of the most common bad smells you might encounter. Remember – always keep your spider senses active!

As you close this book, remember that writing good code is not a one-time effort but a continuous commitment to excellence. Act like a craftsman, constantly refining your code to reflect your evolving understanding of best practices and industry trends.

The concepts you've acquired here will not only result in more readable and efficient Java code but will also empower you to collaborate seamlessly with fellow developers, ultimately contributing to the success of your projects. As you start your coding journey, let the principles of clean code and the art of refactoring be your guiding lights, illuminating a path toward software excellence.

May your code always be clean, your designs elegant, and your ride in the world of Java programming be both fulfilling and rewarding.

Happy coding!

Further reading

- Giuseppe Bonocore, *Hands-On Software Architecture with Java*, Packt Publishing Ltd.
- Robert C. Martin, *Clean Architecture*, Prentice Hall
- Mark Richards, *Software Architecture Patterns*, O'Reilly
- Martin Fowler's work on architecture: `https://martinfowler.com/architecture/`
- *Monorepo Explained*: `https://monorepo.tools/`
- *Intro to Feign*: `https://www.baeldung.com/intro-to-feign`
- *Intro to Apache Kafka*: `https://www.baeldung.com/apache-kafka`
- Akka: `https://www.baeldung.com/akka-actors-java`
- Sam Newman, *Monolith to Microservices*, O'Reilly

Index

A

AAA pattern
  Act phase 90
  Arrange phase 90
  Assert phase 90
abstract syntax tree (AST) 148
accessor methods 152
ACID properties 251
Actor Model 246, 247
Advanced Message Queuing
  Protocol (AMQP) 239
alerts generation 184
all-arguments constructor 151
Allman Style 206
Amazon Web Services (AWS) 235
Apache JMeter 85
Apache Kafka 244
API documentation 223
API gateway 255
  aggregate multiple requests 255
  aggregate responses 255
  authentication and authorization
    processes 255
  caching strategies 255
  monitoring and analytics tools 256
  rate limits 256

application programming
  interface (API) 240
architecture documentation 221
artificial intelligence (AI) 234
automated static analysis tools 174
  Checkstyle 175
  FindBugs 176
  PMD 176, 177
  SonarLint 175
  SonarQube 174
automated testing 249
automated tools 210, 211
automatic protocol generation testing 182

B

Backend for Frontend (BFF) 256, 257
  advantages 257
bad code 52
  Broken Window theory 54
  deadlines 53
  insufficient domain 55
  review process 54
  technical knowledge 55
Boy Scout Rule 11, 12
branch 100

Packtpub.com

Subscribe to our online digital library for full access to over 7,000 books and videos, as well as industry leading tools to help you plan your personal development and advance your career. For more information, please visit our website.

Why subscribe?

- Spend less time learning and more time coding with practical eBooks and Videos from over 4,000 industry professionals

- Improve your learning with Skill Plans built especially for you

- Get a free eBook or video every month

- Fully searchable for easy access to vital information

- Copy and paste, print, and bookmark content

Did you know that Packt offers eBook versions of every book published, with PDF and ePub files available? You can upgrade to the eBook version at packtpub.com and as a print book customer, you are entitled to a discount on the eBook copy. Get in touch with us at customercare@packtpub.com for more details.

At www.packtpub.com, you can also read a collection of free technical articles, sign up for a range of free newsletters, and receive exclusive discounts and offers on Packt books and eBooks.

Other Books You May Enjoy

If you enjoyed this book, you may be interested in these other books by Packt:

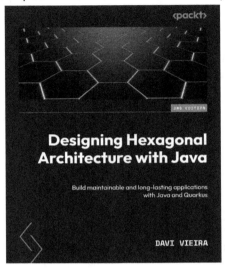

Designing Hexagonal Architecture with Java - Second Edition

Davi Vieira

ISBN: 978-1-83763-511-5

- Apply SOLID principles to the hexagonal architecture
- Assemble business rules algorithms using the specified design pattern
- Combine domain-driven design techniques with hexagonal principles to create powerful domain models
- Employ adapters to enable system compatibility with various protocols such as REST, gRPC, and WebSocket
- Create a module and package structure based on hexagonal principles
- Use Java modules to enforce dependency inversion and ensure software component isolation
- Implement Quarkus DI to manage the life cycle of input and output ports

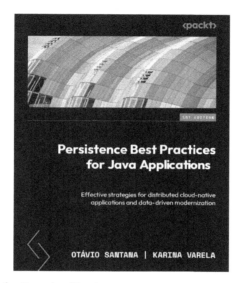

Persistence Best Practices for Java Applications

Otàvio Santana, Karina Varela

ISBN: 978-1-83763-127-8

- Gain insights into data integration in Java services and the inner workings of frameworks
- Apply data design patterns to create a more readable and maintainable design system
- Understand the impact of design patterns on program performance
- Explore the role of cloud-native technologies in modern application persistence
- Optimize database schema designs and leverage indexing strategies for improved performance
- Implement proven strategies to handle data storage, retrieval, and management efficiently

Packt is searching for authors like you

If you're interested in becoming an author for Packt, please visit authors.packtpub.com and apply today. We have worked with thousands of developers and tech professionals, just like you, to help them share their insight with the global tech community. You can make a general application, apply for a specific hot topic that we are recruiting an author for, or submit your own idea.

Share Your Thoughts

Now you've finished *Refactoring in Java*, we'd love to hear your thoughts! Scan the QR code below to go straight to the Amazon review page for this book and share your feedback or leave a review on the site that you purchased it from.

https://packt.link/r/1805126636

Your review is important to us and the tech community and will help us make sure we're delivering excellent quality content.

Download a free PDF copy of this book

Thanks for purchasing this book!

Do you like to read on the go but are unable to carry your print books everywhere?

Is your eBook purchase not compatible with the device of your choice?

Don't worry, now with every Packt book you get a DRM-free PDF version of that book at no cost.

Read anywhere, any place, on any device. Search, copy, and paste code from your favorite technical books directly into your application.

The perks don't stop there, you can get exclusive access to discounts, newsletters, and great free content in your inbox daily

Follow these simple steps to get the benefits:

1. Scan the QR code or visit the link below

https://packt.link/free-ebook/9781805126638

2. Submit your proof of purchase
3. That's it! We'll send your free PDF and other benefits to your email directly

www.ingramcontent.com/pod-product-compliance
Lightning Source LLC
LaVergne TN
LVHW081519050326
832903LV00025B/1542